THE WORKS OF SHAKESPEARE

EDITED FOR THE SYNDICS OF THE
CAMBRIDGE UNIVERSITY PRESS
BY
JOHN DOVER WILSON
ASSISTED IN THIS VOLUME BY
GEORGE IAN DUTHIE

ROMEO AND JULIET

ROMEO & JULIET

CAMBRIDGE UNIVERSITY PRESS

Published by the Syndics of the Cambridge University Press
Bentley House, 200 Euston Road, London, NW1 2DB
American Branch: 32 East 57th Street, New York, N.Y. 10022

ISBNS:

0 521 07554 8 hard covers
0 521 09497 6 paperback

First published 1955
Reprinted 1961
First paperback edition 1969
Reprinted 1971 1973 1974

First printed in Great Britain at the University Press, Cambridge
Reprinted in Great Britain by Hazell Watson & Viney Ltd,
Aylesbury, Bucks

THIS VOLUME IS DEDICATED BY ITS EDITORS
TO THEIR FORMER STUDENTS IN THE
ENGLISH DEPARTMENTS AT
MᶜGILL AND EDINBURGH UNIVERSITIES

CONTENTS

PREFATORY NOTE

The appearance of the present volume leaves another eight or nine to be published in this edition. But for unforeseen accidents, the task might be accomplished single-handed in another eight or nine years. Both the publishers and I are, however, anxious to quicken the pace; my chief reason being the Psalmist's warning to septuagenarians. To this end I have sought help from others, and have been fortunate in securing it from three well-known scholars, Dr Alice Walker, Mr J. C. Maxwell, and Professor Duthie of McGill and Aberdeen; the last consenting to collaborate in two texts, this one and *King Lear*, before setting his hand to *The Oxford Shakespeare*, which he inherits from R. B. McKerrow. The preparation of *King Lear* is well forward, while Dr Walker is engaged with me on *Othello* and Mr Maxwell on *Pericles*, two plays which they will shortly follow, it is hoped, with *Troilus and Cressida* and *Timon of Athens*. Yet, when I observe that Professor Duthie and I began editing *Romeo and Julie* in 1949, subscribers will be wise not to expect too early a completion of the undertaking. One never knows, indeed, what one may find in Shakespeare. And that the settlement of the present text has not proved an exactly easy job will be evident from our Note on the Copy and from the fact that, as the Notes indicate, we have been obliged to leave some points still undecided. It should be stated, in conclusion, that the following Introduction, except for an abridgment of his opening section on the sources, is Professor Duthie's, and the Stage History as usual Mr Young's, while for all the rest—text, Note·on the Copy, Notes, and Glossary—Professor Duthie and I are jointly responsible, though we have found it convenient, necessary indeed in matters of disagreement, to sign a note here and there with our initials.

J.D.W.

1954

INTRODUCTION

In November 1562, Richard Tottel, who a few years earlier had issued that famous 'miscellany' of *Songes and Sonnettes* which now passes under his name, published an octavo volume entitled *The Tragicall Historye of Romeus and Iuliet, written first in Italian by Bandell, and nowe in English by Ar. Br.* This History was a poem of a little over three thousand lines, in 'poulter's measure' (a six-foot iambic line followed by, and rhyming with, a second line of seven feet); a tiresome metre in large quantities, and hardly capable of intense passion, though here handled with some charm and tenderness. That 'Ar. Br.' stands for Arthur Brooke, a young poet who was shortly after drowned while crossing the Channel, we learn from George Turbervile, who printed an epitaph on him in 1570 which makes special reference to the promise shown in a poem on 'Iuliet and her mate'. Most critics agree that this was the poem upon which some thirty years later Shakespeare founded his tragedy, but few, not we think even P. A. Daniel, Brooke's best editor, have appreciated the fullness of Shakespeare's debt. The drama follows the poem not only in incident, but often in word and phrase. Many of these verbal parallels are cited in the Notes below, but no verbal balance-sheet can convey a complete sense of the intimacy of the connexion. It looks as if Shakespeare knew the poem almost by heart, so frequently does he recall some expression or train of thought that occurs in one part of Brooke's story and adapt it to another.

But the tragical history is much older than Brooke's poem or than Bandello's prose version (1554) from

which Brooke professed to draw it, though he actually
went to a French rendering published in 1559 by
Boaistuau, who added to Bandello's straightforward
tale a number of fatalistic and ominous touches, which
Brooke also took over and Shakespeare later turned to
a still better use. One incident indeed which he in-
herited, the heroine's use of a potion to escape an en-
forced marriage, goes right back to the late Greek
novelist Xenophon of Ephesus; while the family names
of Capulet and Montague, in the form Cappelletti and
Montecchi, originally belonged to local branches of the
political factions of the thirteenth century, the one of
the Guelfs in Cremona, the other of the Ghibellines in
Verona, their sole connexion being a line in the sixth
canto of Dante's *Purgatorio*,[1] which mentions them
together as examples of the warring cliques that tore
Italy to pieces at that date. The story in all its essentials
was, however, first found in *Il Novellino* (1476) by
Masuccio Salerintano, who is deeply indebted to
Boccaccio. It was retold some fifty years later by Luigi
da Porto, who seems to have invented the names of
most of the principal characters. And from Porto it
passed to Sevin the earliest writer to give it a French
dress (1542). Sevin was in his turn influenced by
Boccaccio, adopting certain details from the latter's
Filostrato, itself the source of Chaucer's *Troilus and
Criseyde*. That Shakespeare himself went to *Troilus
and Criseyde* direct for inspiration there is no proof,
though he knew the poem, but Brooke certainly
borrowed from it;[2] and thus the two greatest love
poems in our language were doubly linked together.
One of the details Sevin added was the visit to the
apothecary which Boaistuau borrowed in turn from
Bandello. Bandello, however, took it, with the rest of
the story, not direct from Sevin, but through the medium

[1] vi. 105.   [2] See 1. 3. 2 ff. n. for an illustration.

of the Italian pseudonymous poet Clizia, who got it
from Sevin. Finally, five years later than Brooke's,
a second translation from Boaistuau appeared in English, this time in prose from the pen of William Painter,
being one of the tales in his *Palace of Pleasure* (1567).
It seems likely that Shakespeare had read Painter, and
he may also have made use of a lost play on the subject,
which Brooke mentions in his preface, though he does
not tell us whether it was in English or Latin. Such in
bare outline is the tangled history[1] of the expanding
legend of the lovers 'in fair Verona', which when
Shakespeare took it over was one of the best known
stories of Europe, so much so that it 'adorned the
hangings of chambers, and Juliet figures as a tragic
heroine in the sisterhood of Dido and Cleopatra':[2]

> For out of olde feldes, as man seith,
> Cometh al this newe corn froe yeere to yeere;
> And out of olde bokes in good feith,
> Cometh al this newe science that man lere.

Yet each new crop was different from those before;
and features peculiar to Shakespeare's version were
doubtless intended to make the story more powerfully
dramatic than it is in any of the other versions. Brooke's
story extends over a period of several months; Shakespeare's is compressed into a few days.[3] This compres-
sion no doubt represents an attempt (whether fully
successful or not) to induce in the spectator or reader
a feeling of tragic inevitability. Again, in Shakespeare

[1] For a comprehensive study of the sources see Olin H.
Moore, *The Legend of Romeo and Juliet* (Columbus, Ohio,
1950). See also H. B. Charlton in *Proceedings of the British
Academy* (1939), pp. 157 ff., and the citations given by
Georges A. Bonnard in *Review of English Studies*, New
Series, vol. II (1951), pp. 319 ff.

[2] C. H. Herford, *Eversley Shakespeare*, vii, 397.

[3] On this matter see Georges A. Bonnard, *loc. cit.*

Paris comes to the tomb in the last scene of the play.
In no other known version does he do this, and the effect
of the innovation is dramatically powerful. Yet again,
if it is one of Brooke's claims to distinction that he
produced the essentials of the Nurse's character[1] as it
appears in our play, Shakespeare himself, as far as we
know, may claim sole credit for the essentials of the
character of his own Mercutio who is certainly one of
his most vivid creations. The Mercutio of the earlier
versions is hardly a character at all.[2]

*　　*　　*　　*　　*

Coming to the problem of date we have first to
inquire whether Shakespeare composed the play once
for all in a single creative act or whether he worked at it
in stages at different times. It was formerly, for example,
a view widely held, even for a time by one of us,[3] that
the First Quarto represents a first draft by Shakespeare
or some other dramatist, or at least a pirated version of
such a draft. With the advance of our knowledge about
Bad Quartos it has now, however, come to be accepted
that what the First Quarto stands for is a pirated
version of Shakespeare's final Second Quarto text,
corrupted and perverted by certain actors who had
performed it.[4] Or again it might be suggested that
the Second Quarto contains layers of text composed by
Shakespeare at different times. Some passages are
highly ornate, conventional, artificial, full of verbal
ingenuities, full of virtuoso-work, displaying the art of

[1] See note on 1. 3. 2. ff. below.　　[2] See p. 122.
[3] See an article on 'The "stolne and surreptitious"
Shakespearian texts' by A. W. Pollard and J. Dover
Wilson, *Times Literary Supplement*, 14 Aug. 1919.
[4] This view has been skilfully expounded by Professor
Hoppe, *The Bad Quarto of Romeo and Juliet* (Ithaca,
N.Y., 1948). See also *R.E.S.*, vol. xiv (1938), pp. 271 ff.

a verbal acrobat. Other passages are free from this,
seeming to come much more spontaneously from the
poet's heart—and no more astounding example could
be cited than Juliet's terrified soliloquy at 4. 3. 14 ff.
These stylistic differences are obvious. But they should
not be allowed to rush us into any imprudent theory
that the play must be stratified on the assumption that
a highly conceited passage was written at one time, and
a profound passage lacking in conceits was written at
a later period. Harley Granville-Barker, quoting
passages of the one kind and of the other in the first
couple of pages of his Preface to *Romeo and Juliet*,
comments thus:

By all the rules, no doubt, there should be two Shakespeares at work here. But in such a ferment as we now find
him...he may well have been capable of working on
Tuesday in one fashion, on Wednesday in another, capable
of couplet, sonnet, word-juggling, straight sober verse, or
hard-bitten prose, often as the popular story he was turning
to account and the need of the actors for the thing they and
he were so apt at seemed to demand, at times out of the new
strength breeding in him.

Again and again the play suggests an excited Shakespeare and a developing Shakespeare. It might not be
too much to say that at some points he is writing as he
used to write, and at other points he is writing as he is
going to write. At any rate, it is to be emphasized that
the fact that there are different styles at different points
does not necessarily mean that we have to do with pre-
liminary drafting and subsequent revision. On the
contrary, the very character of the 'foul papers' of
which we catch many glimpses behind the Second
Quarto, suggests an imagination working at high
pressure and subject to a single impulse. It is not
unlikely then that Shakespeare wrote this play once
and for all and within a few months. When was this?

Some would put the composition (at any rate of a first draft) in 1591, because in 1. 3 the Nurse refers to an earthquake as having taken place eleven years ago, and there was an actual earthquake in London in 1580. 'This', Sir Edmund Chambers drily remarks, 'is pressing the Nurse's interest in chronology—and Shakespeare's—rather hard.' He himself puts the play in 1595, as belonging to the lyrical group, not long before *Richard II* and *A Midsummer Night's Dream*.[1] And that, unless and until further evidence is forthcoming, is likely to remain its accepted date. We would only add that, if the Nurse's chronology be pressed a little harder, the date 1591 looks still more 'tottered', to use one of Shakespeare's favourite words. For the earthquake that shook her dovecot took place on 'Lammas Eve' (i.e. 31 July) whereas the one that shook London took place on 6 April.

*   *   *   *   *

Whatever a creative writer may take from his source or sources, he makes himself responsible for his total product and for its theme. What then is Shakespeare's *Romeo and Juliet* about?

It is about two wonderful young people who love each other, and it is about two families which hate each other. These two plot-strands are intertwined, and unless we pay due attention to both of them we shall miss the full meaning of the play—or at any rate the meaning which Shakespeare seems to have wished to convey. He may or may not have succeeded in conveying what he wanted to convey. That is a matter which will have to be discussed in due course. Meanwhile we are concerned with Shakespeare's intentions. The story of the two lovers embodies a certain well-known tradi-

[1] *William Shakespeare* (Oxford, 1930), I, pp. 345–6.

tional conception of tragedy. But that was not what Shakespeare finally wanted to leave with us. The story of the lovers is fitted into, is part of, the story of the families; and, as we leave the theatre or close the book, we are aware of quite another conception of tragedy— a more deeply satisfying conception.

THE STORY OF THE LOVERS

Romeo and Juliet are 'star-crossed'. Again and again the dialogue brings out the theme of the malignant influence of the stars on human beings. From quite early in the play we have the expression of premonitions of unhappy doom. The lovers are the predestined victims of a malicious Fate. Fortune is against them. The stars, or Fate, or Destiny, or Fortune, or whatever other specific name may be applied to the cosmic force with which we are concerned, brings the lovers together, gives them supreme happiness and self-fulfillment for a short time, and then casts them down to destruction. The spectator or reader is aware of a devastating sense of waste, and he reacts to the spectacle of the destruction of the lovers with a feeling of deep pity. Their doom is pathetic.

Fate works against the lovers in diverse ways. It works against them by arranging that they are placed in a context of family hostility. It works against them by contriving a deadly series of accidents and coincidences. It works against them through character-flaws in friends and associates of theirs.

The play is full of accident, coincidence, chance. If Friar Lawrence's letter to Romeo had reached Romeo at the time when the Friar was entitled to suppose it would—had not Friar John been unexpectedly detained in a house in Verona suspected of harbouring the plague—then all might have been different. This is but one of the sequence of chance happenings which

extends throughout the play. Shakespeare does not
want us to think of these 'accidents' as merely fortui-
tous. We cannot avoid the impression that he asks us
to think of them as intentionally arranged by Fate.
Fate deliberately works against the lovers by this means.

And then we have the family feud. Romeo with
friends, masked, presents himself at Capulet's ball. Old
Capulet himself is only too ready to forget the feud,
only too ready to take the maskers' visit as a compliment
(as normally, in any given case, it would be taken).
Tybalt hot-headedly objects. Capulet wisely pacifies
Tybalt, albeit with difficulty. But Tybalt's rancour
outlasts the evening. He seeks out Romeo, intent on
avenging what he takes to be a slight on his family's
'honour'. Romeo (with good enough reason, in all
conscience) will not fight. Mercutio—ignorant of
Romeo's love for Juliet, and thus failing to understand
Romeo's attitude—assails Tybalt. This results in
Mercutio's death; and then Romeo must needs avenge
it. Tybalt dies. Romeo is banished. Had Romeo not
been banished, the final catastrophe might never have
taken place.

Fate is here operating against Romeo and Juliet
through the fact that Tybalt and Mercutio have false
ideals, false values. Tybalt is a man whose values are
similar to those of Hotspur in *Henry IV*. He is
obsessed with the notion of 'honour', but it is not
honour in the best sense; it is a mistaken view of honour,
and it leads him into conduct which is contrary to
reason. Mercutio has essentially the same mistaken
sense of honour.

The whole fracas which results in the deaths of
Mercutio and Tybalt, and in the fatal banishment of
Romeo, is a result of the pressing of the claims of
a false sense of honour. Tybalt is to blame initially,
certainly; and Mercutio can hardly be absolved of

blame. Logic may insist that Romeo himself is to some
extent blameworthy. He should not, it may be said,
have given in to the impulse to avenge Mercutio.
Romeo had been pacific when Tybalt challenged him:
Mercutio should have let well alone: Mercutio's fate
was his own fault: and so Romeo, in his turn, should
have let well alone. But we cannot think that Shakespeare wants us to give logic its head absolutely. Romeo
started by being commendably conciliatory when
Tybalt challenged him. He acted violently only when
absolutely forced to do so by the claims of dear friendship. No doubt he should not have allowed himself to
be forced: but at least his error is much more pardonable
than that of Tybalt, and even than that of Mercutio.

Fate works against the lovers by means of the feud,
by means of accident and coincidence, and by means of
character-flaws in others. But are the lovers themselves
in any way responsible for their own doom? Is there
any error in their own behaviour, any fault or faults in
their own characters, which may be regarded as at
least partially responsible for their unhappy end?

From time to time the dialogue invites us to consider
the question, are the lovers too rash, impetuous, reckless? Friar Lawrence thinks they are. Or at any rate he
feels that they must be counselled not to be.

> Wisely and slow. They stumble that run fast.
>
> (2. 3. 95)

> These violent delights have violent ends,...
> Therefore love moderately; long love doth so:
> Too swift arrives as tardy as too slow.
>
> (2. 6. 9, 14–15)

The Friar is a very worthy man. But surely we must
hesitate long before accepting his viewpoint in these
passages as being that of Shakespeare. The Friar is
prudent; he is worldly-wise. He knows what will work

xx ROMEO AND JULIET

and what will not work. Furthermore, we must do him the justice of noting that he is, with genuine religious fervour, anxious to press the claims of the spirit against those of the flesh. But our general impression of the play as a whole forbids us to take the Friar's views as being those which Shakespeare wants to be accepted as valid. We cannot think that Shakespeare wants us to blame these two incomparable young people as being over-hasty; we cannot think that Shakespeare wants us to believe that it would have been better for them, fundamentally, if they had been more prudent, more coolly calculating. We cannot think that Shakespeare wants us to take the Friar's words as indicating the true standard by which we must judge these golden young people. One may, in one's own philosophy, value divine love as infinitely finer than human love. One may, in one's own philosophy, feel that reason, moderation, should prevail over feeling and passion. But surely, if one accepts the assumptions that Shakespeare seems to be implying in this play—if, in other words, one tries to fathom Shakespeare's intentions— one must ask what this well-meaning but dull, timid and unimaginative cleric knows of the ecstasies of a sublime passion which the play, even if it succeeds in doing nothing else, certainly succeeds in glorifying magnificently.

It may, however, be pointed out that it is not only Friar Lawrence who brings up the notion of rashness. Juliet herself says to Romeo—

> Although I joy in thee,
> I have no joy of this contract tonight:
> It is too rash, too unadvised, too sudden,
> Too like the lightning, which doth cease to be
> Ere one can say 'It lightens'. (2. 2. 116–20)

This is one of those touches of premonition by which Shakespeare, as noted above, helps to paint in the

atmosphere of Fate, of oncoming doom, which over-
hangs the play. But we are not to suppose that Juliet
intends it seriously herself or to take it as anything more
than a momentary superstitious utterance of a young
girl who, having suddenly discovered supreme
happiness, is, for a second or two, half-afraid that her
happiness is too great to last. 'Half-afraid', for she goes
on—
Sweet, goodnight:

> This bud of love, by summer's ripening breath,
> May prove a beauteous flower when next we meet.

Her worry has been but the matter of an instant. And
soon, having gone in, she is reappearing and calling
Romeo back for more words of love—not once, but
twice. We cannot think that her 'too rash, too unadvised, too sudden' is meant by Shakespeare to imply
blame.

    Is Romeo to be blamed for over-hastiness in buying
the poison? Is he to be blamed for over-hastiness in
committing his suicide? There is nothing blameworthy
about his believing Balthasar's report of Juliet's 'death'.
Romeo has no reason to doubt the news. And later,
when he sees Juliet in the tomb, she certainly seems
to be dead. It would be quite ridiculous to blame him
for supposing that in fact she is dead. And, since he
has, from his first view of her, regarded her as his
whole life, how can he be blamed by anyone of good
will for killing himself in the belief that she is dead?
There is nothing that we can hold against him here
unless we insist on the (admitted) validity of moral
conceptions that have no meaning for Shakespeare in
this play, such as that under no circumstances should
a man end his own life, or unless we press the claims of
prudent scepticism to the point of insisting that a man
is culpable if he accepts a report from his faithful
servant without verifying it, or if, seeing his loved one

lying motionless in a sepulchre, he fails to say to himself
that perhaps, despite appearances, she is not dead at all
and that perhaps, after all, he had better wait and see.
It is true that when he learns of Juliet's 'death' from
Balthasar Romeo looks 'pale and wild'. There is
emotional unbalance. But, thinking of the magnitude
of the blow he has sustained, how can we blame him?

We do not say that there are no character-flaws in
hero and heroine. On the contrary, there are, as we
shall see later. But it is not part of the basic design of
the story of the lovers that spectator or reader should
regard their fate as directly caused, even partly, by
their own character-flaws.

It seems quite clear that the tragic design which
Shakespeare intends to embody in the story of the
lovers is a design very popular in the Middle Ages—
the conception of tragedy as consisting of the malignant
operation of Fate, or Fortune, against human beings,
these human beings in no way deserving their doom.
The Middle Ages loved their various stories 'de casibus
virorum illustrium'. As Mr Howard Baker says,[1]

Tragedy in the Middle Ages was the story of a great
person's attainment of a special eminence, his brief and
precarious triumph, and his fall. Such a story naturally
took on a definite shape: its first part accounted for the
ascent of the pyramid of worldly success, its second part
viewed the man on the very top, and its final part ushered
him down the inevitable other side: the story recapitulated
in form the image of man's rise and fall upon the Wheel of
Fortune.

While the falls of illustrious men exercised this great
appeal, writers sometimes turned to the stories of

[1] *Induction to Tragedy* (University of Louisiana, 1939),
p. 155. Cf. Introduction to *Richard II* (New Shakespeare),
pp. xix–xxii.

people not of the very highest social eminence, and to private rather than public life. The Troilus and Cressida story is a case in point; and indeed Mr Nevill Coghill has declared[1] that 'the most pervasive influence, one which gave Shakespeare the definable form of tragedy that we see in *Romeo and Juliet*, came from *Troilus and Criseyde*'. Chaucer's poem is, says Mr Coghill, 'a formal tragedy on the Boethian plan'. And he goes on—

The essence of this is...a fall into wretchedness after a transient happiness. The reason given as proper to tragedy for this fall is the operation of Fortune. She turns her wheel and we rise upon it to a fickle joy; she turns it still and we fall into some awaiting Hell-mouth. Our fall has nothing to do with our deserts, for though Fortune may laugh to see pride humbled she is no less delighted to turn her wheel against the innocent. This was the shape of tragedy as Chaucer understood it when he came to write his *Troilus and Criseyde*. He passed no judgement on his faithless heroine; it was the pity of it that struck him:

Iwis, I wolde excuse hire yet for routhe.

And *Romeo and Juliet*, the critic says, is to be classified with Chaucer's poem—they are 'the two perfect examples of this form'. 'It is a form,' he continues, 'peculiarly suited to a story of unfortunate love, for love, of all our passions, seems to us the most manifestly predestined, the most pitiful in its crosses'.

As regards the story of the lovers, then, Shakespeare intends to follow the traditional pattern of the tragedy of Fate or Fortune or Destiny or the Stars, which endow human beings with great happiness (sometimes it is worldly success, power, empire, riches: here it is emotional and spiritual self-fulfilment), and then cast

[1] *The Tragedy of Romeo and Juliet* (Folio Society, London, 1950), pp. 8 ff.

them down to sorrow and to ruin. Their fall is not their own fault. They are the helpless victims of a malevolent, or at least capricious, universal force. The philosophy underlying this conception of tragedy is a profoundly pessimistic philosophy.

But the play deals not only with the lovers but also with the families.

THE STORY OF THE FAMILIES

The play ends with a reconciliation between the two warring families; and it is with the families that it begins—

> Two households, both alike in dignity,
> In fair Verona, where we lay our scene,
> From ancient grudge break to new mutiny,
> Where civil blood makes civil hands unclean.
>
> (Prol. 1–4)

The lovers are set in this context; and the Prologue indicates that, in the all-embracing pattern of the play, the fate of the lovers is meant to be regarded as subsidiary to the fate of the families. The lovers have 'misadventured piteous overthrows', but the final significance of these is that they bury the strife of the parents. The lovers die and must be buried. They are innocent victims, and we feel a sense of pathos. But at the same time the families' strife dies and is buried, and we feel that in the future all is going to be well in Verona. We have, fundamentally, a happy ending, though it is purchased at a sad cost.

If the play concerned nothing but the 'misadventured piteous overthrows' of the two young people who are the innocent victims of a malignant Fate, then we should have to say that it embodied a tragic design that Shakespeare never attempted again. In *King Lear*

there is a point at which the Earl of Gloucester declares
that

> As flies to wanton boys are we to the gods,
> They kill us for their sport.

But this is not the final message with which Shakespeare
leaves us at the end of *King Lear*. If, in *Romeo and
Juliet*, we think of the lovers' story by itself, we shall
no doubt feel that that *is* his final message here. That
pessimistic message is, in fact, the message of any
writer who sets out to deal *simpliciter* with the theme
of Fortune's wheel or with the theme of the malignant
stars which ruin men for no reason connected with
justice. That theme had been dealt with by many writers
before Shakespeare's time, and he was fully aware of it.
But in this play, handling that theme, he wanted it to
fall into place as part of another theme.

The two great protagonists of the drama are the two
families. They belong to the same city, and they should,
in the light of a moral law that we can all accept, be
bound together in a relationship of affection and co-
operation. Actually they are at daggers drawn. The
families sin, then: and they do so before the hero and
heroine are even born. It is a case of 'ancient grudge'.
The hero and heroine, living in this context, are brought
to a fatal doom which they themselves do not deserve.
But their fate brings the two families together, the feud
comes to an end, and the future of Verona looks
bright. Society is redeemed through suffering and loss.
The families are punished for their sin by the loss of
their brightest scions. The final message, then, is that
the gods are just (punishing the families as they do), and
also that the gods are charitable in the highest sense,
wishing to replace hate with love in the world. It
takes the sacrifice of the innocent to purge the guilty of
their sin and to turn strife into amity. But at least the
sacrifice of the innocent is contrived in a total design

which is ultimately regulated by both justice and mercy, in due proportion, in the forces which run the universe.

*　　*　　*　　*　　*

How far was Shakespeare successful in the carrying out of this design? The answer must be: (i) what he actually accomplished is very fine—the play is deservedly one of the most perennially popular of his works; but (ii) he did not quite succeed in doing what he set out to do, so that, in fact, as Professor Charlton has said,[1] the play 'as a pattern of the idea of tragedy... is a failure'.

The story of the two families is vitally important to the intended design, and that of the two lovers is only part of that design: yet, while the design is clearly perceptible, it seems defective, inasmuch as most of the dramatist's attention is concentrated on the lovers, his attention to the families frequently (though not invariably) appearing to be somewhat perfunctory. Thus, while the dramatist is trying to convey a certain great tragic conception (which points forward to his maturity), he succeeds, with many readers, in conveying with full conviction only a fragment of that conception—conveys in fact an impression of tragedy different from that which he finally wanted to convey. The play does not fail because it lacks design. The reason why it fails, to the extent it does, is that the author is profoundly interested in parts of the design, and he is not nearly so much interested in other parts of the design. And so the structure is lop-sided.

Two aspects of this failure which have been noted by critics may be mentioned here. One has been noted by Professor Charlton, the other by Professor Stauffer.

Professor Charlton feels, and others feel with him,

[1] *Shakespearian Tragedy* (Cambridge, 1948), p. 61.

that, while wishing the idea of Fate and the plot-element of the feud to be vitally important components of the design exercising an overwhelming compulsion upon the lovers, Shakespeare has in fact made the feud quite unconvincing and has made of the conception of Fate nothing more important than a matter of sheer bad luck.[1]

In this connexion we must, of course, avoid making the elementary mistake of treating partially non-naturalistic drama as if it were meant to be completely naturalistic. Consider the following point. When Romeo falls in love with Juliet, Shakespeare certainly means us to think, right away, of the feud as the only obstacle in the way of the lover's happiness. But before he fell in love with Juliet Romeo was, or thought he was, in love with Rosaline. It is a critical commonplace that Shakespeare wants us to contrast Romeo's love of Juliet with his earlier love of Rosaline. In the one case Romeo is, to use a convenient cliché, in love with being in love. His feeling for Rosaline, while quite sincere, is not deep, not fundamental. He is going through a fashionable stage of youthful development, thinking, behaving, and speaking in accordance with the well-established conventions that the fashion dictated. In the other case he really is in love, if any man in literature ever was. The distinction is clear. But, in successfully making this distinction, Shakespeare ignores a point which, in the light of a strictly natur-alistic interpretation, may well seem to involve unfortunate inconsistency. Romeo's love-affair with Rosaline meets with frustration. Romeo is a Montague, Rosaline a Capulet. But his frustration is not caused thereby. One may wonder why. If the feud stands in the way of his love of Juliet, why did it not stand

[1] See *Shakespearian Tragedy*, pp. 49 ff., and *Proc. Brit. Acad.* (1939), pp. 143 ff.

in the way of his love of Rosaline? It did not: or, if it did, Shakespeare makes nothing of the point. What, he tells us, actually stands in the way of Romeo's success with Rosaline is her ideal of celibacy. Apparently, despite the feud, Romeo has been able to see Rosaline and to plead his case with her. But she has refused to be moved: she has sworn that she will still (i.e. always) live chaste (i.e. unmarried). She is like Olivia in *Twelfth Night* (though Olivia set a seven-year term to her celibacy). 'She'll not be hit with Cupid's arrow.' Shakespeare disapproves of this attitude in *Twelfth Night*, as he does also (in connexion with a man) in Sonnets 3 and 11. No doubt he disapproves of it in *Romeo and Juliet* too, though he does not allow himself to comment explicitly. Indeed, in Rosaline, who is only mentioned, we have an Olivia-like character who might have been quite an interesting dramatic figure had she actually appeared. But our point is this—that a naturalistic critic may say, on the one hand, that there is an inconsistency here which is an artistic blot on the play, or he may say, on the other hand, that we cannot be expected to take the feud very seriously since it seems to have been no obstacle as regards Romeo's first love-affair. To both criticisms the reply must be that Shakespeare's plays are liable to be only partly naturalistic, and that one should always be on one's guard against applying to them critical criteria which are irrelevant to them.

Nevertheless, allowing for all this, Professor Charlton is right. Our first view of the feud on the stage involves nothing more impressive than a vulgar brawl amongst servants, some at least of whom behave in a distinctly unvalorous and ignoble manner. And then we have the heads of the houses coming in and appearing rather ridiculous. Capulet, attired in a dressing-gown, calls for an absurdly obsolete weapon, and we enjoy his wife's delightful tartness—'A crutch, a crutch! Why call you for a sword?' Montague's wife treats her lord similarly. It all seems rather trivial, rather silly. Professor Charlton notes this, and he feels that the feud is not presented by Shakespeare in such a way as to seem to be a force, working against the lovers, as terrible and as serious as the author apparently wanted it to seem. Admittedly there are places where it at least nearly seems to be such a force. But Shakespeare does not sustain the idea throughout with full conviction.

Now for the point made by Professor Stauffer.[1] Though, as we have said, it was no part of Shakespeare's consciously intended dramatic design that the hero or heroine should be held even partially responsible for their own doom owing to any character-flaws, that is not the end of the matter.

Indubitable weaknesses of character they have, and Shakespeare does not spare them in pointing these out. When the Friar tells him that he is banished, Romeo rants hysterically. He grovels on the floor. He well deserves the rebuke of the Nurse—'Stand up, stand up, stand an you be a man.' Indeed, he shows 'the unreasonable fury of a beast'. He behaves contemptibly. His conduct is infantile. And it must be noted, too, with however much regret, that Juliet is capable of behaving in a similar manner, though this is not shown on the stage. The Nurse tells us that Juliet lies 'blubbering and weeping, weeping and blubbering':

> O, she says nothing, sir, but weeps and weeps,
> And now falls on her bed, and then starts up,
> And Tybalt calls, and then on Romeo cries,
> And then down falls again.   (3. 3. 99–102)

They are two very fine young people, certainly: but

---

[1] *Shakespeare's World of Images* (New York, 1949), pp. 53 ff.

both of them are lacking, at certain points, in mature poise and balance. They are young: they are immature. Thus, while we cannot see that these defects contribute directly and demonstrably to their doom, there they are, and Shakespeare emphasizes them; so that we are left wondering what place, if any, they are supposed to have in the dramatic design. And though some critics pretend to reconcile their apparent inconsistency or obscurity, it can hardly be denied that it spells some degree of failure on Shakespeare's part. As Professor Stauffer puts it:[1]

On the surface, social evil is castigated and purged by 'Fate', which is an extra-human moral order. Yet in contrast to this often declared thesis, and by no means reconciled with it, Shakespeare intrudes a line of thinking which was to become central in his serious philosophy: that the causes of tragedy lie in the sufferers themselves. The doctrines of individual responsibility and of fate as a social Nemesis offer divergent motivations: this play may fail as serious tragedy because Shakespeare blurs the focus and never makes up his mind entirely as to who is being punished, and for what reason. Later he learned to carry differing hypotheses simultaneously, to suggest complex contradictory interactions convincingly; but this is not the effect of the double moral motivations in *Romeo and Juliet*.

Moreover, when he goes on to speak of the lovers' 'extreme rashness', of their 'surging wrong-headed impulses', and refers to the various passages which indicate the desirability of moderation and prudence, he remarks that the passages he cites 'protest too much in words, attest too little in experience'. The truth is, Shakespeare was thinking predominantly in terms of the medieval tragedy of Fortune; but the idea of the hero as partially responsible for his own fate, through defects in himself, an idea to become fundamental in later tragedies, was also present at the back of his mind. He seems to be wanting to bring this idea to the fore at certain points; but he does not succeed in accommodating it to the other theme in a convincing manner. What we actually have then is a drama of Fate involving the destruction of two innocent victims who have defects of character which are not properly worked into the pattern.

But if Shakespeare failed in these ways, wherein consists the success of the play? For, admitting that 'as a pattern of the idea of tragedy it is a failure', the fact remains that in some way or ways it is a resplendent success, being indeed one of the best-loved and most frequently quoted of the author's works.

The answer is that while the play is in certain important respects a dramatic failure, it is a great poetic success. The thing that most powerfully impressed Shakespeare's imagination as he worked on *Romeo and Juliet* was the emotional richness of the lovers' feeling for each other, and he expresses this in lines of incomparable poetic beauty. Professor Charlton and Professor Stauffer both make the same point as regards the nature of Shakespeare's triumph. 'The achievement', says Professor Charlton,[1] 'is due to the magic of Shakespeare's poetic genius and to the intermittent force of his dramatic power rather than to his grasp of the foundations of tragedy.' And he continues—

There is no need here to follow the meetings of Romeo and Juliet through the play, and to recall the spell of Shakespeare's poetry as it transports us along the rushing stream of the lovers' passion, from its sudden outbreak to its consummation in death. Romeo seals his 'dateless bargain to engrossing death', choosing shipwreck on the dashing rocks to secure peace for his 'sea-sick weary bark'. Juliet has but a word: 'I'll be brief. O happy dagger!' There is

[1] *Shakespearian Tragedy*, p. 62.

need for nothing beyond this. Shakespeare, divining their naked passion, lifts them above the world and out of life by the mere force of it. It is the sheer might of poetry.

And here is Professor Stauffer:[1]

The actual ethical energy of the drama resides in its realization of the purity and intensity of ideal love. Here there is no swerving. Both Romeo and Juliet are wholly devoted to their overpowering discovery: from the religious imagery of the wooing to the feasting imagery of the Capulet vault, when Romeo's wit plays its 'lightning before death', the power of love is idealized; and true love, as though it were a hyphenated compound, echoes through the play. Shakespeare has found skill adequate to his ambition. Nothing but the finest part of pure love inhabits his scenes of romantic enchantment.... The sense of triumph descends upon the play from a love so straight, so simple, and so certain that its very bravery transforms death and time and hatred—yes, and the accidents of Fate—into insubstantial shadows. The quick bright things remain shining and alive.

In fact the impression that remains longest in our minds after witnessing or reading the play is not an impression depending on the tragic design that Shakespeare obviously intended to produce. What remains longest in our minds is the feeling that Death has no power to destroy the beauty or the power of the feelings of the lovers for each other. What is totally successful in this play is the poetry which expresses these feelings. As one of the present editors has written elsewhere,

the poetry—it is one of Shakespeare's greatest poems—is as far from the touch of 'Time's injurious hand' as *The Song of Solomon*. And like *The Song* it deals with a situation that never palls; for all mankind love a lover, and every boy and every girl have only to listen to Romeo and Juliet to overhear their own secret thoughts, the things they wish to say

[1] *Op. cit.* p. 57.

INTRODUCTION xxxiii

to each other but can find no words for, expressed in poetry so rapturous that it stills the very beating of the heart.

The expression of the hero's love for the heroine, and of hers for him, is but a part of the fabric of the play. But it is the part that Shakespeare realizes most glowingly; and this was no doubt the reason which led the novelist George Moore to declare, not only that the play is an 'exquisite love-song', but that it is 'no more than a love-song in dialogue'.[1] Had this verdict been presented to Shakespeare himself, he would have had to say, if he accepted it, that he had failed in his artistic intentions. But at any rate, if he failed in these, he certainly succeeded in something else—in that part of his design which, to all spectators and readers since his time, has mattered above all else.

* * * * *

The play has a universal, a timeless appeal. Few remarks made in praise of Shakespeare have been so often repeated as Ben Jonson's declaration that Shakespeare wrote 'not for an age but for all time'. There is truth in this, and *Romeo and Juliet* abundantly attests it. At the same time everyone agrees that a certain amount of qualification is needed. Jonson's great-hearted enthusiasm perhaps led him into the fabrication of a slightly dangerous half-truth. Certainly *Romeo and Juliet*, like most of Shakespeare's plays, contains things that have appealed to all ages since its composition— things that no doubt will never lose their popularity. Yet it might be better to say that Shakespeare wrote, definitely for an age, many things which later ages have treasured and will treasure. For he wrote in the idioms of his own time. Some of these idioms have passed out of vogue, and the danger of the present-day reader mis-understanding certain individual passages is a very real

[1] *Confessions of a Young Man* (London, 1888), p. 233.

danger. It is nowhere more apparent than in *Romeo and Juliet*. As we have already said, some passages in the play are profound and spontaneous, while others abound in conceits and all sorts of verbal ingenuities. We must beware of thinking that passages of the latter sort must necessarily imply shallowness of feeling.

Sometimes it is clear enough that Shakespeare is using an artificial, conventional style with definite dramatic intent. The poetic inanities of the lamentations of Capulet, his wife, and the Nurse in 4. 5 are no doubt intended by Shakespeare to symbolize the poverty of their emotional life and the smallness of their spiritual stature, as contrasted with the richness and the greatness of the emotional and spiritual being of the hero and heroine. But the matter is more complicated than this.

When he wrote Juliet's soliloquy in 4. 3—the marvellous soliloquy she delivers just before taking the potion—Shakespeare was certainly confronting face to face some of the deepest feelings of the human heart, and conveying them spontaneously, profoundly, and without tricks. On the other hand, he was capable of indulging in verbal virtuosity at points where he did not intend his hearers or readers to regard the feelings expressed as in the least degree spurious. 'Some say the lark makes sweet division: This doth not so, for she divideth us.' Juliet puns in this way at a point where her feeling is intended by Shakespeare to stand forth as sincere and genuinely agonized. Many similar examples could be cited. When Juliet strings together a list of oxymorons—'Beautiful tyrant, fiend angelical, Dove-feathered raven, wolvish-ravening lamb'—she is suffering intensely. Her verbal ingenuities express genuine emotional conflict and are not to be taken as evidence of shallow feeling. When a girl in our own age is troubled by the thought that the boy she adores, though delightful to all appearance, may be at root wicked she does not usually express her heart-sick feelings like this:

> Was ever book containing such vile matter
> So fairly bound? O that deceit should dwell
> In such a gorgeous palace!   (3. 2. 83–5)

She speaks more directly, more spontaneously. But that does not mean that Shakespeare meant us to regard Juliet's feeling here as insincere or shallow, or imagined that readers in a later age might do so. Juliet was extremely fond of her cousin Tybalt. Her lover slays her cousin who is very dear to her. For a moment or two she is in the grip of a very serious emotional conflict. Shakespeare does not choose to exploit this conflict for more than a moment or so. But it is there, and while it lasts it is very powerful. In the grip of this terrible conflict Juliet expresses herself in terms that are highly ingenious, highly conceited. But this must not mislead us any more than we must allow ourselves to imagine the two young people insincere because their first conversation consists of a formally perfect sonnet divided between them. The relation of formality of expression to validity of feeling in Shakespeare's age was not in all respects the same as it is commonly taken to be now; and in listening to, or reading, Shakespeare we must be historically minded.

*   *   *   *   *

Beside Romeo Shakespeare sets the vital, irrepressible figure of Mercutio, who is equally ready with a sword, a bawdy jest, or a Queen Mab speech; and beside Juliet he sets the equally vital figure of the Nurse, who is worldly but warm-hearted, realistic and at times cynical but genuinely affectionate, and who, prattling of unseemly things as old village women will, means no harm in the world by it all. We may condemn the quarrel-

someness which impels Mercutio to fight Tybalt with
such dire results; and yet we never cease to like him,
and we readily agree that, though misguided, he meant
well. We may feel tempted to pass a rather severe verdict upon the Nurse for advising Juliet to accept
marriage with Paris; and yet, on reflection, we may
pardon her—for, quite frankly, she could see no other
solution to a grievous problem, and above all things she
desired the welfare and prosperity of her nursling. She
too, though misguided, meant well. And, despite all
her crudities, we can never forget the essential good-
heartedness of this old woman who, vulgar and earthy
as she is, looks back on past days and compresses precious
memories into words which, while brief, suggest
a loving and happy married life, with sorrow philosophically endured:

> God be with his soul,
> 'A was a merry man.
> Well, Susan is with God;
> She was too good for me. (i. 3. 20, 40)

The grief has passed, but the words are still curiously
touching. The speaker is fundamentally good-hearted.
She knows she has faults. When she declares that little
Susan was too good for her, she is speaking partly
jocularly but partly, for a second, seriously, with self-
knowledge. We warm to her here.

They are very bawdy, these two—Mercutio and the
Nurse. Yet the indelicacies, the downright obscenities,
which they and other characters indulge in are not,
properly considered, unhealthy at root. Sometimes—
notably with the Nurse—it is just a way of expressing
a hearty zest and love of life. Sometimes—notably
with Mercutio and his friends who may well reflect
a group of Inns-of-Court students in Shakespeare's
London—it is mainly a matter of sheer mental and
verbal skittishness, the delight which young men, at

all periods of history, especially when together, take in their own brilliance and in the liberty of their new-found maturity. There is not a line in the play that leaves a bad taste in the mouth of one who knows and understands anything about the mind of the Elizabethan Age, or even of the modern undergraduate.

Neither Mercutio nor the Nurse has any real com-prehension of or use for the spiritual element in roman-tic love. The love they understand is of the earth, earthy. There is nothing fundamentally unhealthy about this attitude; but they understand only a fraction, albeit an important fraction, of what Shakespeare means by love. It would be absurd to think that Shakespeare is by implication criticizing Romeo's and Juliet's conception of love, and saying that the best kind of human love is, by contrast, the love that Mer-cutio and the Nurse understand. On the one hand, neither Mercutio nor the Nurse has any knowledge of the emotional and spiritual richness which, fully realized by the hero and heroine, is conveyed by them in passage after passage of exquisite poetry: and, on the other hand, the lovers are not in the least degree refugees from the physical facts of life. Romeo takes delight in speaking golden words to his beloved, but that is not enough; it is the rope-ladder which is the convoy 'to the high topgallant of his joy'. As for Juliet, her 'Gallop apace, you fiery-footed steeds' is clearly, honestly, and passionately expressive of a love that has nothing in the least namby-pamby about it. She is impatient to be taught by Night 'how to lose a winning match'. Both Romeo and Juliet are magnificent in the expression of a love in which spiritual and physical elements are mingled as they should be. Mercutio and the Nurse know only part of the truth: Romeo and Juliet know it all.   G. I. D.

1953

THE STAGE-HISTORY OF *ROMEO AND JULIET*

This play has probably been the most popular after *Hamlet* of all Shakespeare's plays on the English stage, and anything approaching a full chronicle is impossible in a short space.

The title-pages of all the three extant Quartos (1597, 1599, and 1609) speak of many performances by Shakespeare's Company, described as the Lord of Hunsdon's (Q1), the Lord Chamberlain's (Q2), and 'the Kings Maiesties Seruants' (Q3), adding 'at the Globe'. Its popularity, affirmed by Q1's 'with great applause', is attested by the frequent allusions in literature, from Marston's *Scourge of Villany*, 1598, through John Weever's *Epigrams*, 1599, and *The Return from Parnassus*, Part I (?1599), in which a character's misquotation of 2. 4. 41 is hailed as 'Romeo and Juliet', to L. Digges's memorial verses in F1, which declares it 'impossible' for 'some new strain t'outdo | Passions of Juliet and Romeo'.[1] Yet no actual record of performances before the Restoration survives; it is therefore impossible to say how long its vogue lasted before the closing of the theatres in 1642.

At the Restoration a warrant of the Lord Chamberlain of 12 December 1660 gave exclusive acting rights in the play to D'Avenant's Company. They performed it first on 1 March 1662, when Pepys thought it 'a play of itself the worst that ever I heard, and the worst acted

---

[1] v. Chambers, *William Shakespeare; Facts and Problems* (1930), ii. 195, 199, 200 and 232.

[2] Printed in Allardyce Nicoll, *History of Restoration Drama* (1923), pp. 314–15.

that ever I saw these people do'. Yet Betterton was
playing Mercutio to Harris's Romeo, and Miss
Saunderson (Mrs Betterton-to-be) was Juliet. Downes
tells us that 'some time after' it was altered by James
Howard so as to end happily with the lovers alive,
and that when the tragedy was revived again the two
versions were played alternately, 'Tragical one day, and
Tragi-comical another'[1]—a curious side-light on
Pepys's verdict on the true version and contemporary
taste in general. Downes is our only witness even to the
existence of Howard's version, but his mysterious in-
clusion of 'Count Paris' wife, by Mrs Holden' in the
cast may best be explained as indicating further perversions of Shakespeare in Howard's adaptation.

Of the genuine play we hear nothing more for over
eighty years. It was supplanted by a strange hotch-potch
of garbled Shakespeare matter and new invention,
Otway's *Caius Marius*, first shown in Dorset Garden
in 1680. This stole, as the Prologue admitted, half its
material from *Romeo and Juliet*; but the conflict of
Marius and 'Sylla' in Republican Rome took the place
of the Montague-Capulet feud in Verona. The two
lovers are now the son of Marius and Lavinia, daughter
of Metellus, Sylla's chief supporter, who orders her to
marry Sylla; and their tragedy is interwoven into the
larger conflict. The Nurse and a very poor substitute
for Mercutio figure in the play, but there is no equivalent of Tybalt. Betterton played Caius Marius, a far
more important character than Old Montague in
Shakespeare, Smith and Mrs Barry were the lovers, and
James Nokes made a great hit as the Nurse. The whole
is an incongruous mixture in which the 'rifled'
Shakespearian matter is so mangled that it does not
'shine amidst the baser dross', as the Prologue claims

[1] John Downes, *Roscius Anglicanus*, ed. Montague
Summers, p. 22.

it will.[1] Yet it was acted twenty-nine times between 1701 and 1735 to the exclusion from the stage of the original play.

On 11 September 1744 a *Romeo and Juliet* by Theophilus Cibber was shown at the Haymarket; in spite of many alterations of the original, and unhappy reversions from time to time to Otway, it at least approached much nearer to the genuine Shakespeare play. The main independent alterations are in Act 1, where, the lovers being already in love as in Otway, there is no Rosaline, and no ball-room scene. After 2. 3, Shakespearian ordering and wording are largely in control, but lines borrowed from the banished Valentine in *The Two Gentlemen of Verona* are given to Romeo, a longish scene from Otway is interpolated after the lovers' farewell, and Cibber transcribes Otway verbatim in adopting his invention of the awaking of Juliet in the monument before Romeo dies. The play, acted ten times in 1744, proved so popular an item that, the *General Advertiser* tells us, distinguished people were crowded out of the boxes into pit and gallery on the first night. Cibber acted Romeo and his sister Jenny Juliet.[2]

On 29 November 1748 Garrick at Drury Lane put on the first truly Shakespearian *Romeo and Juliet* seen since the initial revival of 1662, though still adapted by himself. He did not act in it himself, but let Spranger Barry play Romeo to Mrs Cibber's Juliet, with Woodward as Mercutio. From this year onwards till the present day the play has never been long off the London stage. From 1750 to 1800 the rival theatre in Covent

[1] For further details see Hazelton Spencer (1927), *Shakespeare Improved*, pp. 292–8; G. C. D. Odell (1921), *Shakespeare from Betterton to Irving*, i. 51–3.

[2] Cf. John Genest, *Some Account of the English Stage, 1660–1830* (1832), iv. 167–9; G. C. D. Odell, *Shakespeare from Betterton to Irving* (1921), i. 341–3.

Garden staged it every year except 1780, a striking
proof of its popularity, since no actor of eminence but
Barry appeared in it there. It was first seen there for
five nights from 1 March 1750, with Lee and Dyer to
play Romeo and Mercutio, and the youthful Miss G.A.
Bellamy making her début as Juliet. This same year
a quarrel of Barry and Mrs Cibber with Garrick and
their desertion to Covent Garden initiated a competition between the two theatres in the play which went
on for many years. On 28 September, Barry and
Mrs Cibber, with Macklin as Mercutio and Mrs
Macklin as the Nurse, were playing the title-roles at
Covent Garden, while Garrick the same night, having
captured Miss Bellamy for his Juliet, acted Romeo at
Drury Lane. For twelve days the contest raged, with
charges and countercharges in the Prologues by
Garrick and Barry; then Covent Garden threw in its
hand, it was said because Mrs Cibber's endurance gave
out, while Garrick added a thirteenth night before
passing to another play.

This victory did not end the competition. Parts
changed hands and actors shifted from theatre to
theatre, while rival productions went on for many
years in both theatres. As manager Garrick put on the
play in November and December, 1750, five times in
1751, and each year later till 1773. In 1753 Mrs
Cibber rejoined Garrick as Juliet at Drury Lane, and
Barry brought in Miss Nossiter at Covent Garden.
In 1754 Barry recaptured Miss Bellamy, who played
the part there each year till 1758. In 1756, Miss
Pritchard, new to the stage, scored a triumph as Juliet
at Drury Lane, and she and Mrs Cibber alternated in
the part each year till 1761. From 1761, Garrick
himself ceased to play Romeo; but in April that year
acted as Mercutio three times. We last hear of Mrs Cibber as Juliet in 1762; but Miss Bellamy continued in

the role at Covent Garden till 1769. Barry, rejoining
Garrick in 1766, brought with him Mrs Dancer,
his Juliet at the Haymarket the next year, and later
his wife; he gave his last Romeo to her Juliet at
Drury Lane in April 1768. Woodward continued his
successes as Mercutio at Covent Garden till 1776,
Dodd being his opposite number at Drury Lane from
1765 on.

Opinion long remained divided on the relative
merits of the chief performers of 1750. Barry possessed
peculiar advantages in a face and voice well suited to
a Romeo, but owed his finest strokes to his previous
pupillage in tragic parts under Garrick. The latter's
'superior grace of attitude, vivacity of countenance, and
fire of expression' made up for the unsuitability of his
figure and heavy features. Miss Bellamy won all hearts
by her naturalness and romantic ardour of love; yet
Mrs Cibber extorted 'admiration' by her forcibleness.
Woodward as Mercutio proved 'a tower of strength',
says Murphy, as his unbroken successes prove. Macklin, however, for all his unattractive face and manner
was, according to Gentleman, 'well received', and he
claimed it as one of his favourite parts.[1]

Garrick's version, though much nearer the original
than any previous, included some alterations, old and
new. It retained Otway's popular innovation of
Juliet's revival before Romeo's death, but entirely
rewrote the dialogue here at much greater length in poor
verse of his own. Gentleman, imagining it Garrick's

---

[1] For quoted remarks, see Francis Gentleman, *Dramatic
Censor* (1770), i. 189, 191, 193; Arthur Murphy, *Life of
Garrick* (1801), i. 193; and cf. also Genest, *op. cit.* iv.
316–17; A. C. Sprague, *Shakespeare and the Actors* (1944),
301–3, 315–16; Margaret Barton, *Garrick* (1948), 122,
134; and McQueen Pope, *Theatre Royal, Drury Lane*
(1945), 171–2.

invention, called it 'a change of infinite merit';[1] it
survived on the English stage till 1845 and was again
used in Charles Wyndham's production at the Crystal
Palace in March 1875. As in Otway and Cibber, the
lovers have fallen for each other before the play begins,
but the ball-room scene is restored.[2] At the end
Garrick added a funeral procession with a dirge for
Juliet: and this too proved so popular as to be retained
for the best part of a century. As late as 1878 Fanny
Kemble can only say she believes that it is at last
finally suppressed.[3]

Garrick's influence on the fortunes of the play did
not quite end with his retirement from the Drury Lane
management at midsummer, 1776. When, in December, Sheridan put on the play there, Garrick not only
chose Mrs Robinson as Juliet, initiating thus her brief
triumphant career, but himself coached her in the part
at the rehearsals, himself acting the whole of Romeo.
But from now on the play remained chiefly in the hands
of relatively lesser lights, among whom Wroughton and
Elliston may be mentioned among the Romeos, and
Miss Farren (first at Drury Lane in May 1781) and
Mrs Jordan (first at Drury Lane in April 1796) as
Juliets. In London, after previous performances in
York and Bath, Elliston's first Romeo was at the Hay-
market in September 1796; he did the part again at
Drury Lane in 1805, 1806 and 1808; but from 1807 to
1822 he played Mercutio instead at five different
revivals. The greatest actors, however, between

---

[1] Gentleman, op. cit. i. 187.
[2] For the Garrick version, v. Genest, op. cit. iv. 262–3;
Odell, op. cit. i. 343–7; for the dialogue on Juliet's awaking,
v. also Furness, Variorum Shakespeare ed. of the play,
395–6, and History of Shakespearean Production (Arts
Council of Great Britain, 1947), p. 13 (no. 33).
[3] Record of a Girlhood (1878), i. 33.

Garrick and Macready largely neglected the play;
J. P. Kemble was only seen thrice, Edmund Kean
twice and Mrs Siddons once in London in the title
parts. As manager, J. P. Kemble put on the play in
1788, 1789 and 1796, though Genest omits the 1788
revival. On 17 and 18 November he acted Romeo to
Mrs Farmer's Juliet,[1] and on 11 May 1789 to Mrs
Siddons's who also played the part some six times in the
provinces. Thereafter both ceased to handle these
parts, in which they were never at their best, both
being, in Boaden's view, of too thoughtful and
dignified a cast of features to express the passionate
abandonment of Shakespeare's young lovers.[2]

Very different was the reception of the younger
brother, Charles, who, in Leigh Hunt's view, was
'the first performer on the stage' in the character of
'the tender lover'.[3] He first appeared in the play as
Paris (April and September 1796 at Drury Lane and
the Haymarket). But when J. P. Kemble, still un-
daunted, presented *Romeo and Juliet* as his first
Shakespeare play on taking over the management of
Covent Garden (19 September 1803), he wisely
handed over Romeo to Charles, with Mrs H. Siddons
as his Juliet; and Charles continued the role in the
many later revivals there from 1805 to 1828, Miss
O'Neill (in 1815, 1816 and 1817) being by far the
greatest of his many Juliets. When, however, on

[1] For the correction of Genest here, v. Herschel Baker,
John Philip Kemble (1942), p. 128; I owe some further
details about Kemble and Mrs Siddons to Mr C. B. Hogan,
to whom I am also indebted for checking the whole of my
account for the eighteenth century.
[2] J. Boaden, *J. P. Kemble* (1825), i. 419, 437; cf. the not
essentially different verdict in Thos. Campbell, *Life of Mrs
Siddons* (1834), ii. 159.
[3] Cited by Joseph Knight in *D.N.B.* x. 1255/1.

5 October 1829, C. Kemble put on the play to help
repair the bankrupt finances of Covent Garden, he
scored a still greater success as Mercutio, 'perhaps his
greatest part', says Joseph Knight, while his youthful
daughter Fanny made a triumphant début on the
stage as Juliet.[1] On 10 March 1836 he again was
Mercutio, when Helen Faucit, another of the great
stage Juliets, first acted this part.

Edmund Kean's one and only Romeo, in January
1815, first with Mrs Bartley and then with Miss Kelly,
as Juliet, was on the whole a failure; after a crowded
house the first night, the audience diminished daily
for the subsequent eight days of its short run. He was
little suited for the part; his rendering, said Hazlitt,
'had nothing of the lover in it'. His production also
suffered from comparison with the Covent Garden
revival the previous October in which Miss O'Neill
first appeared as Juliet. 'Mr Kean,' was Hazlitt's
comment, 'affords a never-failing source of observation
and discussion; we can only *praise* Miss O'Neill.' But
he admired his acting in the scene after Romeo learns
of his banishment, and in 'his dying convulsion'.[2]
Kean never attempted the part again. In December
1828 he handed it to his son Charles, a youth of seventeen, with Miss Phillips as Juliet; and young Kean
again acted the part at the Haymarket the next year
(7 October) to Miss Kelly's Juliet,[3] while in 1841 he
and Ellen Tree again appeared as the lovers at the
Haymarket.[4]

[1] v. *D.N.B.* x. 1254/2; Genest, *op. cit.* ix. 511–12; Fanny
Kemble, *op. cit.* ii. 5–27; and *History of Shakespearean Production*, p. 15 (no. 47).

[2] Hazlitt, *Review of the English Stage*, 1818 (collected
Works, ed. Waller and Glover, vol. viii, pp. 209–10).

[3] Genest, *op. cit.* ix. 491.

[4] v. William Archer, *Macready* (1890), p. 128.

Meanwhile Macready had established himself as
chief successor to Kemble and Kean. It was as Romeo
that he first appeared on the stage, on 7 June 1810,
in Birmingham. Though only seventeen, he acted the
part with conspicuous success, as also again in Bath in
1814–15 and 1816. Yet in London he only played
Romeo twice. He substituted for Charles Kemble
on 15 December 1817 with Miss O'Neill as Juliet
at Covent Garden, and won great applause; while he
sustained the role in his own right there for two nights
in January 1822. He also put on the play (for two
nights from 30 April 1838) as manager of Covent
Garden, but now played Friar Lawrence to J. R.
Anderson's Romeo and Miss Faucit's Juliet.[1] The
latter again played the part with Anderson at Drury
Lane in January 1852, and finally with Barry Sullivan
at the Haymarket in June 1855. A production at the
Haymarket which ran in all to over eighty performances
between 29 December 1845 and 11 July 1846
established Charlotte Cushman's fame when she acted
Romeo to her sister Susan's Juliet, and she played
Romeo there again at the end of January 1855 with
Ada Swanborough as Juliet. The feat of a female
Romeo had been previously performed by Ellen Tree
between 1829 and 1836, and was repeated by
Mrs Davenport (Fanny Vining) at the Theatre Royal,
Marylebone in 1849, and by Ada Swanborough at
the Strand Theatre in April 1864.[2] The Cushman

[1] See for details *Macready's Reminiscences*, ed. Sir
Frederick Pollock (1875), i. 41, 88, 91, 113, 156; Archer,
op. cit. 17, 27, 42–3, 64, 147, 203–4 n.; *Diaries of Macready*
ed. William Toynbee (1912) i. 455.

[2] For Ellen Tree's Romeo, v. F. A. Kemble, *op. cit.*
ii. 27–8 (Covent Garden the only clue to the date); for that
of the others, v. Odell, *op. cit.* ii. 245, 247, 254, 272, 314, and
Who's Who in the Theatre (1947), p. 1710.

sisters' revival was further notable for its restoration
of the Shakespearian text in its entirety, thereby dis-
placing in particular the death-scene with Juliet's
revival before Romeo expires, which had ousted Shakespeare's since Otway's invention of it in 1680. The
claim of doing this before has been made for Madame
Vestris,[1] but if she did, it had no lasting effect. The
example of the Cushmans, however, was followed by
Samuel Phelps in his first production of the play, and
henceforward the Garrick version disappeared from the
stage. Phelps as manager of Sadler Wells gave five
separate revivals of the play there (1846-62); but he
acted Mercutio throughout. The star-crossed lovers in
his first production (for fifteen nights from 16 September
1846 onwards) were Creswick and Miss Addison; in
March 1861 they were Hermann Vezin and Mrs
Vezin. In 1846, Mrs Marston made an admirable
Nurse, and the cast as a whole was a very good one;
but the revival lacked 'the flash of genius' of Charlotte
Cushman's.[2] Phelps's two revivals in February and
September-October 1859 were followed by a com-
mand performance at Windsor Castle on 30 November.
His last production of the play was on 1 February
1862, in the last year of his management of the
theatre.

For the next two decades Adelaide Neilson was the
most popular of the Juliets, first in London in 1865,
and last in 1879; and she created an even greater
furore in America in her four visits from 1872 to
1879, so that to Professor Odell she is 'the great
Juliet' to be set on a par with Mrs Siddons as Lady
Macbeth.[3] Her Romeos in London included George
Rignold at the Queen's Theatre, September 1872, and

---

[1] v. Odell, *op. cit.* ii. 191, 266, 272.
[2] Cf. Odell, *op. cit.* ii. 272.
[3] *Op. cit.* ii. 258.

H. B. Conway and William Terriss at the Haymarket, January 1876, and July 1879. Terriss had previously acted Romeo with Miss Wallis as Juliet at Drury Lane in December 1874. On 8 March 1882 Irving put on the play at the Lyceum, acting Romeo to Ellen Terry's Juliet and William Terriss's Mercutio, with Mrs Stirling as the Nurse, and George Alexander, later followed by F. R. Benson, as Paris. It was Irving's first great Shakespearian production, and the most elaborate of all, with some masterly stage effects; and it ran for over 150 nights in all, going on the whole season, and opening the season of 1882–3. But on the side of acting it was not an outstanding revival, though Mrs Stirling was a superb Nurse; for neither of the principals excelled in their parts, as Ellen Terry realized.[1] More memorable in this respect was the Lyceum production from 1 November 1884 when, Irving being in America, William Terriss and Mary Anderson acted the lovers and won immense praise. Meanwhile Forbes-Robertson had appeared as Romeo at the Court Theatre on 26 March 1881, somewhat handicapped by the Polish accent of Helena Modjeska, otherwise a Juliet of considerable charm. In 1895, when he presented the play at the Lyceum from 21 September, with music by Edward German, he felt himself to have been lacking in 'fire and the buoyance of youth', while Mrs Patrick Campbell, hardly a great Juliet at her best, suffered from illness the first night, and Charles Coghlan, repeating Mercutio after many years' absence from London, was nervous and acted

---

[1] See for all this Ellen Terry, *The Story of my Life*, 2nd ed., pp. 208–15; Percy Fitzgerald, *Henry Irving* (1893), pp. 188–90; Harold Child in *D.N.B.*, 2nd Supplement (1912), ii. 349/2; for the staging, Ellen Terry, *op. cit.* p. 215; Odell, ii. 426–7; *History of Shakespearean Production*, p. 20.

feebly.[1] Yet on the whole the revival was a success. When Forbes-Robertson acted in New York with Mary Anderson in November 1885 Professor Odell declares him to have been 'the best Romeo', and the production 'the finest' he ever saw.[2]

The present century has seen numerous productions. In the early years the Romeos of Lewis Waller (Imperial Theatre, 1905), Matheson Lang (Lyceum, 1908) and Harcourt Williams (New Prince's, 1913) may be mentioned. From America E. H. Sothern came with Julia Marlowe to the Waldorf Theatre in May 1907. On 30 June 1913 Beerbohm Tree produced the play at His Majesty's with his usual lavish splendour, acting Mercutio with Phyllis Neilson-Terry as Juliet and Philip Merivale as Romeo, while at the Lyric on 12 April 1919 Ellen Terry at the age of seventy-one made her last appearance in a Shakespeare play as the Nurse, Leon Quartermaine doing Mercutio. The Norwich Players under Nugent Monck performed the play in 1920 and again in 1925 and 1933; while the last thirty years have seen John Gielgud acting Romeo to the Juliets of Gwen Ffrangcon-Davies (Regent Theatre, 1924), Adèle Dixon ('Old Vic', 1929) and Peggy Ashcroft (New Theatre, 1935). The last of these revivals saw Laurence Olivier as Romeo at the start (17 October) and Gielgud as Mercutio; but in November they exchanged parts.[3] Edith Evans was the Nurse, as she had been in April, 1926 at this theatre, when Frank Vosper was Romeo, Baliol Holloway Mercutio,

[1] Cf. Sir J. Forbes-Robertson, *A Player under Three Reigns* (1925), pp. 103–4; 165–6; Odell, *op. cit.* ii. 377; G. B. Shaw, *Dramatic Opinions and Essays* (1907), i. 185–93.

[2] G. C. D. Odell, *Annals of the New York Stage*, xiii. 20.

[3] Cf. Gordon Crosse, *Shakespearean Playgoing, 1890–1952* (1953), p. 142; *History of Shakespearean Production*, p. 25 (no. 98).

and Nell Carter Juliet. The play had been Gielgud's first production—for the Oxford University Dramatic Society in February, 1932, when Edith Evans had been the Nurse and Peggy Ashcroft Juliet. The latter was seen the next month at the Old Vic in the same role, with Marius Goring as Romeo.[1] The Old Vic also presented the play in 1928 (Eric Portman, Romeo; Ernest Milton, Mercutio; Jean Forbes-Robertson, Juliet). In its latest productions Robert Donat and Constance Cummings in 1939, and in 1952 (in Edinburgh and London) Alan Badel and Claire Bloom were the principals. In 1932 the play was shown at the Kingsway and Embassy theatres as well as at the Old Vic, Joyce Bland, who had previously acted the heroine at Stratford, playing Juliet at the Embassy.

The play had been seen at Stratford in the 1864 tercentenary celebrations before there was a theatre there. After the building of the Memorial Theatre in 1879 it was put on there fifteen times (1882–1919), three times in the Picture House after the fire of 1926, and seven times since has been staged in the New Memorial Theatre. In 1882 Edward Compton played Mercutio to F. W. Wyndham's Romeo and Virginia Bateman's Juliet. For the revivals from 1888 to 1915 Benson was responsible as the Managing Director; he and his wife were the lovers, except in 1893, when George Hippisley took his place during his illness, and in 1908, when Stratford staged a guest production with Henry Ainley and Constance Collier in the title parts. Benson had first acted Romeo in an unsuccessful amateur production got up by himself at the Imperial Theatre in 1881; in Stratford his revivals were a series of popular successes. In 1919 under Bridges-Adams's management Basil Rathbone was Romeo, Joyce Carey

---

[1] *Op. cit.* p. 29 (no. 111); p. 25 (no. 97).

Juliet, and Murray Carrington Mercutio. More recent years have seen many different actors in all the principal parts. The latest production was by Peter Brook in 1947.

In America the play was first acted in New York in January 1754, with Rigby and Mrs Hallam as the lovers. It was not infrequently produced in other cities,[1] though only twelve times in New York, in the eighteenth century; but the nineteenth century saw it in the heyday of its popularity, each year from 1839 to 1894 and two later years yielding revivals in New York, mostly several different ones, and only seven years before 1839 being without any.[2] Its vogue continued in the present century, though with fewer revivals. Booth's Theatre opened with a ten weeks' run of the play from 3 February to 10 April 1869 (Edwin Booth and Mary McVickers in the title parts), and closed with it as its last play (Maurice Barrymore the Romeo and Madame Modjeska the Juliet) on 30 April 1883.[3] Charlotte Cushman (anticipated by Lydia Kelly in 1829) created a rage for female Romeos for over thirty years from 1839, of whom Mrs H. B. Conway, the fourteenth in succession, was the most persistent, while Fay Templeton came at the tail of the procession in 1875. Adelaide Neilson and Mary Anderson stand out among the Juliets of the later years, and Julia Marlowe in the early twentieth century. As in England, there were no quite comparable Romeos, but Edwin Booth

[1] Mr C. B. Hogan (privately).

[2] v. G. C. D. Odell, *Annals of the New York Stage*, *passim*; *Best Plays of 1899–1909* (1944) and *Best Plays of 1909–19* (1945) ed. R. B. Mantell and Garrison Sherwood, *passim*; Mr C. B. Hogan tells me of revivals in 1897, and 1899.

[3] v. Odell, *op. cit.* viii. 424–5; xii. 26; Richard Lockridge, *The Darling of Misfortune* (1932), p. 183.

and Lawrence Barrett were the most successful. The play provided what must have been the oddest of any production in the history of the theatre on 31 May 1877, when George Rignold was billed to act Romeo to seven different Juliets in successive scenes, though Adelaide Neilson failed to appear on the balcony, her place being taken by one of the other six.[1] In 1937, from 2–4 December the Playhouse, Pasadena, California, completed its presentation of the whole Shakespeare canon by staging our play with a sixteen-year-old actor of Romeo and a Juliet aged only fourteen.

C. B. Young

1953

[1] v. Odell, *op. cit.* x. 181; Brander Matthews, *Playwrights and Playmaking, and other Studies of the Stage* (1923), pp. 130–1.

TO THE READER

The following is a brief description of the punctuation and other typographical devices employed in the text, which have been more fully explained in the *Note on Punctuation* and the *Textual Introduction* to be found in *The Tempest* volume:

A single bracket at the beginning of a speech signifies an 'aside.'

Four dots represent a *full stop* in the original, except when it occurs at the end of a speech, and they mark a long pause. Original *colons* or *semicolons*, which denote a somewhat shorter pause, are retained, or represented as three dots when they appear to possess special dramatic significance. Similarly, significant *commas* have been given as dashes.

Round brackets are taken from the original, and mark a significant change of voice; when the original brackets seem to imply little more than the drop in tone accompanying parenthesis, they are conveyed by commas or dashes.

Single inverted commas (' ') are editorial; double ones (" ") derive from the original, where they are used to draw attention to maxims, quotations, etc.

The reference number for the first line is given at the head of each page. Numerals in square brackets are placed at the beginning of the traditional acts and scenes.

THE
MOST EX=
cellent and lamentable
Tragedie, of Romeo
and Iuliet.

Newly corrected, augmented, and
amended:

As it hath bene sundry times publiquely acted, by the
right Honourable the Lord Chamberlaine
his Seruants.

LONDON
Printed by Thomas Creede, for Cuthbert Burby, and are to
be sold at his shop neare the Exchange.
1599.

The scene: Verona and Mantua

CHARACTERS IN THE PLAY

ESCALUS, *prince of Verona*
PARIS, *a young nobleman, kinsman to the prince*
MONTAGUE } *heads of two houses at enmity with each*
CAPULET } *other*
An old man, kinsman to Capulet
ROMEO, *son to Montague*
MERCUTIO, *kinsman to the prince, and friend to Romeo*
BENVOLIO, *nephew to Montague, and friend to Romeo*
TYBALT, *nephew to Lady Capulet*
FRIAR LAWRENCE, *a Franciscan*
FRIAR JOHN, *of the same order*
BALTHASAR, *servant to Romeo*
SAMPSON }
GREGORY } *servants to Capulet*
PETER, *servant to Juliet's Nurse*
ABRAHAM, *servant to Montague*
An Apothecary
Three Musicians
Page to Paris, another Page, an Officer
LADY MONTAGUE, *wife to Montague*
LADY CAPULET, *wife to Capulet*
JULIET, *daughter to Capulet*
Nurse to Juliet

Citizens, Kinsfolk of both houses, Guards, Watchmen, Servants and Attendants

CHORUS

ROMEO AND JULIET

The Prologue

Enter Chorus

Chorus. Two households, both alike in dignity,
  In fair Verona, where we lay our scene,
From ancient grudge break to new mutiny,
  Where civil blood makes civil hands unclean.
From forth the fatal loins of these two foes
  A pair of star-crossed lovers take their life;
Whose misadventured piteous overthrows
  Doth with their death bury their parents' strife.
The fearful passage of their death-marked love,
  And the continuance of their parents' rage,   10
Which, but their children's end, nought could remove,
  Is now the two hours' traffic of our stage;
The which if you with patient ears attend,
What here shall miss, our toil shall strive to mend.

                                                    [*exit*

[I. I.]   *Verona. A public place*

  '*Enter* SAMPSON *and* GREGORY *of the house of*
       CAPULET, *with swords and bucklers*'

  Sampson. Gregory, on my word we'll not carry coals.
  Gregory. No, for then we should be colliers.
  Sampson. I mean, an we be in choler we'll draw.
  Gregory. Ay, while you live draw your neck out of
collar.

Sampson. I strike quickly, being moved.

Gregory. But thou art not quickly moved to strike.

Sampson. A dog of the house of Montague moves me.

Gregory. To move is to stir, and to be valiant is to
10 stand: therefore if thou art moved thou runn'st away.

Sampson. A dog of that house shall move me to stand:
I will take the wall of any man or maid of Montague's.

Gregory. That shows thee a weak slave, for the
weakest goes to the wall.

Sampson. 'Tis true, and therefore women, being the
weaker vessels, are ever thrust to the wall: therefore
I will push Montague's men from the wall, and thrust
his maids to the wall.

Gregory. The quarrel is between our masters, and us
20 their men.

Sampson. 'Tis all one; I will show myself a tyrant:
when I have fought with the men, I will be cruel with
the maids; I will cut off their heads.

Gregory. The heads of the maids?

Sampson. Ay, the heads of the maids, or their maiden-
heads; take it in what sense thou wilt.

Gregory. They must take it in sense that feel it.

Sampson. Me they shall feel while I am able to stand,
and 'tis known I am a pretty piece of flesh.

30 *Gregory.* 'Tis well thou art not fish; if thou hadst,
thou hadst been poor John. Draw thy tool; here comes
two of the house of Montagues.

Enter ABRAHAM and another serving man

Sampson. My naked weapon is out: quarrel; I will
back thee.

Gregory. How? Turn thy back and run?

Sampson. Fear me not.

Gregory. No, marry; I fear thee!

Sampson. Let us take the law of our sides; let them begin.

Gregory. I will frown as I pass by, and let them take it 40
as they list.

Sampson. Nay, as they dare. I will bite my thumb at
them, which is disgrace to them if they bear it.

Abraham. Do you bite your thumb at us, sir?

Sampson. I do bite my thumb, sir.

Abraham. Do you bite your thumb at us, sir?

(*Sampson.* Is the law of our side if I say ay?

(*Gregory.* No.

Sampson. No, sir, I do not bite my thumb at you, sir,
but I bite my thumb, sir.   50

Gregory. Do you quarrel, sir?

Abraham. Quarrel, sir? No, sir.

Sampson. But if you do, sir, I am for you: I serve as
good a man as you.

Abraham. No better.

Sampson. Well, sir.

'*Enter BENVOLIO*' *on one side,* TYBALT *on the other*

(*Gregory* [*seeing Tybalt*]. Say 'better': here comes
one of my master's kinsmen.

Sampson. Yes, better, sir.

Abraham. You lie.   60

Sampson. Draw, if you be men. Gregory, remember
thy washing blow.   ['*they fight*'

Benvolio [*intervening from behind*]. Part, fools!
Put up your swords; you know not what you do.

TYBALT *comes up*

Tybalt. What, art thou drawn among these
        heartless hinds?
Turn thee, Benvolio; look upon thy death.

Benvolio. I do but keep the peace: put up
    thy sword,
Or manage it to part these men with me.
  Tybalt. What, drawn, and talk of peace? I hate
    the word,.
70 As I hate hell, all Montagues, and thee:
Have at thee, coward.

*They fight. Enter several of both houses, joining in the
fray. Then 'enter three or four Citizens with clubs or
partisans', and an Officer*

  Officer. Clubs, bills, and partisans! Strike, beat
    them down.
Down with the Capulets, down with the Montagues!

  '*Enter old* CAPULET *in his gown, and his wife*'

Capulet. What noise is this? Give me my long
    sword, ho!
Lady Capulet. A crutch, a crutch! Why call you for
    a sword?
Capulet. My sword, I say! Old Montague is come,
And flourishes his blade in spite of me.

    '*Enter old* MONTAGUE *and his wife*'

Montague. Thou villain Capulet!—Hold me not, let
    me go.
Lady Montague. Thou shalt not stir one foot to seek
    a foe.

   '*Enter* PRINCE ESCALUS, *with his train*'

80   *Prince.* Rebellious subjects, enemies to peace,
Profaners of this neighbour-stainéd steel,—
Will they not hear? What ho! you men, you beasts,
That quench the fire of your pernicious rage

With purple fountains issuing from your veins,
On pain of torture, from those bloody hands
Throw your mistempered weapons to the ground,
And hear the sentence of your movéd prince.
Three civil brawls, bred of an airy word
By thee, old Capulet, and Montague,
Have thrice disturbed the quiet of our streets,   90
And made Verona's ancient citizens
Cast by their grave beseeming ornaments
To wield old partisans, in hands as old,
Cankered with peace, to part your cankered hate:
If ever you disturb our streets again,
Your lives shall pay the forfeit of the peace.
For this time, all the rest depart away:
You, Capulet, shall go along with me;
And, Montague, come you this afternoon,
To know our farther pleasure in this case,   100
To old Freetown, our common judgement-place.
Once more, on pain of death, all men depart.
[*all but Montague, Lady Montague, and Benvolio depart*
  Montague. Who set this ancient quarrel new abroach?
Speak, nephew, were you by when it began?
  Benvolio. Here were the servants of your adversary
And yours, close fighting ere I did approach:
I drew to part them; in the instant came
The fiery Tybalt, with his sword prepared,
Which, as he breathed defiance to my ears,
He swung about his head, and cut the winds,   110
Who, nothing hurt withal, hissed him in scorn:.
While we were interchanging thrusts and blows,
Came more and more, and fought on part and part,
Till the prince came, who parted either part.
  Lady Montague. O where is Romeo? Saw you
      him today?

Right glad I am he was not at this fray.

  Benvolio. Madam, an hour before the
      worshipped sun
Peered forth the golden window of the east,
A troubled mind drave me to walk abroad,
120 Where, underneath the grove of sycamore
That westward rooteth from this city's side,
So early walking did I see your son:
Towards him I made, but he was ware of me,
And stole into the covert of the wood:
I, measuring his affections by my own,
Which then most sought where most might not
      be found,
Being one too many by my weary self,
Pursued my humour, not pursuing his,
And gladly shunned who gladly fled from me.

130   *Montague.* Many a morning hath he there
      been seen,
With tears augmenting the fresh morning's dew,
Adding to clouds more clouds with his deep sighs;
But all so soon as the all-cheering sun
Should in the farthest east begin to draw
The shady curtains from Aurora's bed,
Away from light steals home my heavy son,
And private in his chamber pens himself,
Shuts up his windows, locks fair daylight out,
And makes himself an artificial night:
140 Black and portentous must this humour prove,
Unless good counsel may the cause remove.

  Benvolio. My noble uncle, do you know the cause?

  Montague. I neither know it, nor can learn
      of him.

  Benvolio. Have you importuned him by
      any means?

Montague. Both by myself and many other friends:
But he, his own affections' counsellor,
Is to himself—I will not say how true—
But to himself so secret and so close,
So far from sounding and discovery,
As is the bud bit with an envious worm,   150
Ere he can spread his sweet leaves to the air,
Or dedicate his beauty to the sun.
Could we but learn from whence his sorrows grow,
We would as willingly give cure as know.

hint of misery to come

'*Enter* ROMEO'

Benvolio. See where he comes: so please you,
    step aside;
I'll know his grievance or be much denied.
Montague. I would thou wert so happy by thy stay
To hear true shrift. Come, madam, let's away.
                              [*Montague and his wife depart*
Benvolio. Good morrow, cousin.
Romeo.   Is the day so young?
Benvolio. But new struck nine.
Romeo.   Ay me, sad hours seem long. 160
Was that my father that went hence so fast?
Benvolio. It was. What sadness lengthens
    Romeo's hours?
Romeo. Not having that which, having, makes
    them short.
Benvolio. In love?
Romeo. Out—
Benvolio. Of love?
Romeo. Out of her favour where I am in love.
Benvolio. Alas that Love, so gentle in his view,
Should be so tyrannous and rough in proof!
Romeo. Alas that Love, whose view is muffled still,   170

Should without eyes see pathways to his will!
Where shall we dine?—O me! What fray
    was here?
Yet tell me not, for I have heard it all:
Here's much to do with hate, but more with love:
Why, then, O brawling love, O loving hate,
O anything of nothing first create!
O heavy lightness, serious vanity,
Misshapen chaos of well-seeming forms,
Feather of lead, bright smoke, cold fire,
    sick health,
180 Still-waking sleep, that is not what it is!
This love feel I, that feel no love in this.
Dost thou not laugh?

Benvolio.   No, coz, I rather weep.

Romeo. Good heart, at what?

Benvolio.   At thy good heart's oppression.

Romeo. Why, such is love's transgression.
Griefs of mine own lie heavy in my breast,
Which thou wilt propagate, to have it pressed
With more of thine. This love that thou hast shown
Doth add more grief to too much of mine own.
Love is a smoke made with the fume of sighs:
190 Being purged, a fire sparkling in lovers' eyes;
Being vexed, a sea nourished with lovers' tears.
What is it else? A madness most discreet,
A choking gall and a preserving sweet.
Farewell, my coz.

Benvolio.   Soft, I will go along:
And if you leave me so, you do me wrong.

Romeo. Tut, I have lost myself, I am not here,
This is not Romeo, he's some other where.

Benvolio. Tell me in sadness, who is that you love?

Romeo. What, shall I groan and tell thee?

Benvolio.   Groan? Why no:
But sadly tell me, who?   200
  Romeo. Bid a sick man in sadness make his will—
A word ill urged to one that is so ill.
In sadness, cousin, I do love a woman.
  Benvolio. I aimed so near when I supposed
        you loved.
  Romeo. A right good markman! And she's fair
        I love.
  Benvolio. A right fair mark, fair coz, is soonest hit.
  Romeo. Well, in that hit you miss. She'll not be hit
With Cupid's arrow: she hath Dian's wit,
And, in strong proof of chastity well armed,
From Love's weak childish bow she lives unharmed..   210
She will not stay the siege of loving terms,
Nor bide th'encounter of assailing eyes,
Nor ope her lap to saint-seducing gold.
O, she is rich in beauty, only poor
That, when she dies, with beauty dies her store.
  Benvolio. Then she hath sworn that she will still
        live chaste?
  Romeo. She hath, and in that sparing makes
        huge waste:
For beauty, starved with her severity,
Cuts beauty off from all posterity.
She is too fair, too wise, wisely too fair.   220
To merit bliss by making me despair:
She hath forsworn to love, and in that vow
Do I live dead, that live to tell it now.
  Benvolio. Be ruled by me; forget to think of her.
  Romeo. O, teach me how I should forget to think.
  Benvolio. By giving liberty unto thine eyes;
Examine other beauties.
  Romeo.   'Tis the way

contrast

To call hers (exquisite) in question more.
These happy masks that kiss fair ladies' brows,
230 Being black, puts us in mind they hide the fair.
He that is strucken blind cannot forget
The precious treasure of his eyesight lost.
Show me a mistress that is passing fair:
What doth her beauty serve but as a note
Where I may read who passed that passing fair?
Farewell, thou canst not teach me to forget.
    Benvolio. I'll pay that doctrine, or else die in debt.
                                     [they go

[I. .2.]   *The same; later in the day*

    '*Enter* CAPULET, *County* PARIS, *and the* CLOWN',
             servant to Capulet

    Capulet. But Montague is bound as well as I,
In penalty alike; and 'tis not hard, I think,
For men so old as we to keep the peace.
    Paris. Of honourable reckoning are you both,
And pity 'tis you lived at odds so long.
But now, my lord, what say you to my suit?
    Capulet. But saying o'er what I have said before:
My child is yet a stranger in the world;
She hath not seen the change of fourteen years:
10 Let two more summers wither in their pride
Ere we may think her ripe to be a bride.
    Paris. Younger than she are happy mothers made.
    Capulet. And too soon marred are those so
        early made.
Earth hath swallowed all my hopes but she;
She is the hopeful lady of my earth.
But woo her, gentle Paris, get her heart;

My will to her consent is but a part:
And, she agreed, within her scope of choice
Lies my consent and fair according voice.
This night I hold an old accustomed feast,   20
Whereto I have invited many a guest,
Such as I love; and you among the store,
One more most welcome, makes my number more.
At my poor house look to behold this night
Earth-treading stars that make dark heaven light.
Such comfort as do lusty young men feel
When well-apparelled April on the heel
Of limping winter treads, even such delight
Among fresh female buds shall you this night
Inherit at my house: hear all, all see,   30
And like her most whose merit most shall be:
Which on more view, of many mine being one
May stand in number, though in reckoning none.
Come, go with me. [*To the Clown*] Go, sirrah,
      trudge about
Through fair Verona; find those persons out
Whose names are written there, [*giving him a paper*]
      and to them say
My house and welcome on their pleasure stay.
                        [*Capulet and Paris go*
  Clown [*turns the paper about*]. Find them out whose
names are written here! It is written that the shoemaker
should meddle with his yard and the tailor with his last, 40
the fisher with his pencil and the painter with his nets.
But I am sent to find those persons whose names are
here writ, and can never find what names the writing
person hath here writ. I must to the learned. In good
time!

'*Enter* Benvolio *and* Romeo'

Benvolio. Tut, man, one fire burns out
     another's burning,
One pain is lessened by another's anguish;
Turn giddy, and be holp by backward turning;
One desperate grief cures with another's languish;
50 Take thou some new infection to thy eye,
And the rank poison of the old will die.
  Romeo. Your plantain leaf is excellent for that.
  Benvolio. For what, I pray thee?
  Romeo.   For your broken shin.
  Benvolio. Why, Romeo, art thou mad?
  Romeo. Not mad, but bound more than a madman is:
Shut up in prison, kept without my food,
Whipped and tormented, and—God-den,
     good fellow.
  Clown. God gi' god-den. I pray, sir, can you read?
  Romeo. Ay, mine own fortune in my misery.
60 *Clown.* Perhaps you have learned it without book:
but, I pray, can you read anything you see?
  Romeo. Ay, if I know the letters and the language.
  Clown. Ye say honestly: rest you merry.
                           [*he turns to go*
  Romeo. Stay, fellow; I can read.   [*he reads the list*
'Signior Martino and his wife and daughters,
County Anselmo and his beauteous sisters,
The lady widow of Vitruvio,
Signior Placentio and his lovely nieces,
Mercutio and his brother Valentine,
70 Mine uncle Capulet, his wife and daughters,
My fair niece Rosaline and Livia,
Signior Valentio and his cousin Tybalt,
Lucio and the lively Helena.'

A fair assembly: whither should they come?

Clown. Up.

Romeo. Whither?

Clown. To supper; to our house.

Romeo. Whose house?

Clown. My master's.

Romeo. Indeed I should have asked thee that before. 80

Clown. Now I'll tell you without asking. My master
is the great rich Capulet; and, if you be not of the house
of Montagues, I pray come and crush a cup of wine.
Rest you merry.   [*goes*

Benvolio. At this same ancient feast of Capulet's
Sups the fair Rosaline whom thou so loves,
With all the admiréd beauties of Verona:
Go thither, and with unattainted eye
Compare her face with some that I shall show,
And I will make thee think thy swan a crow.   90

Romeo. When the devout religion of mine eye
Maintains such falsehood, then turn tears to fires:
And these who, often drowned, could never die,
Transparent heretics, be burnt for liars.
One fairer than my love! The all-seeing sun
Ne'er saw her match since first the world begun.

Benvolio. Tut, you saw her fair, none else being by,
Herself poised with herself in either eye:
But in that crystal scales let there be weighed
Your lady's love against some other maid   100
That I will show you shining at this feast,
And she shall scant show well that now seems best.

Romeo. I'll go along, no such sight to be shown,
But to rejoice in splendour of mine own.   [*they go*

[I. 3.]   *Within Capulet's house*

'Enter Capulet's Wife, and NURSE*'*

Lady Capulet. Nurse, where's my daughter? Call her
    forth to me.
Nurse. Now, by my maidenhead at twelve year old,
I bade her come. What, lamb! What, lady-bird!
God forbid! Where's this girl? What, Juliet!

'Enter JULIET*'*

Juliet. How now, who calls?
Nurse. Your mother.
Juliet. Madam, I am here. What is your will?
Lady Capulet. This is the matter. Nurse, give
    leave awhile:
We must talk in secret. Nurse, come back again:
10 I have remembered me; thou's hear our counsel.
Thou knowest my daughter's of a pretty age.
    Nurse. Faith, I can tell her age unto an hour.
    Lady Capulet. She's not fourteen.
    Nurse.   I'll lay fourteen of my teeth—
And yet, to my teen be it spoken, I have but four—
She's not fourteen. How long is it now
To Lammas-tide?
    Lady Capulet.   A fortnight and odd days.
    Nurse. Even or odd, of all days in the year,
Come Lammas-Eve at night shall she be fourteen.
Susan and she—God rest all Christian souls—
20 Were of an age. Well, Susan is with God;
She was too good for me. But, as I said, .
On Lammas-Eve at night shall she be fourteen:
That shall she, marry; I remember it well.
'Tis since the earthquake now eleven years,

And she was weaned—I never shall forget it—
Of all the days of the year, upon that day:
For I had then laid wormwood to my dug,
Sitting in the sun under the dove-house wall.
My lord and you were then at Mantua—
Nay, I do bear a brain! But, as I said,   30
When it did taste the wormwood on the nipple
Of my dug, and felt it bitter, pretty fool,
To see it tetchy and fall out with the dug!
'Shake,' quoth the dove-house: 'twas no need, I trow,
To bid me trudge.
And since that time it is eleven years:
For then she could stand high-lone; nay, by th' rood,
She could have run and waddled all about:
For even the day before, she broke her brow,
And then my husband—God be with his soul,   40
'A was a merry man—took up the child:
'Yea,' quoth he, 'dost thou fall upon thy face?
Thou wilt fall backward when thou hast more wit;
Wilt thou not, Jule?' And, by my holidame,
The pretty wretch left crying, and said 'Ay'.
To see now how a jest shall come about!
I warrant, an I should live a thousand years,
I never should forget it: 'Wilt thou not, Jule?'
        quoth he;
And, pretty fool, it stinted, and said 'Ay'.
  Lady Capulet. Enough of this; I pray thee hold
        thy peace.   50
  Nurse. Yes, madam, yet I cannot choose but laugh,
To think it should leave crying, and say 'Ay':
And yet, I warrant, it had upon it brow
A bump as big as a young cockerel's stone,
A perilous knock: and it cried bitterly.
'Yea', quoth my husband, 'fallst upon thy face?

Thou wilt fall backward when thou comest to age:
Wilt thou not, Jule?' It stinted, and said 'Ay'.
   Juliet. And stint thou too, I pray thee, Nurse, say I.
60 *Nurse.* Peace, I have done. God mark thee to
     his grace!
.Thou wast the prettiest babe that e'er I nursed:
An I might live to see thee married once,
I have my wish.
   Lady Capulet. Marry, that 'marry' is the very theme
I came to talk of. Tell me, daughter Juliet,
How stands your dispositions to be married?
  ·*Juliet.* It is an honour that I dream not of.
   Nurse. An honour! Were not I thine only nurse,
I would say thou hadst sucked wisdom from thy teat.
70 *Lady Capulet.* Well, think of marriage now; younger
     than you
Here in Verona, ladies of esteem,
Are made already mothers. By my count,
I was your mother much upon these years
That you are now a maid. Thus then in brief:
The valiant Paris seeks you for his love.
   Nurse. A man, young lady! Lady, such a man
As all the world—Why, he's a man of wax.
   Lady Capulet. Verona's summer hath not such
     a flower.
   Nurse. Nay, he's a flower; in faith, a very flower.
80 *Lady Capulet.* What say you? Can you love
     the gentleman?
This night you shall behold him at our feast:
Read o'er the volume of young Paris' face,
And find delight writ there with beauty's pen;
Examine every married lineament,
And see how one another lends content;
And what obscured in this fair volume lies

Find written in the margent of his eyes.
This precious book of love, this unbound lover,
To beautify him, only lacks a cover.
The fish lives in the sea; and 'tis much pride   90
For fair without the fair within to hide.
That book in many's eyes doth share the glory,
That in gold clasps locks in the golden story:
So shall you share all that he doth possess,
By having him making yourself no less.

  Nurse. No less! Nay, bigger women grow by men!
  Lady Capulet. Speak briefly, can you like of
       Paris' love?
  Juliet. I'll look to like, if looking liking move;
But no more deep will I endart mine eye
Than your consent gives strength to make it fly.   100

                    '*Enter Servingman*'

  Servingman. Madam, the guests are come, supper
served up, you called, my young lady asked for, the
nurse cursed in the pantry, and everything in extremity.
I must hence to wait; I beseech you follow straight.
  Lady Capulet. We follow thee. Juliet, the
       County stays.
  Nurse. Go, girl, seek happy nights to happy days.
                                          [*they go*

[1. 4.]   *Without Capulet's house*

   '*Enter* ROMEO, MERCUTIO, BENVOLIO, *with five or
          six other masquers; torch-bearers*'

  Romeo. What, shall this speech be spoke for
       our excuse?
Or shall we on without apology?

Benvolio. The date is out of such prolixity:
We'll have no Cupid hoodwinked with a scarf,
Bearing a Tartar's painted bow of lath,
Scaring the ladies like a crow-keeper:
Nor no without-book prologue, faintly spoke
After the prompter, for our entrance:
But, let them measure us by what they will,
10 We'll measure them a measure and be gone.
  Romeo. Give me a torch: I am not for this ambling;
Being but heavy, I will bear the light.
  Mercutio. Nay, gentle Romeo, we must have
    you dance.
  Romeo. Not I, believe me: you have dancing shoes
With nimble soles; I have a soul of lead
So stakes me to the ground I cannot move.
  Mercutio. You are a lover: borrow Cupid's wings,
And soar with them above a common bound.
  Romeo. I am too sore enpiercéd with his shaft
20 To soar with his light feathers and so bound;
I cannot bound a pitch above dull woe:
Under love's heavy burden do I sink.
  Mercutio. And, to sink in it, should you
    burden love—
Too great oppression for a tender thing.
  Romeo. Is love a tender thing? It is too rough,
Too rude, too boisterous, and it pricks like thorn.
  Mercutio. If love be rough with you, be rough
    with love;
Prick love for pricking, and you beat love down.
Give me a case to put my visage in:
30 A visor for a visor! What care I
What curious eye doth quote deformities?
Here are the beetle-brows shall blush for me.
                  [putting on a mask

Benvolio. Come, knock and enter, and no sooner in
But every man betake him to his legs.

Romeo. A torch for me; let wantons light of heart
Tickle the senseless rushes with their heels.
For I am proverbed with a grandsire phrase,
I'll be a candle-holder, and look on.
The game was ne'er so fair, and I am done.

Mercutio. Tut, dun's the mouse, the constable's
    own word: 40
If thou art Dun, we'll draw thee from the mire,
Or save-your-reverence love, wherein thou stickest
Up to the ears. Come, we burn daylight, ho.

Romeo. Nay, that's not so.

Mercutio.   I mean, sir, in delay
We waste our lights in vain, like lights by day.
Take our good meaning, for our judgement sits
Five times in that ere once in our five wits.

Romeo. And we mean well in going to this masque,
But 'tis no wit to go.

Mercutio.   Why, may one ask?

Romeo. I dreamt a dream tonight.

Mercutio.   And so did I.   50

Romeo. Well, what was yours?

Mercutio.   That dreamers often lie.

Romeo. In bed asleep while they do dream things true.

Mercutio. O then I see Queen Mab hath been
    with you.
She is the fairies' midwife, and she comes
In shape no bigger than an agate-stone
On the fore-finger of an alderman,
Drawn with a team of little atomi
Over men's noses as they lie asleep.
Her chariot is an empty hazel-nut,
Made by the joiner squirrel or old grub   60

Time out o' mind the fairies' coachmakers:
Her waggon-spokes made of long spinners' legs,
The cover of the wings of grasshoppers,
Her traces of the smallest spider-web,
Her collars of the moonshine's watery beams,
Her whip of cricket's bone, the lash of film;
Her waggoner a small grey-coated gnat,
Not half so big as a round little worm
Pricked from the lazy finger of a maid.
70 And in this state she gallops night by night
Through lovers' brains, and then they dream of love;
O'er courtiers' knees, that dream on curtsies straight;
O'er lawyers' fingers who straight dream on fees;
O'er ladies' lips, who straight on kisses dream,
Which oft the angry Mab with blisters plagues
Because their breaths with sweetmeats tainted are.
Sometime she gallops o'er a courtier's nose,
And then dreams he of smelling out a suit:
And sometime comes she with a tithe-pig's tail
80 Tickling a parson's nose as 'a lies asleep,
Then dreams he of another benefice.
Sometime she driveth o'er a soldier's neck,
And then dreams he of cutting foreign throats,
Of breaches, ambuscadoes, Spanish blades,
Of healths five fathom deep; and then anon
Drums in his ear, at which he starts and wakes,
And being thus frighted swears a prayer or two,
And sleeps again. This is that very Mab
That plats the manes of horses in the night,
90 And bakes the elf-locks in foul sluttish hairs,
Which once untangled much misfortune bodes:
This is the hag, when maids lie on their backs,
That presses them and learns them first to bear,
Making them women of good carriage:

This is she—
  Romeo.   Peace, peace, Mercutio, peace!
Thou talkst of nothing.
  Mercutio.   True, I talk of dreams,
Which are the children of an idle brain,
Begot of nothing but vain fantasy,
Which is as thin of substance as the air,
And more inconstant than the wind, who woos   100
Even now the frozen bosom of the north,
And, being angered, puffs away from thence,
Turning his side to the dew-dropping south.
  Benvolio. This wind you talk of blows us
      from ourselves:
Supper is done, and we shall come too late.
  Romeo. I fear, too early: for my mind misgives
Some consequence, yet hanging in the stars,
Shall bitterly begin his fearful date
With this night's revels, and expire the term
Of a despiséd life closed in my breast,   110
By some vile forfeit of untimely death.
But He that hath the steerage of my course
Direct my sail! On, lusty gentlemen.
  Benvolio. Strike, drum.   [*they march into the house*

Foreshadowing of doom

[1. 5.]

*The hall in Capulet's house; musicians waiting. Enter
the masquers, march round the hall, and stand aside.*
    '*Servingmen come forth with napkins*'

  First Servingman. Where's Potpan, that he helps not
to take away? He shift a trencher! He scrape a trencher!
  Second Servingman. When good manners shall lie all
in one or two men's hands, and they unwashed too,
'tis a foul thing.

First Servingman. Away with the joined-stools; remove
the court-cupboard, look to the plate—Good thou,
save me a piece of marchpane; and, as thou loves me,
let the porter let in Susan Grindstone and Nell—
10 Antony and Potpan!

Third Servingman. Ay, boy, ready.

First Servingman. You are looked for and called for,
asked for and sought for, in the great chamber.

Fourth Servingman. We cannot be here and there too.
Cheerly, boys; be brisk a while, and the longer liver
take all.   [*Servingmen withdraw*

'*Enter*' CAPULET, *and* JULIET, *with* '*all the
guests and gentlewomen to the masquers*'

Capulet. Welcome, gentlemen! Ladies that have
      their toes
Unplagued with corns will walk a bout with you.
Ah, my mistresses, which of you all
20 Will now deny to dance? She that makes dainty,
She I'll swear hath corns: am I come near ye now?
Welcome, gentlemen! I have seen the day
That I have worn a visor and could tell
A whispering tale in a fair lady's ear,
Such as would please: 'tis gone, 'tis gone, 'tis gone.
You are welcome, gentlemen! Come, musicians, play.
A hall, a hall! Give room. And foot it, girls.
                        [*'music plays and they dance*'
More light, you knaves, and turn the tables up,
And quench the fire—the room is grown too hot.
30 Ah, sirrah, this unlooked-for sport comes well.—
Nay sit, nay sit, good cousin Capulet,
For you and I are past our dancing days.
How long is't now since last yourself and I
Were in a masque?

Second Capulet.   By'r Lady, thirty years.

Capulet. What, man! 'tis not so much, 'tis not
 so much:
'Tis since the nuptial of Lucentio,
Come Pentecost as quickly as it will,
Some five and twenty years, and then we masqued.

Second Capulet. 'Tis more, 'tis more; his son is
 elder, sir:
His son is thirty.

Capulet.   Will you tell me that?   40
His son was but a ward two years ago.

Romeo. [*to a servingman*] What lady's that which doth
 enrich the hand
Of yonder knight?

Servingman.   I know not, sir.

(*Romeo.* O she doth teach the torches to burn bright!
It seems she hangs upon the cheek of night
As a rich jewel in an Ethiop's ear—
Beauty too rich for use, for earth too dear!
So shows a snowy dove trooping with crows,
As yonder lady o'er her fellows shows.
The measure done, I'll watch her place of stand,   50
And, touching hers, make blessèd my rude hand.
Did my heart love till now? Forswear it, sight!
For I ne'er saw true beauty till this night.

Tybalt. This, by his voice, should be a Montague.
Fetch me my rapier, boy. [*his page goes*] What dares
 the slave
Come hither, covered with an antic face,
To fleer and scorn at our solemnity?
Now, by the stock and honour of my kin,
To strike him dead I hold it not a sin.

Capulet. Why, how now, kinsman! wherefore storm
 you so?   60

Tybalt. Uncle, this is a Montague, our foe:
A villain that is hither come in spite,
To scorn at our solemnity this night.
   Capulet. Young Romeo is it?
   Tybalt.   'Tis he, that villain Romeo.
   Capulet. Content thee, gentle coz, let him alone,
'A bears him like a portly gentleman:
And, to say truth, Verona brags of him
To be a virtuous and well-governed youth.
I would not for the wealth of all this town
70 Here in my house do him disparagement:
Therefore be patient, take no note of him.
It is my will, the which if thou respect,
Show a fair presence and put off these frowns,
An ill-beseeming semblance for a feast.
   Tybalt. It fits when such a villain is a guest:
I'll not endure him.
   Capulet.   He shall be endured.
What, goodman boy? I say he shall. Go to,
Am I the master here, or you? Go to,
You'll not endure him? God shall mend my soul!
80 You'll make a mutiny among my guests!
You will set cock-a-hoop! You'll be the man!
   Tybalt. Why, uncle, 'tis a shame.
   Capulet.   Go to, go to,
You are a saucy boy. Is't so indeed?
This trick may chance to scathe you, I know what.
You must contrary me! Marry, 'tis time—
Well said, my hearts!—You are a princox: go,
Be quiet, or—More light, more light, for shame!—
I'll make you quiet.—What, cheerly, my hearts!
   Tybalt. Patience perforce with wilful
      choler meeting
90 Makes my flesh tremble in their different greeting.

I will withdraw, but this intrusion shall,
Now seeming sweet, convert to bitterest gall. [goes
  Romeo. [*takes Juliet's hand*] If I profane with my
     unworthiest hand
This holy shrine, the gentle sin is this:
My lips, two blushing pilgrims, ready stand
To smooth that rough touch with a tender kiss.
  Juliet. Good pilgrim, you do wrong your hand
     too much,
Which mannerly devotion shows in this:
For saints have hands that pilgrims' hands do touch,
And palm to palm is holy palmers' kiss.   100
  Romeo. Have not saints lips, and holy palmers too?.
  Juliet. Ay, pilgrim, lips that they must use
     in prayer.
  Romeo. O then, dear saint, let lips do what hands do,
They pray: grant thou, lest faith turn to despair.
  Juliet. Saints do not move, though grant for
     prayers' sake.
  Romeo. Then move not, while my prayer's effect
     I take.
Thus from my lips by thine my sin is purged.
                     [*kissing her*
  Juliet. Then have my lips the sin that they
     have took.
  Romeo. Sin from my lips? O trespass sweetly urged!
Give me my sin again.   [*kissing her*
  Juliet.   You kiss by th' book.   110
  Nurse. Madam, your mother craves a word with you.
  Romeo. What is her mother?
  Nurse.   Marry, bachelor,
Her mother is the lady of the house,
And a good lady, and a wise and virtuous.
I nursed her daughter that you talked withal.

I tell you, he that can lay hold of her
Shall have the chinks.

Romeo.   Is she a Capulet?
O dear account! My life is my foe's debt.

Benvolio. Away be gone; the sport is at the best.

120   *Romeo.* Ay, so I fear; the more is my unrest.

Capulet. Nay, gentlemen, prepare not to be gone;
We have a trifling foolish banquet towards.

The masquers excuse themselves, whispering in his ear

Is it e'en so? Why, then, I thank you all:
I thank you, honest gentlemen; good night.
More torches here; come on! then let's to bed.

Servants bring torches to escort the masquers out

Ah, sirrah, by my fay, it waxes late:
I'll to my rest.   [*all leave but Juliet and Nurse*

Juliet. Come hither, nurse. What is yond gentleman?

Nurse. The son and heir of old Tiberio.

130   *Juliet.* What's he that now is going out of door?

Nurse. Marry, that I think be young Petruchio.

Juliet. What's he that follows there, that would
          not dance?

Nurse. I know not.

Juliet. Go ask his name.—If he be marriéd,
My grave is like to be my wedding bed.

Nurse. His name is Romeo, and a Montague,
The only son of your great enemy.

(*Juliet.* My only love sprung from my only hate! Irony
Too early seen unknown, and known too late!

140 Prodigious birth of love it is to me,
That I must love a loathéd enemy.

Nurse. What's this, what's this?

Juliet.   A rhyme I learned even now
Of one I danced withal.

'*One calls within, "Juliet*'"

Nurse.   Anon, anon!
Come, let's away; the strangers all are gone.

[*they go*

[2. *Prologue*]

Enter Chorus

Chorus. Now old desire doth in his deathbed lie,
  And young affection gapes to be his heir;
That fair for which love groaned for and would die,
  With tender Juliet matched, is now not fair.
Now Romeo is beloved and loves again,
  Alike bewitchéd by the charm of looks,
But to his foe supposed he must complain,
  And she steal love's sweet bait from fearful hooks:
Being held a foe, he may not have access
  To breathe such vows as lovers use to swear;   10
And she as much in love, her means much less
  To meet her new belovéd anywhere:
But passion lends them power, time means, to meet,
Tempering extremities with extreme sweet.   [*exi*

[2. 1.]

Capulet's orchard; to the one side the outer wall with a lane beyond, to the other Capulet's house showing an upper window

'*Enter* ROMEO *alone*' *in the lane*

Romeo. Can I go forward when my heart is here?
Turn back, dull earth, and find thy centre out.
  [*he climbs the wall and leaps into the orchard.*

'Enter Benvolio *with* Mercutio' *in the lane.*
Romeo listens behind the wall

Benvolio. Romeo, my cousin Romeo!
Mercutio.   He is wise,
And on my life hath stolen him home to bed.
  Benvolio. He ran this way and leapt this
    orchard wall.
Call, good Mercutio.
  Mercutio.   Nay, I'll conjure too.
Romeo, humours, madman, passion, lover!
Appear thou in the likeness of a sigh;
Speak but one rhyme and I am satisfied:
10 Cry but 'Ay me!', pronounce but 'love' and 'dove';
Speak to my gossip Venus one fair word,
One nickname for her purblind son and heir,
Young Abraham Cupid, he that shot so trim
When King Cophetua loved the beggar maid.
He heareth not, he stirreth not, he moveth not;
The ape is dead, and I must conjure him.
I conjure thee by Rosaline's bright eyes,
By her high forehead and her scarlet lip,
By her fine foot, straight leg, and quivering thigh,
20 And the demesnes that there adjacent lie,
That in thy likeness thou appear to us.
  Benvolio. An if he hear thee, thou wilt anger him.
  Mercutio. This cannot anger him. 'Twould
    anger him
To raise a spirit in his mistress' circle
Of some strange nature, letting it there stand
Till she had laid it and conjured it down;
That were some spite. My invocation
Is fair and honest; in his mistress' name
I conjure only but to raise up him.

  Benvolio. Come! He hath hid himself among
    these trees   30
To be consorted with the humorous night:
Blind is his love and best befits the dark.
  Mercutio. If love be blind, love cannot hit the mark.
Now will he sit under a medlar tree,
And wish his mistress were that kind of fruit
As maids call medlars when they laugh alone.
O Romeo, that she were, O that she were
An open-arse and thou a poperin pear!
Romeo, goodnight. I'll to my truckle-bed;
This field-bed is too cold for me to sleep.   40
Come, shall we go?
  Benvolio.   Go then, for 'tis in vain
To seek him here that means not to be found.
                                   [they go
[2. 2.] *Romeo.* He jests at scars that never felt a wound.

      JULIET appears aloft at the window

But soft! What light through yonder window breaks?
It is the east, and Juliet is the sun.
Arise, fair sun, and kill the envious moon,
Who is already sick and pale with grief
That thou, her maid, art far more fair than she.
Be not her maid, since she is envious.
Her vestal livery is but sick and green,
And none but fools do wear it: cast it off.
It is my lady, O it is my love;   10
O that she knew she were.
She speaks, yet she says nothing. What of that?
Her eye discourses: I will answer it.
I am too bold: 'tis not to me she speaks.
Two of the fairest stars in all the heaven,
Having some business, do entreat her eyes

To twinkle in their spheres till they return.
What if her eyes were there, they in her head?
The brightness of her cheek would shame those stars
20 As daylight doth a lamp; her eyes in heaven
Would through the airy region stream so bright
That birds would sing and think it were not night.
See how she leans her cheek upon her hand!
O that I were a glove upon that hand,
That I might touch that cheek.

    Juliet.   Ay me!
    (*Romeo.*   She speaks.

O speak again, bright angel, for thou art
As glorious to this night, being o'er my head,
As is a wingéd messenger of heaven
Unto the white-upturnéd wondering eyes
30 Of mortals that fall back to gaze on him
When he bestrides the lazy-passing clouds
And sails upon the bosom of the air.

    Juliet. O Romeo, Romeo! Wherefore art
        thou Romeo?
Deny thy father and refuse thy name:
Or, if thou wilt not, be but sworn my love,
And I'll no longer be a Capulet.

    (*Romeo.* Shall I hear more, or shall I speak at this?
    Juliet. 'Tis but thy name that is my enemy.
Thou art thy self, though not a Montague.
40 O be some other name! What's Montague?
It is nor hand, nor foot, nor arm, nor face,
Nor any part belonging to a man.
What's in a name? That which we call a rose
By any other name would smell as sweet.
So Romeo would, were he not Romeo called,
Retain that dear perfection which he owes,
Without that title. Romeo, doff thy name;

And for thy name, which is no part of thee,
Take all myself.

 Romeo.   I take thee at thy word.
Call me but love, and I'll be new baptized;   50
Henceforth I never will be Romeo.

 Juliet. What man art thou that, thus bescreened
   in night,
So stumblest on my counsel?

 Romeo.   By a name
I know not how to tell thee who I am.
My name, dear saint, is hateful to myself
Because it is an enemy to thee.
Had I it written, I would tear the word.

 Juliet. My ears have yet not drunk a
   hundred words
Of thy tongue's uttering, yet I know the sound.
Art thou not Romeo, and a Montague?   60

 Romeo. Neither, fair maid, if either thee dislike.

 Juliet. How camest thou hither, tell me,
   and wherefore?
The orchard walls are high and hard to climb,
And the place death, considering who thou art,
If any of my kinsmen find thee here.

 Romeo. With love's light wings did I o'erperch
   these walls;
For stony limits cannot hold love out,
And what love can do, that dares love attempt:
Therefore thy kinsmen are no stop to me.

 Juliet. If they do see thee, they will murther thee.   70

 Romeo. Alack, there lies more peril in thine eye
Than twenty of their swords. Look thou but sweet,
And I am proof against their enmity.

 Juliet. I would not for the world they saw
   thee here.

Romeo. I have night's cloak to hide me from
    their eyes;
And but thou love me, let them find me here:
My life were better ended by their hate
Than death proroguéd, wanting of thy love.
    Juliet. By whose direction foundst thou out
        this place?
80 *Romeo.* By love, that first did prompt me to enquire.
He lent me counsel, and I lent him eyes.
I am no pilot; yet, wert thou as far
As that vast shore washed with the farthest sea,   *Tempest*
I should adventure for such merchandise.
    Juliet. Thou knowest the mask of night is on
        my face;
Else would a maiden blush bepaint my cheek,
For that which thou hast heard me speak tonight.
Fain would I dwell on form; fain, fain deny
What I have spoke: but farewell compliment!
90 Dost thou love me? I know thou wilt say 'Ay',
And I will take thy word. Yet, if thou swearst,
Thou mayst prove false. At lovers' perjuries
They say Jove laughs. O gentle Romeo,
If thou dost love, pronounce it faithfully.
Or, if thou think'st I am too quickly won,
I'll frown and be perverse and say thee nay,
So thou wilt woo; but else, not for the world.
In truth, fair Montague, I am too fond,
And therefore thou mayst think my haviour light;
100 But trust me, gentleman, I'll prove more true
Than those that have more cunning to be strange.
I should have been more strange, I must confess,
But that thou overheardst, ere I was ware,
My true-love passion. Therefore pardon me,
And not impute this yielding to light love,

Which the dark night hath so discov12ed.

Romeo. Lady, by yonder blessèd moon I vow, ⎫ *Too dainty' for*
That tips with silver all these fruit tree tops— ⎭ *Juliet.*

Juliet. O swear not by the moon, th'incon-
    stant moon,
That monthly changes in her circled orb,   110
Lest that thy love prove likewise variable.

Romeo. What shall I swear by?

Juliet.   Do not swear at all: *She proves*
Or, if thou wilt, swear by thy gracious self,   *her strength here*
Which is the god of my idolatry,   *Romeo is hesitant*
And I'll believe thee.

Romeo.   If my heart's dear love—

Juliet. Well, do not swear. Although I joy in thee,
I have no joy of this contract tonight:
It is too rash, too unadvised, too sudden,
Too like the lightning, which doth cease to be
Ere one can say 'It lightens'. Sweet, goodnight: 120
This bud of love, by summer's ripening breath,
May prove a beauteous flower when next we meet.
Goodnight, goodnight! As sweet repose and rest
Come to thy heart as that within my breast.

Romeo. O wilt thou leave me so unsatisfied?

Juliet. What satisfaction canst thou have tonight?

Romeo. Th'exchange of thy love's faithful vow
    for mine.

Juliet. I gave thee mine before thou didst
    request it:
And yet I would it were to give again.

Romeo. Would'st thou withdraw it? For what
    purpose, love?   130

Juliet. But to be frank and give it thee again:
And yet I wish but for the thing I have.
My bounty is as boundless as the sea,

My love as deep: the more I give to thee,
The more I have: for both are infinite.
I hear some noise within. Dear love, adieu—

                         [Nurse calls within

Anon, good nurse!—sweet Montague, be true.
Stay but a little; I will come again.   *[Juliet goes in*
  Romeo. O blessed, blessed night! I am afeared,
140 Being in night, all this is but a dream,
Too flattering sweet to be substantial.

      JULIET reappears at the window

  Juliet. Three words, dear Romeo, and good
     night indeed.
If that thy bent of love be honourable,
Thy purpose marriage, send me word tomorrow,
By one that I'll procure to come to thee,
Where and what time thou wilt perform the rite;
And all my fortunes at thy foot I'll lay,
And follow thee my lord throughout the world.
  Nurse. [*within*] Madam!
150 *Juliet.* I come, anon.—But if thou meanest not well,
I do beseech thee—
  Nurse. [*within*]   Madam!
  Juliet.   By and by I come—
To cease thy suit, and leave me to my grief.
Tomorrow will I send.
  Romeo. So thrive my soul—
  Juliet.   A thousand times good night!

                         [she goes in

  Romeo. A thousand times the worse, to want
     thy light!
Love goes toward love as schoolboys from
     their books,
But love from love, toward school with heavy looks.

JULIET returns to the window

Juliet. Hist, Romeo, hist! O for a falconer's voice
To lure this tassel-gentle back again!
Bondage is hoarse and may not speak aloud,   160
Else would I tear the cave where Echo lies,
And make her airy tongue more hoarse than mine
With repetition of my "Romeo!"
    Romeo. It is my soul that calls upon my name.
How silver-sweet sound lovers' tongues by night,
Like softest music to attending ears!
    Juliet. Romeo!
    Romeo.   My niëss!
    Juliet.   What o'clock tomorrow
Shall I send to thee?
    Romeo.   By the hour of nine.
    Juliet. I will not fail. 'Tis twenty year till then.
I have forgot why I did call thee back.   170
    Romeo. Let me stand here till thou remember it.
    Juliet. I shall forget, to have thee still stand there,
Rememb'ring how I love thy company.
    Romeo. And I'll still stay, to have thee still forget,
Forgetting any other home but this.
    Juliet. 'Tis almost morning. I would have
        thee gone,
And yet no farther than a wanton's bird,
That lets it hop a little from her hand,
Like a poor prisoner in his twisted gyves,
And with a silk thread plucks it back again,   180
So loving-jealous of his liberty.
    Romeo. I would I were thy bird.
    Juliet.   Sweet, so would I;
Yet I should kill thee with much cherishing.
Goodnight, goodnight! Parting is such sweet sorrow,

That I shall say goodnight till it be morrow.
  Romeo. Sleep dwell upon thine eyes, peace in
    thy breast!
Would I were sleep and peace, so sweet to rest!

                        [*she goes in*

Hence will I to my ghostly sire's close cell,
His help to crave, and my dear hap to tell.   [*he goes*

[2. 3.]   *Friar Lawrence's cell*

'*Enter* FRIAR *alone with a basket*'

  Friar. The grey-eyed morn smiles on the
    frowning night,
Check'ring the eastern clouds with streaks of light:
And darkness flecked like a drunkard reels
From forth day's pathway, made by Titan's wheels:
Now ere the sun advance his burning eye,
The day to cheer and night's dank dew to dry,
I must upfill this osier cage of ours,
With baleful weeds and precious-juicéd flowers.
The earth that's nature's mother is her tomb;
10. What is her burying grave, that is her womb;
And from her womb children of divers kind
We sucking on her natural bosom find:
Many for many virtues excellent,
None but for some, and yet all different.
O mickle is the powerful grace that lies
In plants, herbs, stones, and their true qualities:
For nought so vile that on the earth doth live
But to the earth some special good doth give:
Nor aught so good but, strained from that
    fair use,
20 Revolts from true birth, stumbling on abuse.

Virtue itself turns vice, being misapplied,
And vice sometime by action dignified.

ROMEO approaches, unseen by the Friar

Within the infant rind of this weak flower
Poison hath residence, and medicine power:
For this, being smelt, with that part cheers each part;
Being tasted, stays all senses with the heart.
Two such opposéd kings encamp them still
In man as well as herbs—grace and rude will:
And where the worser is predominant,
Full soon the canker death eats up that plant.   30
  Romeo. Good morrow, father.
  Friar.   Benedicite!
What early tongue so sweet saluteth me?
Young son, it argues a distempered head,
So soon to bid goodmorrow to thy bed.
Care keeps his watch in every old man's eye,
And where care lodges sleep will never lie:
But where unbruiséd youth with unstuffed brain
Doth couch his limbs, there golden sleep doth reign.
Therefore thy earliness doth me assure
Thou art uproused with some distemperature: 40
Or if not so, then here I hit it right—
Our Romeo hath not been in bed tonight.
  Romeo. That last is true—the sweeter rest was mine
  Friar. God pardon sin! Wast thou with Rosaline?
  Romeo. With Rosaline? My ghostly father, no;
I have forgot that name, and that name's woe.
  Friar. That's my good son! But where hast thou
    been then?
  Romeo. I'll tell thee ere thou ask it me again.
I have been feasting with mine enemy,
Where on a sudden one hath wounded me   50

That's by me wounded. Both our remedies
Within thy help and holy physic lies.
I bear no hatred, blessed man, for lo,
My intercession likewise steads my foe.
   Friar. Be plain, good son, and homely in thy drift.
Riddling confession finds but riddling shrift.
   Romeo. Then plainly know my heart's dear love
      is set
On the fair daughter of rich Capulet:
As mine on hers, so hers is set on mine,
60 And all combined save what thou must combine
By holy marriage: when and where and how
We met, we wooed, and made exchange of vow
I'll tell thee as we pass; but this I pray,
That thou consent to marry us today.
   Friar. Holy Saint Francis, what a change is here!
Is Rosaline, that thou didst love so dear,
So soon forsaken? Young men's love then lies
Not truly in their hearts but in their eyes.
Jesu Maria, what a deal of brine
70 Hath washed thy sallow cheeks for Rosaline!
How much salt water thrown away in waste
To season love, that of it doth not taste!
The sun not yet thy sighs from heaven clears,
Thy old groans ring yet in mine ancient ears;
Lo, here upon thy cheek the stain doth sit
Of an old tear that is not washed off yet.
If e'er thou wast thyself, and these woes thine,
Thou and these woes were all for Rosaline.
And art thou changed? Pronounce this sentence, then—
80 Women may fall, when there's no strength in men.
   Romeo. Thou chid'st me oft for loving Rosaline.
   Friar. For doting, not for loving, pupil mine.
   Romeo. And bad'st me bury love.

Friar.   Not in a grave
To lay one in, another out to have.
  Romeo. I pray thee chide me not. Her I love now
Doth grace for grace and love for love allow:
The other did not so.
  Friar.   O, she knew well
Thy love did read by rote, that could not spell.
But come, young waverer, come go with me;
In one respect I'll thy assistant be: 90
For this alliance may so happy prove
To turn your households' rancour to pure love.
  Romeo. O let us hence! I stand on sudden haste.
  Friar. Wisely and slow. They stumble that run fast.
                                              [*they go*

[2. 4.]   *A public place*
                '*Enter* BENVOLIO *and* MERCUTIO'

  Mercutio. Where the devil should this Romeo be?
Came he not home tonight?
  Benvolio. Not to his father's; I spoke with his man.
  Mercutio. Why, that same pale hard-hearted wench,
        that Rosaline,
Torments him so, that he will sure run mad.
  Benvolio. Tybalt, the kinsman to old Capulet,
Hath sent a letter to his father's house.
  Mercutio. A challenge, on my life.
  Benvolio. Romeo will answer it.
  Mercutio. Any man that can write may answer a letter. 10
  Benvolio. Nay, he will answer the letter's master, how
he dares being dared.
  Mercutio. Alas, poor Romeo, he is already dead—
stabbed with a white wench's black eye, run through
the ear with a love-song, the very pin of his heart

Perfect
follow on of
imagery.

cleft with the blind bow-boy's butt-shaft; and is he a
man to encounter Tybalt?

Benvolio. Why, what is Tybalt?

Mercutio. More than Prince of Cats. O, he's the
20 courageous captain of compliments. He fights as you
sing pricksong—keeps time, distance, and proportion; he
rests his minim rests—one, two, and the third in your
bosom. The very butcher of a silk button, a duellist, a
duellist, a gentleman of the very first house, of the first
and second cause! Ah, the immortal passado, the punto
reverso, the hai!

Benvolio. The what?

Mercutio. The pox of such antic, lisping, affecting
fantasticoes, these new tuners of accent! 'By Jesu, a
30 very good blade! a very tall man! a very good whore!'
Why, is not this a lamentable thing, grandsire, that we
should be thus afflicted with these strange flies, these
fashion-mongers, these pardon-me's, who stand so much
on the new form that they cannot sit at ease on the old
bench? O, their bones, their bones!

'Enter ROMEO'

Benvolio. Here comes Romeo, here comes Romeo!

Mercutio. Without his roe, like a dried herring. O
flesh, flesh, how art thou fishified! Now is he for the
numbers that Petrarch flowed in. Laura to his lady
40 was a kitchen wench—marry, she had a better love to
be-rhyme her!—Dido a dowdy, Cleopatra a gipsy,
Helen and Hero hildings and harlots, Thisbe a gray
eye or so, but not to the purpose. Signior Romeo, bon
jour! There's a French salutation to your French slop.
You gave us the counterfeit fairly last night.

Romeo. Good morrow to you both. What counterfeit
did I give you?

Mercutio. The slip, sir, the slip. Can you not conceive?

Romeo. Pardon, good Mercutio. My business was great, and in such a case as mine a man may strain courtesy. 50

Mercutio. That's as much as to say, such a case as yours constrains a man to bow in the hams.

Romeo. Meaning to curtsy?

Mercutio. Thou hast most kindly hit it.

Romeo. A most courteous exposition.

Mercutio. Nay, I am the very pink of courtesy.

Romeo. Pink for flower?

Mercutio. Right.

Romeo. Why, then is my pump well flowered. 60

Mercutio. Sure wit! Follow me this jest now till thou hast worn out thy pump, that, when the single sole of it is worn, the jest may remain, after the wearing, solely singular.

Romeo. O single-soled jest, solely singular for the singleness!

Mercutio. Come between us, good Benvolio; my wits faints.

Romeo. Switch and spurs, switch and spurs; or I'll cry a match. 70

Mercutio. Nay, if our wits run the wild-goose chase, I am done: for thou hast more of the wild goose in one of thy wits than, I am sure, I have in my whole five. Was I with you there for the goose?

Romeo. Thou wast never with me for anything when thou wast not there for the goose.

Mercutio. I will bite thee by the ear for that jest.

Romeo. Nay, good goose, bite not.

Mercutio. Thy wit is a very bitter sweeting; it is a most sharp sauce. 80

Romeo. And is it not then well served in to a sweet goose?

Mercutio. O, here's a wit of cheveril, that stretches from an inch narrow to an ell broad.

Romeo. I stretch it out for that word 'broad', which, added to the goose, proves thee far and wide a broad goose.

Mercutio. Why, is not this better now than groaning for love? Now art thou sociable, now art thou Romeo: now art thou what thou art, by art as well as by nature. For this drivelling love is like a great natural that runs 90 lolling up and down to hide his bauble in a hole.

Benvolio. Stop there, stop there!

Mercutio. Thou desirest me to stop in my tale, against the hair?

Benvolio. Thou wouldst else have made thy tale large.

Mercutio. O, thou art deceived! I would have made it short, for I was come to the whole depth of my tale, and meant indeed to occupy the argument no longer.

The NURSE *in her best array is seen
approaching with her man* PETER

Romeo. Here's goodly gear! A sail, a sail!

Mercutio. Two, two! a shirt and a smock.

100 *Nurse.* Peter!

Peter. Anon.

Nurse. My fan, Peter.

(*Mercutio.* Good Peter, to hide her face; for her fan's the fairer face.

Nurse. God ye good morrow, gentlemen.

Mercutio. God ye good-den, fair gentlewoman.

Nurse. Is it good-den?

Mercutio. 'Tis no less, I tell ye; for the bawdy hand of the dial is now upon the prick of noon.

110 *Nurse.* Out upon you! What a man are you?

Romeo. One, gentlewoman, that God hath made, himself to mar.

Nurse. By my troth, it is well said. 'For himself to mar,' quoth 'a? Gentlemen, can any of you tell me where I may find the young Romeo?

Romeo. I can tell you; but young Romeo will be older when you have found him than he was when you sought him. I am the youngest of that name, for fault of a worse.

Nurse. You say well.

Mercutio. Yea, is the worst well? Very well took, 120 i' faith! Wisely, wisely!

Nurse. If you be he, sir, I desire some confidence with you.

Benvolio. She will indite him to some supper.

(*Mercutio.* A bawd, a bawd, a bawd! So ho!

Romeo. What, hast thou found?

Mercutio. No hare, sir; unless a hare, sir, in a lenten pie, that is something stale and hoar ere it be spent.

'*He walks by them and sings*'

　　An old hare hoar
　　And an old hare hoar
　Is very good meat in Lent.　　　　　130
　　But a hare that is hoar
　　Is too much for a score
When it hoars ere it be spent.

Romeo, will you come to your father's? We'll to dinner thither.

Romeo. I will follow you.

Mercutio. Farewell, ancient lady; farewell, [*singing*] 'lady, lady, lady'.　　　　　[*Mercutio and Benvolio go off*

Nurse. I pray you, sir, what saucy merchant was this 140 that was so full of his ropery?

Romeo. A gentleman, Nurse, that loves to hear himself talk, and will speak more in a minute than he will stand to in a month.

Nurse. And 'a speak anything against me, I'll take him down and 'a were lustier than he is, and twenty such Jacks: and if I cannot, I'll find those that shall. Scurvy knave! I am none of his flirt-gills, I am none of his skains-mates. [*To Peter*] And thou must stand by

150 too, and suffer every knave to use me at his pleasure!

Peter. I saw no man use you at his pleasure. If I had, my weapon should quickly have been out. I warrant you I dare draw as soon as another man, if I see occasion in a good quarrel, and the law on my side.

Nurse. Now afore God, I am so vexed that every part about me quivers. Scurvy knave! Pray you, sir, a word. And as I told you, my young lady bid me enquire you out. What she bid me say I will keep to myself: but first let me tell ye, if ye should lead her in a fool's paradise,

160 as they say, it were a very gross kind of behaviour, as they say: for the gentlewoman is young; and therefore, if you should deal double with her, truly it were an ill thing to be offered to any gentlewoman, and very weak dealing.

Romeo. Nurse, commend me to thy lady and mistress. I protest unto thee—

Nurse. Good heart! and i' faith I will tell her as much. Lord, Lord! she will be a joyful woman.

Romeo. What wilt thou tell her, Nurse? Thou dost not

170 mark me!

Nurse. I will tell her, sir, that you do protest, which, as I take it, is a gentlemanlike offer.

Romeo. Bid her devise

Some means to come to shrift this afternoon,

And there she shall at Friar Lawrence' cell

Be shrived and married. Here is for thy pains.

Nurse. No, truly, sir; not a penny.

Romeo. Go to, I say you shall.

Nurse. This afternoon, sir; well, she shall be there.

Romeo. And stay, good Nurse, behind the abbey wall. 180
Within this hour my man shall be with thee
And bring thee cords made like a tackled stair,
Which to the high topgallant of my joy
Must be my convoy in the secret night.
Farewell. Be trusty, and I'll quit thy pains.
Farewell. Commend me to thy mistress.

Nurse. Now God in heaven bless thee! Hark you, sir.

Romeo. What sayst thou, my dear Nurse?

Nurse. Is your man secret? Did you ne'er hear say,
'Two may keep counsel, putting one away'?   190

Romeo. I warrant thee my man's as true as steel.

Nurse. Well, sir, my mistress is the sweetest lady.
Lord, Lord! when 'twas a little prating thing—O, there
is a nobleman in town, one Paris, that would fain lay
knife aboard: but she, good soul, had as lief see a toad,
a very toad, as see him. I anger her sometimes, and
tell her that Paris is the properer man; but I'll warrant
you, when I say so, she looks as pale as any clout in the
versal world. Doth not rosemary and Romeo begin both
with a letter?   200

Romeo. Ay, Nurse; what of that? Both with an R.

Nurse. Ah, mocker, that's the dog-name; R is for
the—No; I know it begins with some other letter; and
she hath the prettiest sententious of it, of you and
rosemary, that it would do you good to hear it.

Romeo. Commend me to thy lady.

Nurse. Ay, a thousand times. [*Romeo goes*] Peter!

Peter. Anon.

Nurse. Before and apace.   [*they go*

[2. 5.]   *Capulet's orchard*

'*Enter* JULIET'

Juliet. The clock struck nine when I did send
    the Nurse;
.In half an hour she promised to return.
Perchance she cannot meet him. That's not so.
O, she is lame! Love's heralds should be thoughts,
Which ten times faster glides than the sun's beams
Driving back shadows over louring hills.
Therefore do nimble-pinioned doves draw Love,
And therefore hath the wind-swift Cupid wings.
Now is the sun upon the highmost hill
10 Of this day's journey, and from nine till twelve
Is three long hours; yet she is not come.
Had she affections and warm youthful blood,
She would be swift in motion as a ball;
My words would bandy her to my sweet love,
And his to me.
But old folks, many feign as they were dead—
Unwieldy, slow, heavy, and pale as lead.

'*Enter* NURSE', *with* PETER

O God, she comes! O honey Nurse, what news?
Hast thou met with him? Send thy man away.
20   *Nurse.* Peter, stay at the gate.   [*Peter withdraws*
  Juliet. Now good sweet Nurse—O Lord, why
    look'st thou sad?
Though news be sad, yet tell them merrily;
If good, thou shamest the music of sweet news
By playing it to me with so sour a face.
  Nurse. I am aweary, give me leave a while.
Fie, how my bones ache! What a jaunce have I!

Juliet. I would thou hadst my bones, and I
 thy news:
Nay, come, I pray thee speak; good, good
 Nurse, speak.
Nurse. Jesu, what haste! Can you not stay awhile?
Do you not see that I am out of breath? 30
 Juliet. How art thou out of breath when thou
 hast breath
To say to me that thou art out of breath?
The excuse that thou dost make in this delay
Is longer than the tale thou dost excuse.
Is thy news good or bad? Answer to that.
Say either, and I'll stay the circumstance.
Let me be satisfied; is't good or bad?
 Nurse. Well, you have made a simple choice; you
know not how to choose a man. Romeo? No, not he.
Though his face be better than any man's, yet his leg 40
excels all men's; and for a hand and a foot and a body,
though they be not to be talked on, yet they are past
compare. He is not the flower of courtesy, but, I'll
warrant him, as gentle as a lamb. Go thy ways, wench;
serve God. What, have you dined at home?
 Juliet. No, no. But all this did I know before.
What says he of our marriage, what of that?
 Nurse. Lord, how my head aches! what a head have I!
It beats as it would fall in twenty pieces.
My back o' t'other side; ah, my back, my back! 50
Beshrew your heart for sending me about
To catch my death with jauncing up and down.
 Juliet. I' faith, I am sorry that thou art not well.
Sweet, sweet, sweet Nurse, tell me, what says my love?
 Nurse. Your love says, like an honest gentleman, and a
courteous, and a kind, and a handsome, and, I warrant,
a virtuous—Where is your mother?

Juliet. Where is my mother? Why, she is within.
Where should she be? How oddly thou repliest:
60 'Your love says, like an honest gentleman,
"Where is your mother?"'
   Nurse.   O God's Lady dear!
Are you so hot? Marry come up, I trow!
Is this the poultice for my aching bones?
Henceforward do your messages yourself.
   Juliet. Here's such a coil! Come, what says Romeo?
   Nurse. Have you got leave to go to shrift today?
   Juliet. I have.
   Nurse. Then hie you hence to Friar Lawrence' cell;
There stays a husband to make you a wife.
70 Now comes the wanton blood up in your cheeks;
They'll be in scarlet straight at any news.
Hie you to church; I must another way,
To fetch a ladder, by the which your love
Must climb a bird's nest soon when it is dark.
I am the drudge, and toil in your delight:
But you shall bear the burden soon at night.
Go; I'll to dinner; hie you to the cell.
   Juliet. Hie to high fortune! Honest Nurse, farewell.
                             [they go

[2. 6.]   *Friar Lawrence's cell*

'*Enter* FRIAR *and* ROMEO'

   Friar. So smile the heavens upon this holy act
That after-hours with sorrow chide us not.
   Romeo. Amen, amen. But come what sorrow can,
It cannot countervail the exchange of joy
That one short minute gives me in her sight.
Do thou but close our hands with holy words,

Then love-devouring death do what he dare;
It is enough I may but call her mine.

 Friar. These violent delights have violent ends, } Foreshadowing
And in their triumph die like fire and powder   10
Which, as they kiss, consume. The sweetest honey
Is loathsome in his own deliciousness,
And in the taste confounds the appetite.
Therefore love moderately; long love doth so:
Too swift arrives as tardy as too slow.
Here comes the lady.

                    '*Enter JULIET*'

                    O, so light a foot
Will ne'er wear out the everlasting flint!
A lover may bestride the gossamers
That idles in the wanton summer air,
And yet not fall; so light is vanity.   20

 Juliet. Good even to my ghostly confessor.

 Friar. Romeo shall thank thee, daughter, for
  us both.

 Juliet. As much to him, else is his thanks too much.
                    [*they embrace*

 Romeo. Ah, Juliet, if the measure of thy joy
Be heaped like mine, and that thy skill be more
To blazon it, then sweeten with thy breath
This neighbour air, and let rich music's tongue
Unfold the imagined happiness that both
Receive in either by this dear encounter.

 Juliet. Conceit, more rich in matter than
  in words,   30
Brags of his substance, not of ornament.
They are but beggars that can count their worth;
But my true love is grown to such excess
I cannot sum up sum of half my wealth.

Friar. Come, come with me, and we will make
    short work;
For, by your leaves, you shall not stay alone
Till Holy Church incorporate two in one.   *[they go*

[3. 1.]   *A public place*

'*Enter* MERCUTIO, BENVOLIO, *and*' *their* '*men*'

Benvolio. I pray thee, good Mercutio, let's retire;
The day is hot, the Capels are abroad:
And if we meet we shall not scape a brawl,
For now, these hot days, is the mad blood stirring.

Mercutio. Thou art like one of these fellows that, when
he enters the confines of a tavern, claps me his sword
upon the table and says 'God send me no need of thee';
and, by the operation of the second cup, draws him on
the drawer, when indeed there is no need.

10   *Benvolio.* Am I like such a fellow?

Mercutio. Come, come, thou art as hot a Jack in thy
mood as any in Italy; and as soon moved to be moody,
and as soon moody to be moved.

Benvolio. And what to?

Mercutio. Nay, an there were two such, we should
have none shortly, for one would kill the other. Thou?
Why, thou wilt quarrel with a man that hath a hair
more or a hair less in his beard than thou hast. Thou
wilt quarrel with a man for cracking nuts, having no

20   other reason but because thou hast hazel eyes. What
eye but such an eye would spy out such a quarrel? Thy
head is as full of quarrels as an egg is full of meat, and
yet thy head hath been beaten as addle as an egg for
quarrelling. Thou hast quarrelled with a man for

coughing in the street, because he hath wakened thy
dog that hath lain asleep in the sun. Didst thou not fall
out with a tailor for wearing his new doublet before
Easter? With another for tying his new shoes with old
riband? And yet thou wilt tutor me from quarrelling?

Benvolio. An I were so apt to quarrel as thou art, 30
any man should buy the fee-simple of my life for an
hour and a quarter.

Mercutio. The fee-simple? O simple!

'*Enter* TYBALT,' '*and others*'

Benvolio. By my head, here comes the Capulets.

Mercutio. By my heel, I care not.

Tybalt. Follow me close, for I will speak to them.
Gentlemen, good-den: a word with one of you.

Mercutio. And but one word with one of us? Couple
it with something; make it a word and a blow.

Tybalt. You shall find me apt enough to that, sir, an 40
you will give me occasion.

Mercutio. Could you not take some occasion without
giving?

Tybalt. Mercutio, thou consort'st with Romeo—

Mercutio. Consort? What, dost thou make us minstrels? An thou make minstrels of us, look to hear
nothing but discords. Here's my fiddlestick; here's that
shall make you dance. Zounds, consort!

Benvolio. We talk here in the public haunt
    of men.
Either withdraw unto some private place   50
And reason coldly of your grievances,
Or else depart: here all eyes gaze on us.

Mercutio. Men's eyes were made to look, and let
    them gaze.
I will not budge for no man's pleasure, I.

'Enter ROMEO'

Tybalt. Well, peace be with you, sir; here comes
    my man.

Mercutio. But I'll be hanged, sir, if he wears
    your livery.

Marry, go before to field, he'll be your follower!
Your worship in that sense may call him man.

Tybalt. Romeo, the love I bear thee can afford
60 No better term than this: thou art a villain.

Romeo. Tybalt, the reason that I have to love thee
Doth much excuse the appertaining rage
To such a greeting. Villain am I none—
Therefore farewell; I see thou knowest me not.

Tybalt. Boy, this shall not excuse the injuries
That thou hast done me; therefore turn and draw.

Romeo. I do protest I never injured thee,
But love thee better than thou canst devise
Till thou shalt know the reason of my love:
70 And so, good Capulet, which name I tender
As dearly as mine own, be satisfied.

Mercutio. O calm, dishonourable, vile submission!
'Alla stoccata' carries it away.   [*draws*
Tybalt, you rat-catcher, will you walk?

Tybalt. What wouldst thou have with me?

Mercutio. Good King of Cats, nothing but one of
your nine lives that I mean to make bold withal and,
as you shall use me hereafter, dry-beat the rest of the
eight. Will you pluck your sword out of his pilcher by
80 the ears? Make haste, lest mine be about your ears ere
it be out.

Tybalt. I am for you.   [*draws*

Romeo. Gentle Mercutio, put thy rapier up.

Mercutio. Come, sir, your passado.   [*they fight*

Romeo. Draw, Benvolio; beat down their weapons.
Gentlemen, for shame forbear this outrage.
Tybalt, Mercutio, the prince expressly hath
Forbid this bandying in Verona streets.
Hold, Tybalt! good Mercutio!

'*Tybalt under Romeo's arm thrusts Mercutio in
and flies*'.

Mercutio.   I am hurt.
A plague o' both your houses! I am sped.   90
Is he gone and hath nothing?
Benvolio.   What, art thou hurt?
Mercutio. Ay, ay, a scratch, a scratch; marry,
    'tis enough.
Where is my page? Go, villain, fetch a surgeon.
                              [*Page goes*
Romeo. Courage, man; the hurt cannot be much.
Mercutio. No, 'tis not so deep as a well, nor so wide as
a church door, but 'tis enough, 'twill serve. Ask for me
tomorrow and you shall find me a grave man. I am
peppered, I warrant, for this world. A plague o' both
your houses! Zounds! A dog, a rat, a mouse, a cat, to
scratch a man to death! A braggart, a rogue, a villain, 100
that fights by the book of arithmetic! Why the devil
came you between us? I was hurt under your arm.
Romeo. I thought all for the best.
Mercutio. Help me into some house, Benvolio,
Or I shall faint. A plague o' both your houses!
They have made worms' meat of me. I have it,
And soundly too. Your houses!
                         [*Benvolio helps him away*
Romeo. This gentleman, the prince's near ally,
My very friend, hath got this mortal hurt
In my behalf, my reputation stained   110

With Tybalt's slander—Tybalt that an hour
Hath been my cousin. O sweet Juliet,
Thy beauty hath made me effeminate,
And in my temper softened valour's steel!

BENVOLIO *returns*

Benvolio. O Romeo, Romeo, brave Mercutio's
    dead.
That gallant spirit hath aspired the clouds,
Which too untimely here did scorn the earth.
    Romeo. This day's black fate on moe days
       doth depend;
This but begins the woe others must end.

TYBALT *returns*

120 *Benvolio.* Here comes the furious Tybalt
       back again.
    Romeo. Again! in triumph, and Mercutio slain!
Away to heaven, respective lenity,
And fire-eyed fury be my conduct now!
Now, Tybalt, take the 'villain' back again
That late thou gavest me, for Mercutio's soul
Is but a little way above our heads,
Staying for thine to keep him company.
Either thou or I, or both, must go with him.
    Tybalt. Thou wretched boy that didst consort
       him here
130 Shalt with him hence.
    Romeo.   This shall determine that.
               ['*they fight, Tybalt falls*'
    Benvolio. Romeo, away, be gone!
The citizens are up, and Tybalt slain.
Stand not amazed. The prince will doom thee death
If thou art taken. Hence, be gone, away!

Romeo. O, I am Fortune's fool.

Benvolio.   Why dost thou stay?

                            [*Romeo goes*

'*Enter Citizens*'

A Citizen. Which way ran he that killed Mercutio?
Tybalt, that murderer, which way ran he?

Benvolio. There lies that Tybalt.

A Citizen.   Up, sir, go with me:
I charge thee in the prince's name obey.

'*Enter* PRINCE, *old* MONTAGUE, CAPULET, *their wives and all*'

Prince. Where are the vile beginners of this fray?   140

Benvolio. O noble Prince, I can discover all
The unlucky manage of this fatal brawl.
There lies the man, slain by young Romeo,
That slew thy kinsman, brave Mercutio.

Lady Capulet. Tybalt, my cousin, O my
     brother's child!
O prince! O husband! O, the blood is spilled
Of my dear kinsman. Prince, as thou art true,
For blood of ours shed blood of Montague.
O cousin, cousin!

Prince. Benvolio, who began this bloody fray?   150

Benvolio. Tybalt, here slain, whom Romeo's hand
     did slay.
Romeo, that spoke him fair, bid him bethink
How nice the quarrel was, and urged withal
Your high displeasure. All this—utteréd
With gentle breath, calm look, knees humbly bowed—
Could not take truce with the unruly spleen
Of Tybalt deaf to peace, but that he tilts
With piercing steel at bold Mercutio's breast,

Who, all as hot, turns deadly point to point,
160 And, with a martial scorn, with one hand beats
Cold death aside and with the other sends
It back to Tybalt, whose dexterity
Retorts it. Romeo he cries aloud,
'Hold, friends! friends, part!' and, swifter than
      his tongue,
His agile arm beats down their fatal points,
And 'twixt them rushes; underneath whose arm
An envious thrust from Tybalt hit the life
Of stout Mercutio, and then Tybalt fled,
But by and by comes back to Romeo
170 Who had but newly entertained revenge,
And to 't they go like lightning; for, ere I
Could draw to part them, was stout Tybalt slain,
And, as he fell, did Romeo turn and fly:
This is the truth, or let Benvolio die.

   Lady Capulet. He is a kinsman to the Montague;
Affection makes him false, he speaks not true.
Some twenty of them fought in this black strife,
And all those twenty could but kill one life.
I beg for justice, which thou, Prince, must give:
180 Romeo slew Tybalt; Romeo must not live.

   Prince. Romeo slew him; he slew Mercutio.
Who now the price of his dear blood doth owe?

   Montague. Not Romeo, Prince; he was
      Mercutio's friend;
His fault concludes but what the law should end—
The life of Tybalt.

   Prince.   And for that offence
Immediately we do exile him hence.
I have an interest in your hearts' proceeding:
My blood for your rude brawls doth lie a-bleeding.
But I'll amerce you with so strong a fine

That you shall all repent the loss of mine.   190
I will be deaf to pleading and excuses;
Nor tears nor prayers shall purchase out abuses.
Therefore use none. Let Romeo hence in haste,
Else, when he is found, that hour is his last. *foreshadowing*
Bear hence this body, and attend our will.
Mercy but murders, pardoning those that kill.

                                        [*they go*

[3. 2.]   *Capulet's house*

                '*Enter* JULIET *alone*'

Juliet. Gallop apace, you fiery-footed steeds,
Towards Phoebus' lodging! Such a waggoner
As Phaëton would whip you to the west
And bring in cloudy night immediately.
Spread thy close curtain, love-performing night,
†That runaways' eyes may wink, and Romeo
Leap to these arms untalked of and unseen.
Lovers can see to do their amorous rites
By their own beauties; or, if love be blind,
It best agrees with night. Come, civil Night,   10
Thou sober-suited matron all in black,
And learn me how to lose a winning match,
Played for a pair of stainless maidenhoods.
Hood my unmanned blood, bating in my cheeks,
With thy black mantle till strange love, grown bold,
Think true love acted simple modesty.
Come, Night! Come, Romeo! Come, thou day *black/white*
    in night;   *contrast*
For thou wilt lie upon the wings of night
Whiter than snow upon a raven's back.
Come, gentle Night; come, loving, black-
    browed Night: 20

Give me my Romeo; and, when he shall die,
Take him and cut him out in little stars,
And he will make the face of heaven so fine
That all the world will be in love with night
And pay no worship to the garish sun.
O, I have bought the mansion of a love,
But not possessed it; and though I am sold,
Not yet enjoyed. So tedious is this day
As is the night before some festival
30 To an impatient child that hath new robes
And may not wear them. O, here comes my nurse,

'*Enter Nurse with cords*'

And she brings news; and every tongue that speaks
But Romeo's name speaks heavenly eloquence.
Now, Nurse, what news? What hast thou there? The cords
That Romeo bid thee fetch?
    Nurse.   Ay, ay, the cords.
                        [*throws them down*
    Juliet. Ay me, what news? Why dost thou wring
        thy hands?
    Nurse. Ah, weraday! He's dead, he's dead,
        he's dead!
We are undone, lady, we are undone.
Alack the day, he's gone, he's killed, he's dead!
40 *Juliet.* Can heaven be so envious?
    Nurse.   Romeo can,
Though heaven cannot. O Romeo, Romeo!
Who ever would have thought it? Romeo!
    Juliet. What devil art thou that dost torment
        me thus?
This torture should be roared in dismal hell.
Hath Romeo slain himself? Say thou but 'ay',

And that bare vowel 'I' shall poison more
Than the death-darting eye of cockatrice.
I am not I if there be such an 'I',
Or those eyes shut that makes thee answer 'ay'.
If he be slain, say 'ay', or, if not, 'no'.   50
Brief sounds determine of my weal or woe.

Nurse. I saw the wound, I saw it with mine eyes,
(God save the mark!) here on his manly breast.
A piteous corse, a bloody piteous corse,
Pale, pale as ashes, all bedaubed in blood,   "black/white"
All in gore blood; I swounded at the sight.

Juliet. O break, my heart! Poor bankrout, break
     at once!
To prison, eyes; ne'er look on liberty.
Vile earth, to earth resign, end motion here,
And thou and Romeo press one heavy bier!   60

Nurse. O Tybalt, Tybalt, the best friend I had!
O courteous Tybalt, honest gentleman,
That ever I should live to see thee dead!

Juliet. What storm is this that blows so contrary?
Is Romeo slaught'red? and is Tybalt dead?
My dearest cousin, and my dearer lord?
Then, dreadful trumpet, sound the general doom;
For who is living if those two are gone?

Nurse. Tybalt is gone and Romeo banishéd;
Romeo that killed him, he is banishéd.   70

Juliet. O God! did Romeo's hand shed
     Tybalt's blood?

Nurse. It did, it did! alas the day, it did!

Juliet. O serpent heart, hid with a flowering face!
Did ever dragon keep so fair a cave?
Beautiful tyrant, fiend angelical,   Contrast
Dove-feathered raven, wolvish-ravening lamb!
Despiséd substance of divinest show,

(left margin, handwritten:) we of the word that was apt to the passage. Brilliant apposite

Just opposite to what thou justly seemst—
A damnéd saint, an honourable villain!
80 O nature, what hadst thou to do in hell
When thou didst bower the spirit of a fiend
In mortal paradise of such sweet flesh?
Was ever book containing such vile matter
So fairly bound? O that deceit should dwell
In such a gorgeous palace!
    Nurse.   There's no trust,
No faith, no honesty in men; all perjured,
All forsworn, all naught, all dissemblers.
Ah, where's my man? Give me some aqua vitae.
These griefs, these woes, these sorrows make me old.
90 Shame come to Romeo!
    Juliet.   Blistered be thy tongue
For such a wish! He was not born to shame.
Upon his brow shame is ashamed to sit:
For 'tis a throne where honour may be crowned
Sole monarch of the universal earth.
O what a beast was I to chide at him!
    Nurse. Will you speak well of him that killed
        your cousin?
    Juliet. Shall I speak ill of him that is my husband?
Ah, poor my lord, what tongue shall smooth
        thy name
When I, thy three-hours wife, have mangled it?
100 But wherefore, villain, didst thou kill my cousin?
That villain cousin would have killed my husband.
Back, foolish tears, back to your native spring!
Your tributary drops belong to woe
Which you, mistaking, offer up to joy.
My husband lives, that Tybalt would have slain,
And Tybalt's dead that would have slain my husband:
All this is comfort; wherefore weep I then?

(right margin, handwritten:) foreshadow

(left margin, handwritten:) Tybalt or Romeo Juliet realizes one must die: Rather it be Romeo.

Some word there was, worser than Tybalt's death,
That murd'red me. I would forget it fain,
But oh, it presses to my memory   110
Like damnéd guilty deeds to sinners' minds—
'Tybalt is dead and Romeo banishéd'.
That 'banishéd', that one word 'banishéd',
Hath slain ten thousand Tybalts. Tybalt's death
Was woe enough if it had ended there:
Or, if sour woe delights in fellowship
And needly will be ranked with other griefs,
Why followed not, when she said 'Tybalt's dead',
'Thy father', or 'thy mother', nay, or both,
Which modern lamentation might have moved?   120
But, with a rearward following Tybalt's death,
'Romeo is banishéd'! To speak that word
Is father, mother, Tybalt, Romeo, Juliet,
All slain, all dead: 'Romeo is banishéd'!
There is no end, no limit, measure, bound,
In that word's death; no words can that
        woe sound.
Where is my father and my mother, Nurse?
  Nurse. Weeping and wailing over Tybalt's corse.
Will you go to them? I will bring you thither.
  Juliet. Wash they his wounds with tears? Mine
        shall be spent,   130
When theirs are dry, for Romeo's banishment.
Take up those cords. Poor ropes, you are beguiled,
Both you and I, for Romeo is exiled.
He made you for a highway to my bed,
But I, a maid, die maiden-widowéd.
Come, cords; come, Nurse: I'll to my wedding bed,
And death, not Romeo, take my maidenhead!
  Nurse. Hie to your chamber. I'll find Romeo
To comfort you: I wot well where he is.

140 Hark ye, your Romeo will be here at night:
I'll to him; he is hid at Lawrence' cell.
    Juliet. O find him! Give this ring to my true knight
And bid him come to take his last farewell.

                                              [*they go*

    [3. 3.]   *Friar Lawrence's cell with his
                    study at the back*

                    Enter FRIAR

    Friar. Romeo, come forth; come forth, thou
        fearful man.
Affliction is enamoured of thy parts,
And thou art wedded to calamity.   Foreshadowing

                Enter ROMEO *from the study*

    Romeo. Father, what news? What is the
        prince's doom?
What sorrow craves acquaintance at my hand
That I yet know not?
    Friar.   Too familiar
Is my dear son with such sour company!
I bring thee tidings of the prince's doom.
    Romeo. What less than doomsday is the
        prince's doom?
10 *Friar.* A gentler judgment vanished from his lips;
Not body's death, but body's banishment.
    Romeo. Ha, banishment? Be merciful, say 'death':
For exile hath more terror in his look,
Much more than death: do not say 'banishment'.
    Friar. Hence from Verona art thou banishéd.
Be patient, for the world is broad and wide.
    Romeo. There is no world without Verona walls,
But purgatory, torture, hell itself:

Hence banishéd is banished from the world,
And world's exile is death. Then 'banishéd'   20
Is death mis-termed. Calling death 'banishéd',
Thou cut'st my head off with a golden axe,
And smilest upon the stroke that murders me.

  Friar. O deadly sin! O rude unthankfulness!
Thy fault our law calls death, but the kind Prince,
Taking thy part, hath rushed aside the law,
And turned that black word 'death' to 'banishment'.
This is dear mercy, and thou seest it not.

  Romeo. 'Tis torture and not mercy. Heaven is here
Where Juliet lives, and every cat and dog   30
And little mouse, every unworthy thing,
Live here in heaven and may look on her,
But Romeo may not. More validity,
More honourable state, more courtship, lives
In carrion flies than Romeo: they may seize
On the white wonder of dear Juliet's hand,
And steal immortal blessing from her lips,
Who even in pure and vestal modesty
Still blush, as thinking their own kisses sin;
This may flies do, when I from this must fly;   40
And say'st thou yet that exile is not death?
⌈But Romeo may not—he is banishéd.
|Flies may do this, but I from this must fly:
⌊They are free men, but I am banishéd.
Hadst thou no poison mixed, no sharp-ground knife,
No sudden mean of death, though ne'er so mean,
But 'banishéd' to kill me? 'Banishéd'!
O friar, the damnéd use that word in hell:
Howling attends it. How hast thou the heart,
Being a divine, a ghostly confessor,   50
A sin-absolver, and my friend professed,
To mangle me with that word 'banishéd'?

Friar. Thou fond mad man, hear me a little speak.

Romeo. O thou wilt speak again of banishment.

Friar. I'll give thee armour to keep off that word—
Adversity's sweet milk, philosophy,
To comfort thee though thou art banishéd.

Romeo. Yet 'banishéd'? Hang up philosophy!
Unless philosophy can make a Juliet,
60 Displant a town, reverse a prince's doom,
It helps not, it prevails not; talk no more.

Friar. O then I see that madmen have no ears.

Romeo. How should they, when that wise men have
    no eyes?

Friar. Let me dispute with thee of thy estate.

Romeo. Thou canst not speak of that thou dost
    not feel.
Wert thou as young as I, Juliet thy love,
An hour but married, Tybalt murderéd,
Doting like me, and like me banishéd,
Then mightst thou speak, then mightst thou tear
    thy hair,
70 And fall upon the ground as I do now,
Taking the measure of an unmade grave.
                    [*knocking without*

Friar. Arise; one knocks. Good Romeo, hide thyself.

Romeo. Not I, unless the breath of heartsick groans
Mist-like infold me from the search of eyes.
                    [*knocking again*

Friar. Hark, how they knock!—Who's there?—
    Romeo, arise;
Thou wilt be taken.—Stay awhile!—Stand up;
                    [*louder knocking*
Run to my study.—By and by!—God's will,
What simpleness is this?—I come, I come!
                    [*knocking yet again*

Who knocks so hard? Whence come you? What's
    your will?
  Nurse. [*from without*] Let me come in and you shall
    know my errand: 80
I come from Lady Juliet.
  Friar.   Welcome then.

'*Enter* NURSE'

  Nurse. O holy friar, O tell me, holy friar,
Where is my lady's lord? Where's Romeo?
  Friar. There on the ground, with his own tears
    made drunk.
  Nurse. O he is even in my mistress' case,
Just in her case.
  Friar.   O woeful sympathy:
Piteous predicament!
  Nurse.   Even so lies she,
Blubbering and weeping, weeping and blubbering.
Stand up, stand up! Stand an you be a man;
For Juliet's sake, for her sake rise and stand: 90
Why should you fall into so deep an O?
  Romeo. [*rising*] Nurse!
  Nurse.   Ah sir, ah sir, death's the end of all.
  Romeo. Spakest thou of Juliet? How is it with her?
Doth not she think me an old murderer,
Now I have stained the childhood of our joy
With blood removed but little from her own?
Where is she? and how doth she? and what says
My concealed lady to our cancelled love?
  Nurse. O she says nothing, sir, but weeps and weeps,
And now falls on her bed, and then starts up,   100
And Tybalt calls, and then on Romeo cries,
And then down falls again.
  Romeo.   As if that name,

Shot from the deadly level of a gun,
Did murder her, as that name's curséd hand
Murdered her kinsman. O tell me, friar, tell me,
In what vile part of this anatomy
Doth my name lodge? Tell me, that I may sack
The hateful mansion.   ['*he offers to stab himself, and*
                                      Nurse snatches the dagger away'

  Friar.   Hold thy desperate hand!
Art thou a man? Thy form cries out thou art:
110 Thy tears are womanish, thy wild acts denote
The unreasonable fury of a beast.
Unseemly woman in a seeming man,
And ill-beseeming beast in seeming both!
Thou hast amazed me. By my holy order,
I thought thy disposition better tempered.
Hast thou slain Tybalt? Wilt thou slay thyself?
And slay thy lady, that in thy life lives,
By doing damnéd hate upon thyself?
Why rail'st thou on thy birth, the heaven, and earth,
120 Since birth, and heaven, and earth, all three do meet
In thee at once, which thou at once wouldst lose?
Fie, fie! thou sham'st thy shape, thy love, thy wit,
Which like a usurer abound'st in all,
And usest none in that true use indeed
Which should bedeck thy shape, thy love, thy wit.
Thy noble shape is but a form of wax,
Digressing from the valour of a man;
Thy dear love sworn but hollow perjury,
Killing that love which thou hast vowed to cherish;
130 Thy wit, that ornament to shape and love,
Misshapen in the conduct of them both,
Like powder in a skilless soldier's flask
Is set afire by thine own ignorance,
And thou dismembered with thine own defence.

What, rouse thee, man! Thy Juliet is alive,
For whose dear sake thou wast but lately dead.
There art thou happy. Tybalt would kill thee,
But thou slewest Tybalt. There art thou happy.
The law that threatened death becomes thy friend,
And turns it to exile. There art thou happy too.   140
A pack of blessings light upon thy back;
Happiness courts thee in her best array;
But, like a misbehaved and sullen wench,
Thou pouts upon thy fortune and thy love.
Take heed, take heed, for such die miserable.
Go get thee to thy love, as was decreed;
Ascend her chamber; hence and comfort her.
But look thou stay not till the watch be set,
For then thou canst not pass to Mantua,
Where thou shalt live till we can find a time   150
To blaze your marriage, reconcile your friends,
Beg pardon of the prince, and call thee back
With twenty hundred thousand times more joy
Than thou wentst forth in lamentation.
Go before, Nurse. Commend me to thy lady,
And bid her hasten all the house to bed,
Which heavy sorrow makes them apt unto.
Romeo is coming.
  Nurse. O Lord, I could have stayed here all
     the night
To hear good counsel; O what learning is!   160
My lord, I'll tell my lady you will come.
  Romeo. Do so, and bid my sweet prepare to chide.

     '*Nurse offers to go in and turns again*'

  Nurse. Here, sir, a ring she bid me give you, sir.
Hie you, make haste, for it grows very late. [*she goes*
  Romeo. How well my comfort is revived by this.

Friar. Go hence; goodnight; and here stands all
    your state:
Either be gone before the watch be set,
Or by the break of day disguised from hence.
Sojourn in Mantua. I'll find out your man,
170 And he shall signify from time to time
Every good hap to you that chances here.
Give me thy hand. 'Tis late; farewell, goodnight.
  Romeo. But that a joy past joy calls out on me,
It were a grief so brief to part with thee.
Farewell.   [*they go*

[3. 4.]   *Capulet's house*

'*Enter old* CAPULET, *his wife, and* PARIS'

  Capulet. Things have fall'n out, sir, so unluckily
That we have had no time to move our daughter.
Look you, she loved her kinsman Tybalt dearly,
And so did I. Well, we were born to die.
'Tis very late; she'll not come down tonight.
I promise you, but for your company,
I would have been abed an hour ago.
  Paris. These times of woe afford no times
    to woo.
Madam, goodnight; commend me to your daughter.
10 *Lady Capulet.* I will, and know her mind
    early tomorrow;
Tonight she's mewed up to her heaviness.

Paris offers to go; Capulet calls him again

  Capulet. Sir Paris, I will make a desperate tender
Of my child's love: I think she will be ruled heavy
In all respects by me: nay more, I doubt it not. father
Wife, go you to her ere you go to bed;

Acquaint her ear of my son Paris' love,
And bid her, mark you me, on Wednesday next—
But soft, what day is this?
  Paris.   Monday, my lord.
  Capulet. Monday, ha, ha; well, Wednesday is
    too soon;
O' Thursday let it be— O' Thursday, tell her,   20
She shall be married to this noble earl—
Will you be ready? Do you like this haste?
We'll keep no great ado; a friend or two:
For hark you, Tybalt being slain so late,
It may be thought we held him carelessly,
Being our kinsman, if we revel much:
Therefore we'll have some half a dozen friends,
And there an end. But what say you to Thursday?
  Paris. My lord, I would that Thursday
    were tomorrow.
  Capulet. Well, get you gone. O' Thursday be
    it then.   30
Go you to Juliet ere you go to bed;
Prepare her, wife, against this wedding day.
Farewell, my lord. Light to my chamber, ho!
Afore me, 'tis so very late, that we
May call it early by and by. Goodnight.   *[they go*

[3. 5.]   *Juliet's bedroom: to one side the
      window above the Orchard; to the other a door*

     ROMEO and JULIET stand by the window

  Juliet. Wilt thou be gone? It is not yet near day.
It was the nightingale, and not the lark,
That pierced the fearful hollow of thine ear.
Nightly she sings on yond pomegranate tree.

Believe me, love, it was the nightingale.

Romeo. It was the lark, the herald of the morn;
No nightingale. Look, love, what envious streaks
Do lace the severing clouds in yonder east.
Night's candles are burnt out, and jocund day
10 Stands tiptoe on the misty mountain tops.
I must be gone and live, or stay and die. choice of two extremes

Juliet. Yond light is not daylight; I know it, I:
It is some meteor that the sun exhaled
To be to thee this night a torchbearer
And light thee on thy way to Mantua.
Therefore stay yet; thou needst not to be gone.

Romeo. Let me be ta'en, let me be put
   to death;
I am content, so thou wilt have it so.
I'll say yon gray is not the morning's eye,
20 'Tis but the pale reflex of Cynthia's brow;
Nor that is not the lark whose notes do beat
The vaulty heaven so high above our heads.
I have more care to stay than will to go:
Come, death, and welcome! Juliet wills it so.
How is't, my soul? Let's talk; it is not day.

Juliet. It is, it is! Hie hence, be gone, away!
It is the lark that sings so out of tune,   Unpleasing sound
Straining harsh discords and unpleasing sharps. from circumflow
Some say the lark makes sweet division:
30 This doth not so, for she divideth us.
Some say the lark and loathèd toad changed eyes;
O now I would they had changed voices too,
Since arm from arm that voice doth us affray,
Hunting thee hence with hunt's-up to the day.
O now be gone! More light and light it grows.

Romeo. More light and light, more dark and dark
   our woes.

b/w

'*Enter NURSE hastily*'

Nurse. Madam!

Juliet. Nurse?

Nurse. Your lady mother is coming to your chamber.
The day is broke; be wary, look about.   40

> [*she goes; Juliet bolts the door*

Juliet. Then, window, let day in and let life out.

Romeo. Farewell, farewell; one kiss, and I'll descend.

> [*he lowers the ladder and descends*

Juliet. Art thou gone so, love, lord, ay
    husband, friend?
I must hear from thee every day in the hour,
For in a minute there are many days.
O, by this count I shall be much in years
Ere I again behold my Romeo.

Romeo. [*from the orchard*] Farewell!
I will omit no opportunity
That may convey my greetings, love, to thee.   50

Juliet. O, think'st thou we shall ever meet again?

Romeo. I doubt it not; and all these woes shall serve
For sweet discourses in our times to come.

Juliet. O God, I have an ill-divining soul!
Methinks I see thee, now thou art so low,
As one dead in the bottom of a tomb.
Either my eyesight fails or thou look'st pale.

Romeo. And trust me, love, in my eye so do you.
Dry sorrow drinks our blood. Adieu, adieu!

> [*he goes*

Juliet. O Fortune, Fortune, all men call thee fickle; 60
If thou art fickle, what dost thou with him
That is renowned for faith? Be fickle, Fortune:
For then I hope thou wilt not keep him long,
But send him back.

Lady Capulet. [*without the door*] Ho, daughter, are
    you up?
Juliet. [*pulls up and conceals the ladder*]
Who is't that calls? It is my lady mother.
Is she not down so late, or up so early?
What unaccustomed cause procures her hither?
                         [*she unlocks the door*

Enter LADY CAPULET

Lady Capulet. Why, how now, Juliet?
Juliet.   Madam, I am not well.
Lady Capulet. Evermore weeping for your
    cousin's death?
70 What, wilt thou wash him from his grave with tears?
An if thou couldst, thou couldst not make him live:
Therefore have done—some grief shows much
      of love,
But much of grief shows still some want of wit.
Juliet. Yet let me weep for such a feeling loss.
Lady Capulet. So shall you feel the loss, but not
    the friend
Which you weep for.
Juliet.   Feeling so the loss,
I cannot choose but ever weep the friend.
Lady Capulet. Well, girl, thou weep'st not so much
    for his death,
As that the villain lives which slaughtered him.
80 *Juliet.* What villain, madam?
Lady Capulet.   That same villain Romeo.
(*Juliet.* Villain and he be many miles asunder.
[*aloud*] God pardon him; I do, with all my heart:
And yet no man like he doth grieve my heart.
Lady Capulet. That is because the traitor
    murderer lives.

Juliet. Ay, madam, from the reach of these
    my hands.
Would none but I might venge my cousin's death!
  Lady Capulet. We will have vengeance for it, fear
    thou not.
Then weep no more. I'll send to one in Mantua,
Where that same banished runagate doth live,
Shall give him such an unaccustomed dram   90
That he shall soon keep Tybalt company;
And then I hope thou wilt be satisfied.
  Juliet. Indeed I never shall be satisfied
With Romeo till I behold him—dead—
Is my poor heart so for a kinsman vexed.
Madam, if you could find out but a man
To bear a poison, I would temper it
That Romeo should upon receipt thereof
Soon sleep in quiet. O how my heart abhors
To hear him named and cannot come to him   100
To wreak the love I bore my cousin
Upon his body that hath slaughtered him.
  Lady Capulet. Find thou the means and I'll find such
    a man.
But now I'll tell thee joyful tidings, girl.
  Juliet. And joy comes well in such a
    needy time.
What are they, I beseech your ladyship?
  Lady Capulet. Well, well, thou hast a careful
    father, child;
One who, to put thee from thy heaviness,
Hath sorted out a sudden day of joy
That thou expects not, nor I looked not for.   110
  Juliet. Madam, in happy time! What day is that?
  Lady Capulet. Marry, my child, early next
    Thursday morn

The gallant, young, and noble gentleman,
The County Paris, at Saint Peter's Church
Shall happily make thee there a joyful bride.
  Juliet. Now by Saint Peter's Church, and
      Peter too,
He shall not make me there a joyful bride.
I wonder at this haste, that I must wed
Ere he that should be husband comes to woo.
120 I pray you tell my lord and father, madam,
I will not marry yet; and when I do, I swear
It shall be Romeo, whom you know I hate,
Rather than Paris. These are news indeed!
  Lady Capulet. Here comes your father; tell him
      so yourself,
And see how he will take it at your hands.

      '*Enter* CAPULET *and* NURSE'

  Capulet. When the sun sets, the air doth
      drizzle dew;
But for the sunset of my brother's son
It rains downright.
How now, a conduit, girl? What, still in tears?
130 Evermore showering? In one little body
Thou counterfeits a bark, a sea, a wind:
For still thy eyes, which I may call the sea,
Do ebb and flow with tears; the bark thy body is,
Sailing in this salt flood; the winds thy sighs,
Who raging with thy tears, and they with them,
Without a sudden calm will overset
Thy tempest-tossèd body. How now, wife?
Have you delivered to her our decree?
  Lady Capulet. Ay, sir; but she will none, she gives
      you thanks.
140 I would the fool were married to her grave!

Capulet. Soft, take me with you, take me with
     you, wife.
How? Will she none? Doth she not give us thanks?
Is she not proud? Doth she not count her blest,
Unworthy as she is, that we have wrought
So worthy a gentleman to be her bride?
   Juliet. Not proud you have, but thankful that
     you have.
Proud can I never be of what I hate,
But thankful even for hate that is meant love.
   Capulet. How how! how how, chop-logic! what
     is this?
'Proud', and 'I thank you', and 'I thank you not',   150
And yet 'not proud', mistress minion you?
Thank me no thankings nor proud me no prouds,
But fettle your fine joints 'gainst Thursday next
To go with Paris to Saint Peter's Church,
Or I will drag thee on a hurdle thither.
Out, you green-sickness carrion! out, you baggage!
You tallow-face!
   Lady Capulet.   Fie, fie! what, are you mad?
   Juliet. [*kneeling*] Good father, I beseech you on
     my knees,
Hear me with patience but to speak a word.
   Capulet. Hang thee, young baggage!
     disobedient wretch!   160
I tell thee what; get thee to church o' Thursday,
Or never after look me in the face.
Speak not, reply not, do not answer me!
My fingers itch. Wife, we scarce thought us blest
That God had lent us but this only child;
But now I see this one is one too much,
And that we have a curse in having her.
Out on her, hilding!

Nurse.   God in heaven bless her!
You are to blame, my lord, to rate her so.
170 *Capulet.* And why, my Lady Wisdom? Hold
    your tongue,
Good Prudence. Smatter with your gossips, go!
Nurse. I speak no treason.
Capulet.   O Godigoden!
Nurse. May not one speak?
Capulet.   Peace, you mumbling fool!
Utter your gravity o'er a gossip's bowl,
For here we need it not.
Lady Capulet.   You are too hot.
Capulet. God's bread! it makes me mad. Day, night,
    work, play,
Alone, in company, still my care hath been
To have her matched; and having now provided
A gentleman of noble parentage,
180 Of fair demesnes, youthful and nobly trained,
Stuffed, as they say, with honourable parts,
Proportioned as one's thought would wish a man—
And then to have a wretched puling fool,
A whining mammet, in her fortune's tender,
To answer 'I'll not wed, I cannot love;
I am too young, I pray you pardon me'.
But, an you will not wed, I'll pardon you—
Graze where you will; you shall not house with me.
Look to't, think on't; I do not use to jest.
190 Thursday is near. Lay hand on heart; advise.
An you be mine, I'll give you to my friend;
An you be not, hang, beg, starve, die in the streets,
For by my soul I'll ne'er acknowledge thee,
Nor what is mine shall never do thee good:
Trust to 't; bethink you; I'll not be forsworn.

                                        [*he goes*

Juliet. Is there no pity sitting in the clouds
That sees into the bottom of my grief?
O sweet my mother, cast me not away!
Delay this marriage for a month, a week;
Or, if you do not, make the bridal bed   200
In that dim monument where Tybalt lies.

  Lady Capulet. Talk not to me, for I'll not speak
        a word;
Do as thou wilt, for I have done with thee.

                                        [*she goes*

  Juliet. O God!—O nurse, how shall this
        be prevented?
My husband is on earth, my faith in heaven;   *christian again*
How shall that faith return again to earth,
Unless that husband send it me from heaven
By leaving earth? Comfort me, counsel me.
Alack, alack, that heaven should practise stratagems   *Fate?*
Upon so soft a subject as myself!   210
What sayst thou? Hast thou not a word of joy?
Some comfort, nurse.

  Nurse.   Faith, here it is. Romeo
Is banishéd; and all the world to nothing
That he dares ne'er come back to challenge you;
Or, if he do, it needs must be by stealth.
Then, since the case so stands as now it doth,
I think it best you married with the County.
O, he's a lovely gentleman!
Romeo's a dishclout to him. An eagle, madam,
Hath not so green, so quick, so fair an eye   220
As Paris hath. Beshrew my very heart,
I think you are happy in this second match,
For it excels your first; or, if it did not,
Your first is dead—or 'twere as good he were   *Realist view*
As living here and you no use of him.

Juliet. Speakst thou from thy heart?

Nurse. And from my soul too; else beshrew
    them both.

Juliet. Amen!

Nurse. What?

230 *Juliet.* Well, thou hast comforted me
    marvellous much.

Go in and tell my lady I am gone,

Having displeased my father, to Lawrence' cell

To make confession and to be absolved.

    Nurse. Marry, I will; and this is wisely done.

                       [*she goes*

    Juliet. Ancient damnation! O most wicked fiend!

Is it more sin to wish me thus forsworn,

Or to dispraise my lord with that same tongue

Which she hath praised him with above compare

So many thousand times? Go, counsellor!

240 Thou and my bosom henceforth shall be twain.

I'll to the friar to know his remedy.

If all else fail, myself have power to die.   [*she goes*

[4. 1.]   *Friar Lawrence's cell*

'*Enter* FRIAR *and County* PARIS'

Friar. On Thursday, sir? The time is very short.

Paris. My father Capulet will have it so,

And I am nothing slow to slack his haste.

Friar. You say you do not know the lady's mind?

Uneven is the course; I like it not.

Paris. Immoderately she weeps for Tybalt's death,

And therefore have I little talked of love,

For Venus smiles not in a house of tears.

Now, sir, her father counts it dangerous

That she do give her sorrow so much sway,   10
And in his wisdom hastes our marriage
To stop the inundation of her tears,
Which, too much minded by herself alone,
May be put from her by society.
Now do you know the reason of this haste.
    (*Friar.* I would I knew not why it should
        be slowed—
Look, sir, here comes the lady toward my cell.

'Enter JULIET'

Paris. Happily met, my lady and my wife!
Juliet. That may be, sir, when I may be a wife.
Paris. That 'may be' must be, love, on
        Thursday next.   20
Juliet. What must be shall be.   *mimic play on words*
Friar.   That's a certain text.
Paris. Come you to make confession to this father?
Juliet. To answer that, I should confess to you.
Paris. Do not deny to him that you love me.
Juliet. I will confess to you that I love him.
Paris. So will ye, I am sure, that you love me.
Juliet. If I do so, it will be of more price,
Being spoke behind your back, than to your face.
Paris. Poor soul, thy face is much abused with tears.
Juliet. The tears have got small victory by that,   30
For it was bad enough before their spite.
Paris. Thou wrong'st it more than tears with
        that report.
Juliet. That is no slander, sir, which is a truth;
And what I spake, I spake it to my face.
Paris. Thy face is mine, and thou hast sland'red it.
Juliet. It may be so, for it is not mine own.—
Are you at leisure, holy father, now,

Or shall I come to you at evening mass?
 Friar. My leisure serves me, pensive daughter, now.
40 My lord, we must entreat the time alone.
 Paris. God shield I should disturb devotion!
Juliet, on Thursday early will I rouse ye;
Till then adieu, and keep this holy kiss.
      [kisses her, and departs
 Juliet. O shut the door, and, when thou hast
  done so,
Come weep with me—past hope, past cure, past help.
 Friar. O Juliet, I already know thy grief;
It strains me past the compass of my wits.
I hear thou must, and nothing may prorogue it,
On Thursday next be married to this County.
50 *Juliet*. Tell me not, friar, that thou hearest of this,
Unless thou tell me how I may prevent it.
If in thy wisdom thou canst give no help,
Do thou but call my resolution wise
And with this knife I'll help it presently.
God joined my heart and Romeo's, thou our hands;
And ere this hand, by thee to Romeo's sealed,
Shall be the label to another deed,
Or my true heart with treacherous revolt
Turn to another, this shall slay them both:
60 Therefore, out of thy long-experienced time,
Give me some present counsel; or, behold,
'Twixt my extremes and me this bloody knife
Shall play the umpire, arbitrating that
Which the commission of thy years and art
Could to no issue of true honour bring.
Be not so long to speak: I long to die
If what thou speak'st speak not of remedy.
 Friar. Hold, daughter. I do spy a kind of hope,
Which craves as desperate an execution

As that is desperate which we would prevent.   70
If, rather than to marry County Paris,
Thou hast the strength of will to slay thyself,
Then is it likely thou wilt undertake
A thing like death to chide away this shame,
That copest with death himself to scape from it;
And, if thou darest, I'll give thee remedy.
   Juliet. O bid me leap, rather than marry Paris,
From off the battlements of any tower,
Or walk in thievish ways, or bid me lurk
Where serpents are; chain me with roaring bears,   80
Or hide me nightly in a charnel house,
O'ercovered quite with dead men's rattling bones,
With reeky shanks and yellow chapless skulls;
Or bid me go into a new-made grave
And lay me with a dead man in his shroud—
Things that, to hear them told, have made
    me tremble—
And I will do it without fear or doubt,
To live an unstained wife to my sweet love.
  Friar. Hold, then. Go home, be merry,
    give consent
To marry Paris. Wednesday is tomorrow.   90
Tomorrow night look that thou lie alone;
Let not the nurse lie with thee in thy chamber.
Take thou this vial, being then in bed,
And this distilléd liquor drink thou off,
When presently through all thy veins shall run
A cold and drowsy humour, for no pulse
Shall keep his native progress, but surcease;
No warmth, no breath, shall testify thou livest;
The roses in thy lips and cheeks shall fade
To wanny ashes, thy eyes' windows fall   100
Like death when he shuts up the day of life.

Each part, deprived of supple government,
Shall stiff and stark and cold appear like death;
And in this borrowed likeness of shrunk death
Thou shalt continue two and forty hours,
And then awake as from a pleasant sleep.
Now, when the bridegroom in the morning comes
To rouse thee from thy bed, there art thou dead.
Then, as the manner of our country is,
110 In thy best robes, uncovered on the bier,
Thou shalt be borne to that same ancient vault
Where all the kindred of the Capulets lie.
In the meantime, against thou shalt awake,
Shall Romeo by my letters know our drift,
And hither shall he come; and he and I
Will watch thy waking, and that very night
Shall Romeo bear thee hence to Mantua.
And this shall free thee from this present shame,
If no inconstant toy nor womanish fear
120 Abate thy valour in the acting it.
    Juliet. Give me, give me! O tell not me of fear!
    Friar. Hold, get you gone! Be strong
        and prosperous
In this resolve. I'll send a friar with speed
To Mantua with my letters to thy lord.
    Juliet. Love give me strength! and strength shall
        help afford.
Farewell, dear father.   *[they go*

[4. 2.] *Capulet's house*

Enter CAPULET, LADY CAPULET, NURSE
and two or three Servingmen

Capulet [*giving a paper*]. So many guests invite as here
    are writ.   [*servingman goes out with it*
[*to another*] Sirrah, go hire me twenty cunning cooks.
  Servingman. You shall have none ill, sir; for I'll try
if they can lick their fingers.
  Capulet. How canst thou try them so?
  Servingman. Marry, sir, 'tis an ill cook that cannot
lick his own fingers: therefore he that cannot lick his
fingers goes not with me.
  Capulet. Go, be gone.   [*he goes*
We shall be much unfurnished for this time.   10
What, is my daughter gone to Friar Lawrence?
  Nurse. Ay, forsooth.
  Capulet. Well, he may chance to do some good
    on her.
A peevish self-willed harlotry it is. *Seems to loath Juliet*

'*Enter* JULIET'

  Nurse. See where she comes from shrift with
    merry look.
  Capulet. How now, my headstrong? Where have you
    been gadding?
  Juliet. Where I have learned me to repent the sin
Of disobedient opposition
To you and your behests, and am enjoined *easy deceit*
By holy Lawrence to fall prostrate here   20
To beg your pardon. [*abasing herself*] Pardon,
    I beseech you!
Henceforward I am ever ruled by you.

Capulet. Send for the County: go tell him of this.
I'll have this knot knit up tomorrow morning.

Juliet. I met the youthful lord at Lawrence' cell
And gave him what becoméd love I might,
Not stepping o'er the bounds of modesty.

Capulet. Why, I am glad on't; this is well.
    Stand up.
This is as 't should be. Let me see, the County:
30 Ay, marry, go, I say, and fetch him hither.
Now, afore God, this reverend holy friar,
All our whole city is much bound to him.

Juliet. Nurse, will you go with me into my closet
To help me sort such needful ornaments
As you think fit to furnish me tomorrow?

Lady Capulet. No, not till Thursday; there is
    time enough.

Capulet. Go, nurse, go with her; we'll to
    church tomorrow.   [*Nurse departs with Juliet*

Lady Capulet. We shall be short in our provision;
'Tis now near night.

Capulet.   Tush, I will stir about,
40 And all things shall be well, I warrant thee, wife.
Go thou to Juliet; help to deck up her.
I'll not to bed tonight. Let me alone;
I'll play the housewife for this once. What, ho!
They are all forth; well, I will walk myself
To County Paris, to prepare up him
Against tomorrow. My heart is wondrous light
Since this same wayward girl is so reclaimed.   [*they go*

[4. 3.] *Juliet's chamber; at the back a bed*
with curtains

'*Enter* JULIET *and* NURSE'

Juliet. Ay, those attires are best. But,
    gentle nurse,
I pray thee leave me to myself tonight:
For I have need of many orisons
To move the heavens to smile upon my state,
Which well thou knowest is cross and full of sin.

Enter LADY CAPULET

Lady Capulet. What, are you busy, ho? Need you
    my help?
Juliet. No, madam, we have culled such necessaries
As are behoveful for our state tomorrow.
So please you, let me now be left alone,
And let the nurse this night sit up with you,   10
For I am sure you have your hands full all
In this so sudden business.
Lady Capulet.   Good night.
Get thee to bed and rest, for thou hast need.
                    [*she departs with the Nurse*
Juliet. Farewell! God knows when we shall
    meet again.
I have a faint cold fear thrills through my veins
That almost freezes up the heat of life.
I'll call them back again to comfort me.
Nurse!—What should she do here?
My dismal scene I needs must act alone.
Come, vial!
What if this mixture do not work at all?
Shall I be married then tomorrow morning?

No, no! This shall forbid it. Lie thou there.

[laying down her knife

What if it be a poison which the friar
Subtly hath minist'red to have me dead,
Lest in this marriage he should be dishonoured
Because he married me before to Romeo?
I fear it is; and yet methinks it should not,
For he hath still been tried a holy man.

30 How if, when I am laid into the tomb,
I wake before the time that Romeo
Come to redeem me? There's a fearful point!
Shall I not then be stifled in the vault,
To whose foul mouth no healthsome air breathes in,
And there die strangled ere my Romeo comes?
Or, if I live, is it not very like
The horrible conceit of death and night,
Together with the terror of the place—
As in a vault, an ancient receptacle

40 Where for this many hundred years the bones
Of all my buried ancestors are packed;
Where bloody Tybalt, yet but green in earth,
Lies festering in his shroud; where, as they say,
At some hours in the night spirits resort—
Alack, alack, is it not like that I,
So early waking—what with loathsome smells,
And shrieks like mandrakes' torn out of
      the earth,
That living mortals, hearing them, run mad—
O, if I wake, shall I not be distraught,

50 Environéd with all these hideous fears,
And madly play with my forefathers' joints,
And pluck the mangled Tybalt from his shroud,
And, in this rage, with some great kinsman's bone,
As with a club, dash out my desp'rate brains?

O, look! Methinks I see my cousin's ghost
Seeking out Romeo, that did spit his body
Upon a rapier's point. Stay, Tybalt, stay!
Romeo, I come! this do I drink to thee.

[*'she falls upon her bed within*
the curtains'

[4. 4.]   *Hall in Capulet's house*

Enter LADY CAPULET *and* 'NURSE,
with herbs'

Lady Capulet. Hold, take these keys and fetch more
    spices, nurse.
Nurse. They call for dates and quinces in the pastry.

'*Enter old* CAPULET'

Capulet. Come, stir, stir, stir! The second cock
    hath crowed:
The curfew bell hath rung, 'tis three o'clock.
Look to the baked meats, good Angelica;
Spare not for cost.
    Nurse.   Go, you cot-quean, go,
Get you to bed. Faith, you'll be sick tomorrow
For this night's watching.
    Capulet. No, not a whit. What, I have watched
    ere now
All night for lesser cause, and ne'er been sick.   10
    Lady Capulet. Ay, you have been a mouse-hunt in
    your time,
But I will watch you from such watching now.

[*she hurries out with Nurse*
    Capulet. A jealous hood, a jealous hood!

*'Enter three or four with spits and
logs and baskets'*

Now, fellow, what is there?

First Servingman. Things for the cook, sir; but I
know not what.

Capulet. Make haste, make haste. [1 *servingman goes*]
Sirrah, fetch drier logs.

Call Peter; he will show thee where they are.

Second Servingman. I have a head, sir, that will find
out logs

And never trouble Peter for the matter.

Capulet. Mass, and well said; a merry whoreson, ha!

20 Thou shalt be loggerhead.   [2 *servingman goes*]
Good faith, 'tis day!

The County will be here with music straight,
For so he said he would. [*music*] I hear him near.
Nurse! Wife! What, ho! What, nurse, I say!

'Enter NURSE'

Go waken Juliet; go and trim her up.
I'll go and chat with Paris. Hie, make haste,
Make haste! The bridegroom he is come already:
Make haste, I say.   [*they go*

[4. 5.]   *Juliet's chamber; the curtains
closed about the bed*

Enter NURSE

Nurse. Mistress! what, mistress! Juliet! Fast, I warrant
her, she.

Why, lamb! why, lady! Fie, you slug-a-bed!
Why, love, I say! madam! sweetheart! why, bride!

What, not a word? You take your pennyworths now!
Sleep for a week; for the next night, I warrant,
The County Paris hath set up his rest
That you shall rest but little. God forgive me!
Marry, and amen! How sound is she asleep!
I needs must wake her. Madam, madam, madam!
Ay, let the County take you in your bed,   10
He'll fright you up, i'faith! Will it not be?
                          [*draws back the curtains*
What, dressed, and in your clothes, and down again?
I must needs wake you. Lady, lady, lady! [*shakes her*
Alas, alas! Help, help! My lady's dead!
O weraday that ever I was born!
Some aqua-vitae, ho! My lord! my lady!

Enter LADY CAPULET

Lady Capulet. What noise is here?
Nurse.   O lamentable day!
Lady Capulet. What is the matter?
Nurse.   Look, look! O heavy day!
Lady Capulet. O me, O me! My child, my only life!
Revive, look up, or I will die with thee!   20
Help, help! Call help.

Enter CAPULET

Capulet. For shame, bring Juliet forth; her lord
    is come.
Nurse. She's dead, deceased: she's dead, alack
    the day!
Lady Capulet. Alack the day, she's dead, she's dead,
    she's dead!
Capulet. Ha, let me see her. Out, alas! She's cold,
Her blood is settled, and her joints are stiff:
Life and these lips have long been separated;

Death lies on her like an untimely frost
Upon the sweetest flower of all the field.
30 *Nurse*. O lamentable day!
 Lady Capulet.   O woeful time!
 Capulet. Death, that hath ta'en her hence to make
  me wail,
Ties up my tongue and will not let me speak.

 '*Enter* FRIAR *and the* COUNTY' *with Musicians*

 Friar. Come, is the bride ready to go to church?
 Capulet. Ready to go, but never to return.
O son, the night before thy wedding day
Hath Death lain with thy wife. There she lies,
Flower as she was, defloweréd by him.
Death is my son-in-law, Death is my heir;
My daughter he hath wedded! I will die
40 And leave him all; life, living, all is Death's.
 Paris. Have I thought long to see this morning's face,
And doth it give me such a sight as this?
 Lady Capulet. Accursed, unhappy, wretched,
  hateful day!
Most miserable hour that e'er time saw
In lasting labour of his pilgrimage!
But one, poor one, one poor and loving child,
But one thing to rejoice and solace in,
And cruel Death hath catched it from my sight!
 Nurse. O woe! O woeful, woeful, woeful day!
.50 Most lamentable day, most woeful day
That ever, ever I did yet behold!
O day, O day, O day, O hateful day!
Never was seen so black a day as this.
O woeful day, O woeful day!
 Paris. Beguiled, divorcéd, wrongéd, spited, slain!
Most detestable Death, by thee beguiled,

By cruel, cruel thee quite overthrown!
O love! O life! Not life, but love in death!
  Capulet. Despised, distresséd, hated,
     martyred, killed!
Uncomfortable time, why cam'st thou now   60
To murder, murder our solemnity?
O child, O child! my soul, and not my child!
Dead art thou. Alack, my child is dead,
And with my child my joys are buriéd!
  Friar. Peace, ho, for shame! Confusion's cure
     lives not
In these confusions. Heaven and yourself
Had part in this fair maid; now heaven hath all,
And all the better is it for the maid.
Your part in her you could not keep from death,
But heaven keeps his part in eternal life.   70
The most you sought was her promotion,
For 'twas your heaven she should be advanced;
And weep ye now, seeing she is advanced
Above the clouds as high as heaven itself?
O, in this love you love your child so ill
That you run mad, seeing that she is well.
She's not well married that lives married long,
But she's best married that dies married young.
Dry up your tears and stick your rosemary
On this fair corse, and as the custom is,   80
All in her best array, bear her to church:
For though fond nature bids us all lament,
Yet nature's tears are reason's merriment.
  Capulet. All things that we ordainéd festival
Turn from their office to black funeral,
Our instruments to melancholy bells,
Our wedding cheer to a sad burial feast;
Our solemn hymns to sullen dirges change,

Our bridal flowers serve for a buried corse,
90 And all things change them to the contrary.

Friar. Sir, go you in; and, madam, go
    with him;
And go, Sir Paris. Everyone prepare
To follow this fair corse unto her grave.
The heavens do lour upon you for some ill;
Move them no more by crossing their high will.

[*'all but the Nurse' and the Musicians 'go forth, casting*
    rosemary upon her and shutting the curtains'

1 *Musician.* Faith, we may put up our pipes and
    be gone.

Nurse. Honest good fellows, ah, put up, put up!
For well you know this is a pitiful case.

1 *Musician.* Ay, by my troth, the case may
    be amended. [*Nurse goes*

Enter PETER

100 *Peter.* Musicians, O musicians, 'Heart's ease',
'Heart's ease'! O, an you will have me live, play
'Heart's ease'.

1 *Musician.* Why 'Heart's ease'?

Peter. O musicians, because my heart itself plays
'My heart is full of woe'. O play me some merry dump
to comfort me.

1 *Musician.* Not a dump we! 'Tis no time to play
now.

Peter. You will not then?

110 1 *Musician.* No.

Peter. I will then give it you soundly.

1 *Musician.* What will you give us?

Peter. No money, on my faith, but the gleek. I will
give you the minstrel.

1 *Musician.* Then will I give you the serving-creature.

Peter. Then will I lay the serving-creature's dagger on your pate. I will carry no crotchets. I'll re you, I'll fa you. Do you note me?

1 *Musician.* An you re us and fa us, you note us.

2 *Musician.* Pray you put up your dagger, and put 120 out your wit.

Peter. Then have at you with my wit! I will dry-beat you with an iron wit, and put up my iron dagger. Answer me like men:

 'When griping grief the heart doth wound,
  And doleful dumps the mind oppress,
  Then music with her silver sound—'
Why 'silver sound'? Why 'music with her silver sound'? What say you, Simon Catling?

1 *Musician.* Marry, sir, because silver hath a sweet 130 sound.

Peter. Pretty! What say you, Hugh Rebeck?

2 *Musician.* I say 'silver sound', because musicians sound for silver.

Peter. Pretty too! What say you, James Soundpost?

3 *Musician.* Faith, I know not what to say.

Peter. O, I cry you mercy! You are the singer. I will say for you. It is 'music with her silver sound', because musicians have no gold for sounding.

 'Then music with her silver sound   140
  With speedy help doth lend redress.'

           [he goes

1 *Musician.* What a pestilent knave is this same!

2 *Musician.* Hang him, Jack! Come, we'll in here, tarry for the mourners, and stay dinner.

           [they go also

[5. 1.] *Mantua. A street with shops*

'*Enter* ROMEO'

Romeo. If I may trust the flattering truth of sleep,
My dreams presage some joyful news at hand.
My bosom's lord sits lightly in his throne,
And all this day an unaccustomed spirit
Lifts me above the ground with cheerful thoughts.
I dreamt my lady came and found me dead—
Strange dream that gives a dead man leave
        to think!—
And breathed such life with kisses in my lips
That I revived and was an emperor.
10 Ah me! how sweet is love itself possessed,
When but love's shadows are so rich in joy!

Enter BALTHASAR, *Romeo's man, booted*

News from Verona! How now, Balthasar?
Dost thou not bring me letters from the friar?
How doth my lady? Is my father well?
How fares my Juliet? That I ask again,
For nothing can be ill if she be well.
    Balthasar. Then she is well, and nothing can
        be ill.
Her body sleeps in Capel's monument,
And her immortal part with angels lives.
20 I saw her laid low in her kindred's vault,
And presently took post to tell it you.
O pardon me for bringing these ill news,
Since you did leave it for my office, sir.
    Romeo. Is it e'en so? Then I defy you, stars!
Thou know'st my lodging. Get me ink and paper,
And hire post-horses; I will hence tonight.

Balthasar. I do beseech you, sir, have patience.
Your looks are pale and wild and do import
Some misadventure.

Romeo.   Tush, thou art deceived.
Leave me, and do the thing I bid thee do.   30
Hast thou no letters to me from the friar?

Balthasar. No, my good lord.

Romeo.   No matter. Get thee gone,
And hire those horses; I'll be with thee straight.

                              [*Balthasar goes*

Well, Juliet, I will lie with thee tonight.
Let's see for means. O mischief, thou art swift
To enter in the thoughts of desperate men!
I do remember an apothecary,
And hereabouts 'a dwells, which late I noted
In tatt'red weeds, with overwhelming brows,
Culling of simples. Meagre were his looks;   40
Sharp misery had worn him to the bones:
And in his needy shop a tortoise hung,
An alligator stuffed, and other skins
Of ill-shaped fishes; and about his shelves
A beggarly account of empty boxes,
Green earthen pots, bladders, and musty seeds,
Remnants of packthread, and old cakes of roses
Were thinly scattered, to make up a show.
Noting this penury, to myself I said,
'An if a man did need a poison now,   50
Whose sale is present death in Mantua,
Here lives a caitiff wretch would sell it him'.
O, this same thought did but forerun my need,
And this same needy man must sell it me.
As I remember, this should be the house.
Being holiday, the beggar's shop is shut.
What ho, apothecary!

Enter Apothecary

Apothecary.   Who calls so loud?

Romeo. Come hither, man. I see that thou art poor.
Hold, there is forty ducats; let me have
60 A dram of poison, such soon-speeding gear
As will disperse itself through all the veins
That the life-weary taker may fall dead,
And that the trunk may be discharged of breath
As violently as hasty powder fired
Doth hurry from the fatal cannon's womb.

Apothecary. Such mortal drugs I have, but
          Mantua's law
Is death to any he that utters them.

Romeo. Art thou so bare and full of wretchedness
And fear'st to die? Famine is in thy cheeks,
70 Need and oppression starveth in thy eyes,
Contempt and beggary hangs upon thy back:
The world is not thy friend, nor the world's law;
The world affords no law to make thee rich:
Then be not poor, but break it and take this.

Apothecary. My poverty but not my will consents.

Romeo. I pay thy poverty and not thy will.

Apothecary. [*giving a phial*] Put this in any liquid
          thing you will
And drink it off, and if you had the strength
Of twenty men it would dispatch you straight.

80 *Romeo.* There is thy gold—worse poison to
          men's souls,
Doing more murder in this loathsome world,
Than these poor compounds that thou mayst not sell.
I sell thee poison; thou hast sold me none.
Farewell; buy food and get thyself in flesh.
                              [*Apothecary goes in*

Come, cordial and not poison, go with me
To Juliet's grave, for there must I use thee.

[*he passes on*

[5. 2.]   *Verona. Friar Lawrence's cell*

Enter Friar JOHN

Friar John. Holy Franciscan friar, brother, ho!

Enter Friar LAWRENCE

Friar Lawrence. This same should be the voice of
     Friar John.
Welcome from Mantua. What says Romeo?
Or, if his mind be writ, give me his letter.
  Friar John. Going to find a barefoot brother out,
One of our order, to associate me,
Here in this city visiting the sick,
And finding him, the searchers of the town,
Suspecting that we both were in a house
Where the infectious pestilence did reign,   10
Sealed up the doors, and would not let us forth,
So that my speed to Mantua there was stayed.
  Friar Lawrence. Who bare my letter then to Romeo?
  Friar John. I could not send it—here it is again—
Nor get a messenger to bring it thee,
So fearful were they of infection.
  Friar Lawrence. Unhappy fortune! By
     my brotherhood,
The letter was not nice, but full of charge,
Of dear import; and the neglecting it
May do much danger. Friar John, go hence,   20
Get me an iron crow and bring it straight
Unto my cell.
     R. & J.—9

Friar John. Brother, I'll go and bring it thee. [*goes*
Friar Lawrence. Now must I to the monument alone.
Within this three hours will fair Juliet wake.
She will beshrew me much that Romeo
Hath had no notice of these accidents;
But I will write again to Mantua,
And keep her at my cell till Romeo come.
30 Poor living corse, closed in a dead man's tomb!
                                        [*he goes*

[5. 3.]   *Verona. A churchyard; in it the
          monument of the Capulets*

'*Enter* PARIS *and his* PAGE', *bearing
          flowers and a torch*

Paris. Give me thy torch, boy. Hence, and
          stand aloof.
Yet put it out, for I would not be seen.
Under yond yew-trees lay thee all along,
Holding thine ear close to the hollow ground;
So shall no foot upon the churchyard tread,
Being loose, unfirm with digging up of graves,
But thou shalt hear it. Whistle then to me
As signal that thou hear'st some thing approach.
Give me those flowers. Do as I bid thee; go.
10 (*Page.* I am almost afraid to stand alone
Here in the churchyard, yet I will adventure.
                                        [*retires*

Paris. Sweet flower, with flowers thy bridal bed
          I strew—
O woe, thy canopy is dust and stones!—
Which with sweet water nightly I will dew,
Or, wanting that, with tears distilled by moans.

The obsequies that I for thee will keep
Nightly shall be to strew thy grave and weep.

                          [Page whistles

The boy gives warning something doth approach.
What curséd foot wanders this way tonight
To cross my obsequies and true love's rite?   20
What, with a torch? Muffle me, night, awhile.

                                [retires

'*Enter* ROMEO *and* BALTHASAR, *with a torch,
a mattock, and a crow of iron*'

Romeo. Give me that mattock and the wrenching iron.
Hold, take this letter. Early in the morning
See thou deliver it to my lord and father.
Give me the light. Upon thy life I charge thee,
Whate'er thou hear'st or seest, stand all aloof
And do not interrupt me in my course.
Why I descend into this bed of death
Is partly to behold my lady's face,
But chiefly to take thence from her dead finger   30
A precious ring, a ring that I must use
In dear employment. Therefore hence, be gone.
But if thou, jealous, dost return to pry
In what I farther shall intend to do,
By heaven, I will tear thee joint by joint
And strew this hungry churchyard with thy limbs.
The time and my intents are savage-wild,
More fierce and more inexorable far
Than empty tigers or the roaring sea.
  Balthasar. I will be gone, sir, and not trouble ye.   40
  Romeo. So shalt thou show me friendship. Take
      thou that;   *[gives money*
Live and be prosperous; and farewell, good fellow.
  (*Balthasar.* For all this same, I'll hide me hereabout.

His looks I fear, and his intents I doubt.   [*retires*

Romeo. Thou detestable maw, thou womb of death,
Gorged with the dearest morsel of the earth,
Thus I enforce thy rotten jaws to open,
                         [*begins to open the tomb*
And in despite I'll cram thee with more food.

(*Paris.* This is that banished haughty Montague
50 That murd'red my love's cousin—with which grief
It is supposéd the fair creature died—
And here is come to do some villainous shame
To the dead bodies: I will apprehend him.—
                         [*comes forward*

Stop thy unhallowed toil, vile Montague!
Can vengeance be pursued further than death?
Condemnéd villain, I do apprehend thee.
Obey, and go with me, for thou must die.

Romeo. I must indeed, and therefore came I hither.
Good gentle youth, tempt not a desp'rate man.
60 Fly hence and leave me. Think upon these gone;
Let them affright thee. I beseech thee, youth,
Put not another sin upon my head
By urging me to fury. O be gone!
By heaven, I love thee better than myself,
For I come hither armed against myself.
Stay not, be gone. Live, and hereafter say
A madman's mercy bid thee run away.

Paris. I do defy thy conjuration,
And apprehend thee for a felon here.

70 *Romeo.* Wilt thou provoke me? Then have at thee, boy!
                         [*they fight*

Page. O Lord, they fight! I will go call the watch.
                         [*runs off*

Paris. O, I am slain! [*falls*] If thou be merciful,
Open the tomb, lay me with Juliet.   [*dies*

Romeo. In faith, I will. Let me peruse this face.
Mercutio's kinsman, noble County Paris!
What said my man when my betosséd soul
Did not attend him as we rode? I think
He told me Paris should have married Juliet.
Said he not so? Or did I dream it so?
Or am I mad, hearing him talk of Juliet,   80
To think it was so? O give me thy hand,   *death brings these*
One writ with me in sour misfortune's book!   *opposites together*
I'll bury thee in a triumphant grave.
A grave? O no!—a lanthorn, slaught'red youth:
For here lies Juliet, and her beauty makes
This vault a feasting presence full of light.
Dead, lie thou there, by a dead man interred.

                        [*lays Paris within the tomb*

How oft when men are at the point of death   } *dramatic contrast*
Have they been merry, which their keepers call
A light'ning before death! O how may I   90
Call this a light'ning? O my love, my wife!
Death, that hath sucked the honey of thy breath,
Hath had no power yet upon thy beauty.
Thou art not conquered; beauty's ensign yet
Is crimson in thy lips and in thy cheeks,
And death's pale flag is not advancéd there.
Tybalt, liest thou there in thy bloody sheet?
O, what more favour can I do to thee
Than with that hand that cut thy youth in twain
To sunder his that was thine enemy?   100
Forgive me, cousin! Ah, dear Juliet,
Why art thou yet so fair? Shall I believe
That unsubstantial Death is amorous,   *Image of rapine Death*
And that the lean abhorréd monster keeps
Thee here in dark to be his paramour?
For fear of that I still will stay with thee,

And never from this palace of dim night
Depart again. Here, here will I remain
With worms that are thy chambermaids. O, here
110 Will I set up my everlasting rest,
And shake the yoke of inauspicious stars   ill-fated
From this world-wearied flesh. Eyes, look your last!
Arms, take your last embrace! and lips, O you,
The doors of breath, seal with a righteous kiss
A dateless bargain to engrossing Death!   The final ed.
Come, bitter conduct; come, unsavoury guide!
Thou desperate pilot, now at once run on
The dashing rocks thy seasick weary bark!
Here's to my love! [drinks] O true apothecary!
120 Thy drugs are quick. Thus with a kiss I die.   [dies

'Enter Friar' LAWRENCE 'with lanthorn,
crow, and spade'

Friar. Saint Francis be my speed! how oft tonight
Have my old feet stumbled at graves! Who's there?
Balthasar. Here's one, a friend, and one that knows
    you well.
Friar. Bliss be upon you! Tell me, good my friend,
What torch is yond that vainly lends his light
To grubs and eyeless skulls? As I discern,
It burneth in the Capels' monument.
Balthasar. It doth so, holy sir; and there's
    my master,
One that you love.
Friar.   Who is it?
Balthasar.   Romeo.
130 Friar. How long hath he been there?
Balthasar.   Full half an hour.
Friar. Go with me to the vault.
Balthasar.   I dare not, sir.

My master knows not but I am gone hence,
And fearfully did menace me with death
If I did stay to look on his intents.

  Friar. Stay then; I'll go alone. Fear comes upon me.
O, much I fear some ill unthrifty thing.

  Balthasar. As I did sleep under this yew-tree here,
I dreamt my master and another fought,
And that my master slew him.

  Friar.   Romeo!   *[advances*
Alack, alack, what blood is this which stains   140
The stony entrance of this sepulchre?
What mean these masterless and gory swords
To lie discoloured by this place of peace?
                           [enters the tomb
Romeo! O, pale! Who else? What, Paris too?
And steeped in blood? Ah, what an unkind hour
Is guilty of this lamentable chance!
The lady stirs.   *[Juliet wakes*

  Juliet. O comfortable friar, where is my lord?
I do remember well where I should be,
And there I am. Where is my Romeo? *[voices afar off* 150

  Friar. I hear some noise, lady. Come from that nest
Of death, contagion, and unnatural sleep.
A greater power than we can contradict
Hath thwarted our intents. Come, come away.
Thy husband in thy bosom there lies dead:
And Paris too. Come, I'll dispose of thee
Among a sisterhood of holy nuns.
Stay not to question, for the watch is coming.
Come, go, good Juliet; I dare no longer stay.

  Juliet. Go, get thee hence, for I will not away.   160
                           [he goes
What's here? A cup, closed in my true love's hand?
Poison, I see, hath been his timeless end,

O churl! drunk all, and left no friendly drop
To help me after? I will kiss thy lips.
Haply some poison yet doth hang on them
To make me die with a restorative.   [*kisses him*
Thy lips are warm!

The Page of Paris enters the graveyard
with Watch

1 *Watchman.* Lead, boy. Which way?
Juliet. Yea, noise? Then I'll be brief. O happy
        dagger,   [*snatching Romeo's dagger*
170 This is thy sheath [*stabs herself*]; there rest, and let
        me die.   [*falls on Romeo's body and dies*
Page. This is the place, there where the torch
        doth burn.
1 *Watchman.* The ground is bloody. Search about
        the churchyard.
Go, some of you; whoe'er you find attach.
                [*some Watchmen depart*
Pitiful sight! Here lies the County slain:
And Juliet bleeding, warm and newly dead,
Who here hath lain this two days buriéd.
Go tell the Prince; run to the Capulets;
Raise up the Montagues; some others search.
                [*other Watchmen depart*
We see the ground whereon these woes do lie,
180 But the true ground of all these piteous woes
We cannot without circumstance descry.

Re-enter some of the Watch, with BALTHASAR

2 *Watchman.* Here's Romeo's man; we found him in
        the churchyard.
1 *Watchman.* Hold him in safety till the Prince
        come hither.

Re-enter another Watchman, with Friar LAWRENCE

3 *Watchman.* Here is a friar that trembles, sighs,
   and weeps.
We took this mattock and this spade from him
As he was coming from this churchyard's side.
   1 *Watchman.* A great suspicion! Stay the friar too.

   'Enter the Prince' and attendants

Prince. What misadventure is so early up,
That calls our person from our morning rest?

   Enter CAPULET *and his wife*

Capulet. What should it be that is so
   shrieked abroad?
Lady Capulet. O, the people in the street
   cry 'Romeo',   190
Some 'Juliet', and some 'Paris', and all run
With open outcry toward our monument.
   Prince. What fear is this which startles in our ears?
   1 *Watchman.* Sovereign, here lies the County
      Paris slain;
And Romeo dead; and Juliet, dead before,
Warm and new killed.
   Prince. Search, seek, and know how this foul
      murder comes.
   1 *Watchman.* Here is a friar, and slaughtered
      Romeo's man,
With instruments upon them fit to open   200
These dead men's tombs.
   Capulet. O heaven! O wife, look how our
      daughter bleeds!
This dagger hath mista'en, for, lo, his house
Is empty on the back of Montague,

And it mis-sheathéd in my daughter's bosom.

   Lady Capulet. O me! this sight of death is as a bell
That warns my old age to a sepulchre.

           '*Enter* MONTAGUE'

   Prince. Come Montague; for thou art early up
To see thy son and heir more early down.

210   *Montague.* Alas, my liege, my wife is dead tonight;
Grief of my son's exile hath stopped her breath.
What further woe conspires against mine age?

   Prince. Look and thou shalt see.

   Montague. O thou untaught! what manners is
     in this,
To press before thy father to a grave?

   Prince. Seal up the mouth of outrage for a while,
Till we can clear these ambiguities,
And know their spring, their head, their true descent;
And then will I be general of your woes,

220 And lead you even to death. Meantime forbear,
And let mischance be slave to patience.
Bring forth the parties of suspicion.

          [*Watchmen bring forward Friar Lawrence*
                          and Balthasar

   Friar. I am the greatest; able to do least,
Yet most suspected, as the time and place
Doth make against me, of this direful murder:
And here I stand both to impeach and purge
Myself condemnéd and myself excused.

   Prince. Then say at once what thou dost know
     in this.

   Friar. I will be brief, for my short date of breath

230 Is not so long as is a tedious tale.
Romeo there dead was husband to that Juliet;
And she, there dead, that Romeo's faithful wife.

I married them; and their stol'n marriage day
Was Tybalt's doomsday, whose untimely death
Banished the new-made bridegroom from this city;
For whom, and not for Tybalt, Juliet pined.
You, to remove that siege of grief from her,
Betrothed and would have married her perforce
To County Paris. Then comes she to me,
And with wild looks bid me devise some mean   240
To rid her from this second marriage,
Or in my cell there would she kill herself.
Then gave I her (so tutored by my art)
A sleeping potion; which so took effect
As I intended, for it wrought on her
The form of death. Meantime I writ to Romeo
That he should hither come as this dire night
To help to take her from her borrowed grave,
Being the time the potion's force should cease.
But he which bore my letter, Friar John,   250
Was stayed by accident, and yesternight
Returned my letter back. Then all alone
At the prefixéd hour of her waking
Came I to take her from her kindred's vault,
Meaning to keep her closely at my cell
Till I conveniently could send to Romeo.
But when I came, some minute ere the time
Of her awakening, here untimely lay
The noble Paris and true Romeo dead.
She wakes; and I entreated her come forth,   260
And bear this work of heaven with patience;
But then a noise did scare me from the tomb,
And she, too desperate, would not go with me,
But, as it seems, did violence on herself.
All this I know; and to the marriage
Her nurse is privy: and if aught in this

Miscarried by my fault, let my old life
Be sacrificed, some hour before his time,
Unto the rigour of severest law.

270   *Prince.* We still have known thee for a holy man.
Where's Romeo's man? What can he say to this?

Balthasar. I brought my master news of
    Juliet's death,
And then in post he came from Mantua
To this same place, to this same monument.
This letter he early bid me give his father,
And threat'ned me with death, going in the vault,
If I departed not and left him there.

Prince. Give me the letter; I will look on it.
Where is the County's page, that raised the watch?

                              [Page comes forward

280 Sirrah, what made your master in this place?

Page. He came with flowers to strew his
    lady's grave,
And bid me stand aloof, and so I did.
Anon comes one with light to ope the tomb,
And by and by my master drew on him,
And then I ran away to call the watch.

Prince. This letter doth make good the
    friar's words,
Their course of love, the tidings of her death;
And here he writes that he did buy a poison
Of a poor pothecary, and therewithal

290 Came to this vault to die, and lie with Juliet.
Where be these enemies? Capulet, Montague?
See what a scourge is laid upon your hate,
That heaven finds means to kill your joys with love!
And I, for winking at your discords too,
Have lost a brace of kinsmen. All are punished.

Capulet. O brother Montague, give me thy hand.

This is my daughter's jointure, for no more
Can I demand.

   Montague.   But I can give thee more;
For I will raise her statue in pure gold,
That, whiles Verona by that name is known,   300
There shall no figure at such rate be set
As that of true and faithful Juliet.

   Capulet. As rich shall Romeo's by his lady's lie—
Poor sacrifices of our enmity!

   Prince. A glooming peace this morning with
      it brings;
   The sun for sorrow will not show his head.
Go hence, to have more talk of these sad things.
   Some shall be pardoned, and some punishéd;
For never was a story of more woe
Than this of Juliet and her Romeo.   [*they go* 310

THE COPY FOR
ROMEO AND JULIET, 1599

As the F *Romeo and Juliet* was a mere reprint of Q2
(1599), an editor has only to take Q2 into account
together with its predecessor, Q1 (1597); and, as Q2
is now acknowledged by all to be a 'good' quarto and Q1
to be a 'bad' quarto, his task would at first sight appear
an easy one. But in matters textual appearances are
often deceptive. And the trouble here is not so much
that Q2 is one of the worst of the Shakespearian 'good'
quartos and Q1 one of the best of the 'bad', as that the
relations between the two have so far never been
satisfactorily defined. This Note is the latest of many
attempts. A full account of the issues involved and of
the reasons for the solution we ourselves offer would,
however, take more space than a volume of this size
allows; and what follows is therefore but a summary of
our conclusions. These are discussed at length in an
article entitled 'Recent work on the text of *Romeo and
Juliet*' (*Shakespeare Survey*, 1955), to which the
reader may be referred.

Q1 is 'bad' because it is undoubtedly derived from
a text reconstructed from memory by an actor or actors
who had taken part in performances of the authentic
play, though for some reason not yet explained the
reconstruction is remarkably good in the first two acts
and becomes progressively less successful afterwards.[1]
And Q2 is 'good' because it is as undoubtedly closely
related to a Shakespearian MS., which the capriciously

---

[1] See H. R. Hoppe, *The Bad Quarto of Romeo and Juliet*
(Cornell University Press, 1948).

varied designation of the characters in speech-headings
and stage-directions,[1] the occurrence of what are
evidently Shakespeare's 'first shots' as he composed side
by side with his final decisions,[2] and the presence of
a good many other confusions and duplications, all
combine to define as his rough draft or 'foul papers'.[3]
Yet as a German critic pointed out as long ago as 1879,[4]
Q 2 was printed, in one passage at least, not from any
Shakespearian MS. but from Q 1. This passage
extends from 1. 2. 58 to 1. 3. 36, between which
points the two Qq are not only identical in substance
but linked together by similarities of spelling, misprint
and type. The Nurse's speeches, for example, appear in
italic in Q 1, though the rest of the text is in roman; an
eccentricity which Q 2 repeats throughout a whole
sheet, at the end of which, however, the compositor
seemed to realize its irrelevancy, since thenceforward
he set up her speeches in roman like those of other
characters.

So far all critics are agreed. What lies in dispute is the
area or amount of Q 2 which was derived from Q 1;
and there are three schools of thought in this matter:
(*a*) that Q 2 was entirely printed from the MS. except
between 1. 2. 58 and 1. 3. 36, where the MS. being
presumably defective or illegible the printer had to
fall back upon Q 1;[5] (*b*) that it was printed in the main
from the MS. but in parts also from a *corrected* copy
of Q 1 which was probably at times consulted as well

[1] See *Stage-directions*, pp. 122–3, and, for speech-headings,
notes 1. 3. *Entry*; 3. 5. 172; 4. 2. 37, etc.
[2] See notes 2. 2. 10–11; 3. 2. 19, 76; 3. 3. 40–44; 3. 5.
176; 4. 1. 110; 5. 3. 102–3, 107–8.
[3] See Greg, *Editorial Problem in Shakespeare*, pp. 61–2.
[4] Robert Gericke, *Shakespeare Jahrbuch*, xiv. 207–73.
[5] See Sidney Thomas, *Review of English Studies*, xxv
(1949), 110–14.

elsewhere;[1] (*c*) that it was printed entirely from a copy of Q1, corrected and added to by a scribe who had collated it with the MS.[2] Obviously the first is the solution an editor would most desire, since it admits of only one agent, the Q2 compositor, between us and Shakespeare's original, whereas (*b*) and (*c*) not only introduce a second intermediary in the collating scribe but involve the serious possibility that Q2 may transmit corrupt readings from the 'bad' Q1. We were nevertheless in the end compelled to adopt this, in its extremer form (*c*), as the most likely hypothesis. One of us indeed published a paper on these lines in 1951, contending that the copy for Q2 probably consisted partly of leaves of Q1 edited by comparison with the foul papers and partly of leaves or slips of foolscap directly transcribed from the same MS.[3] But the main reason then found for postulating transcription proved illusory, and we accordingly attempted for some months to work from the middle position, held by Greg, viz. that Q2 was mostly printed from the foul papers with the help in difficult or illegible passages of a corrected Q1 supplemented by transcription from the MS. Yet as our editing went forward and we grew more familiar with the facts of the Q2 text, this theory came to satisfy us less and less. It failed, for one thing, to explain the extensive corruption, often of a type for which a compositor is unlikely to have been responsible, or even some of those glaring

[1] Approximately Greg's present position, *op. cit.* pp. 61–2.

[2] First advanced by Greta Hjort, *Modern Language Review*, xxi (1926), 140–6 and tentatively by Greg in *Aspects of Shakespeare* (1933), pp. 144–7, 175–81.

[3] G. I. Duthie, 'The Text of Shakespeare's *Romeo and Juliet*', in *Studies in Bibliography* (University of Virginia Bibliographical Society), iv (1951–2).

examples of confusion which Greg claims as pointing
to the use of foul papers.[1] But what finally led us back
to the belief that a scribe collating Q1 with the foul
papers had furnished the entire copy for Q2 were the
bibliographical links with Q2 we detected, or thought
we detected, in about half the printed pages of Q1;
and we found such pages in each of its ten sheets.[2]

Absolute proof is out of the question. But this was
the working hypothesis we were compelled to adopt,
which means that we assumed we were editing a text,
ultimately derived from a Shakespearian MS., but
transmitted first by a scribe of unknown quality and
then by the printers. It was a situation that at best
doubled the chances of corruption. And unhappily
the best was not to be hoped for. On the contrary, our
analysis of the text convinced us that the scribe was on
the one hand so careless in his collation of the MS. that
he overlooked a number of errors in Q1 which he
ought to have corrected, and on the other hand so
unintelligently meticulous in his transcription that he
reproduced Shakespeare's first and second shots together, replaced obviously correct literary stage-
directions in Q1 by such purely theatrical ones as
'Enter Will Kemp', and, when he found one of
Shakespeare's words difficult to read, as he often did,
spelt it out *literatim* with little or no regard for the
sense of the passage. Nor was that the end of our
troubles. The compositor who handled this muddled
and already much corrupted copy in Creede's office
was, we were again forced to admit, either a very
slovenly or a much overdriven mechanic. The 'literals',
the frequent omissions, e.g. of small words, or the equally
common substitution of one synonym for another, the

[1] See notes on 1. 4. 54–91; 2. 2. 38–43; 2. 2. 187–88.
[2] Pages on which we think these links occur are briefly
indicated in the Notes below.

occurrence of dittographs, of literal assimilations, and of misprints which suggested an inattention to the endings of words, all point to Q 2 as the product of a compositor (we think there was only one) who was attempting throughout to carry too many words in his head at a time. And, like other printers of Shakespearian Qq, he was also inclined to expand or normalize contracted or colloquial forms, often to the ruin of the verse. Many errors may of course be attributed either to the compositor or to the collator. For example, *e*:*d* misprints, which are fairly common,[1] may be misreadings either of Shakespeare's hand or of the scribe's, while the strange, and surely most careless, error of 'kisman' for 'kinsman', found four times in Q 2,[2] must be a reproduction of 'kīsman' in script, though in whose script once again we cannot tell.

In his endeavour to extract from Q 2 a true text, i.e. one corresponding as far as possible with Shakespeare's final intentions, an editor must, we therefore conclude, be on the lookout for four different sources of possible corruption: (i) the duplications, confusions, and inconsistencies incident to the dramatist's rough draft, (ii) the actor's perversions in Q 1 overlooked by the collator, (iii) the collator's own misunderstandings and mistranscriptions, together with the words and passages from Q 1 which he has corrected but forgotten to delete, so that both get into print,[3] and (iv) the misprints and misunderstandings of Creede's compositor. Thus, though its causes are different, the situation facing an editor is not unlike that we had to encounter

[1] v. notes 2. 2. 110; 3. 2. 79; 3. 3. 168; 3. 5. 31; 4. 1. 7; 4. 5. 82; 5. 3. 190, 199.   [2] v. notes 2. 4. 6; 3. 1. 144.

[3] Possible or probable common errors of this sort are noted below under 1. 2. 29, 64 S.D., 66, 67, 92; 2. 2. 5, 160; 2. 4. 149; 3. 3. 10, 26, 86-7; 3. 5. 13, 31; 4. 4. 27 S.D.; 5. 3. 87.

in *Richard III*, the text previously published in this edition; and conservatism is no more a virtue here than it was there.

This does not imply a return to the pre-Pollardian eclecticism. The old editors, for instance, ignorant of its provenance, borrowed far too freely from Q1. We now realize that an editor has no right to accept a reading from that text unless (*a*) he feels confident that Q2 is wrong, and (*b*) what Q1 offers is as good as or better than anything he can himself arrive at by emending Q2. For though the only authority behind Q1 is an actor's memory, that authority is not entirely negligible: indeed there are some passages even late in the play where it affords the only light we have, while, in the earlier acts mostly, it offers at times evidence of a quasi-objective character which encourages us to follow it. When, that is to say, the Q1 readings, written out in a 'secretary' hand, present graphical outlines similar to those of their variants in Q2, and when the latter are nonsense or even suspiciously awkward, the reported text may well be correct, and even accepted, if justifiable on other grounds. A few examples will show how this works:

1. 1. 210	Q2	vncharmd	Q1	vnharm'd
1. 2. 29	Q2	fennell	Q1	female
1. 4. 39	Q2	dum	Q1	done
1. 4. 113	Q2	sute	Q1	saile
2. 1. 10	Q2	prouaunt	Q1	pronounce
2. 1. 13	Q2	true	Q1	trim
3. 1. 123	Q2	fire end	Q1	fier eyed
3. 1. 165	Q2	aged	Q1	agile
3. 5. 180	Q2	liand	Q1	trainde
4. 1. 45	Q2	care	Q1	cure
4. 5. 82	Q2	some	Q1	fond
5. 3. 209	Q2	now	Q1	more

It will be conceded also that, when Q1 seems to correct one of the faults noted above as characteristic of the Q2 compositor, its reading should be carefully weighed, and if sufficiently attractive may also be accepted.

Obviously, of course, very much depends in all this upon the judgement and taste of the editor concerned, and there is much room therefore for differences of opinion. During the five years of collaboration in the preparation of this text we have ourselves not seldom differed, both on matters of principle and on the readings we ought to adopt. Some sixty-five of the latter were at one time in debate between us; and though all but a handful of these, recorded in the notes, have since been decided, we do not delude ourselves with the hope that other students of this troublesome text will necessarily agree with us.

J. D. W.
G. I. D.

1954.

NOTES

All significant departures from Q 2 are recorded, the source of the accepted reading being indicated in brackets. Line-numeration for references to plays not yet issued in this edition is that found in Bartlett's *Concordance* and the *Globe Shakespeare*.

Q 1, Q 2, Q 3, etc., stand for the Quarto editions, first, second, third, etc.; F or F 1 for the First Folio; F 2, F 3, F 4 for the second, third, and fourth Folios; Qq., Ff. for 'Quartos' and 'Folios' respectively; G. for Glossary; O.E.D. for *The Oxford English Dictionary*; S.D. for stage-direction; Sh. for Shakespeare or Shakespearian. Common words are also usually abbreviated; e.g. sp. = spelling or spelt, prob. = probable or probably, comp. = compositor, etc.

The following is a list of works cited with abridged titles: Abbott = *A Shakespearian Grammar*, by E. A. Abbott, 1886; Adams = *The Globe Theatre*, 1943, by J. C. Adams; *Aspects* = *Aspects of Sh.* (British Academy Lectures), 1933; A. W. = Miss Alice Walker (private communications); Barker = *Prefaces to Sh., 2nd Series*, by Harley Granville-Barker, 1946; Brooke = *The Tragicall Historye of Romeus and Iuliet, written first in Italian by Bandell, and nowe in Englishe by Ar. Br.*, 1562; ed. by P. A. Daniel (New Sh. Soc.), 1875; *Camb.* = *The Cambridge Sh.* (2nd ed. 1892); Capell = ed. of Sh. by Edward Capell, 1768; Castle = *Schools and Masters of Fence* by Egerton Castle, 1885; C.B.Y. = C. B. Young; Chambers, *Med. St.* = *The Mediaeval Stage*, by E. K. Chambers, 1903; Chambers, *Eliz. St.* = *The Elizabethan Stage*, by E. K. Chambers, 1923; Chambers, *Wm. Sh.* = *William Shakespeare: Facts and Problems*, by E. K. Chambers, 1930; Cotgrave = *A Dictionary of the French and English Tongues*,

1611; Creizenach = *The English Drama in the Age of Shakespeare*, 1916; D.D. = *The English Dialect Dictionary*, ed. Joseph Wright; Daniel = ed. by P. A. Daniel (New Sh. Soc.), 1875; Delius = ed. by Nicholaus Delius in *Shakesperes Werke* (Bd. 11), 1872; *Dict. Slang* = *Dictionary of Slang* by Farmer and Henley, 1921; Dowden = ed. by Edward Dowden (*Arden Sh.*), 1900; Dyce = ed. of Sh. by Alexander Dyce, 1857; *F.Q.* = *The Faerie Queene*, by Edmund Spenser, Bks i–iii, 1590; Franz = *Die Sprache Shakespeares* (4th ed.), by W. Franz, 1939; Furness = The *Variorum* ed. by H. H. Furness, 1871; G.I.D. = G. I. Duthie; Golding, *Ovid* = Ovid's *Metamorphoses*, *by Arthur Golding*, 1565 [cited from ed. by W. H. D. Rouse, 1904]; Greg, *Ed. Prob.* = *The Editorial Problem in Sh.*, by W. W. Greg, 1942 (2nd ed. 1951); Grosart = *The Works of Robert Greene* (The Huth Library), 15 vols, 1881–3; G.S. = the ed. by George Sampson (*Pitt Press Sh.*), 1936; Hanmer = ed. of Sh. by Sir Thomas Hanmer, 1743; Harrison = ed. by G. B. Harrison (*Penguin Sh.*); Herford = the ed. by C. H. Herford (*Eversley Sh.*), 1900; Hoppe = ed. by H. R. Hoppe (*Crofts Classics*), New York, 1947; Hosley = article by Richard Hosley on 'The corrupting influence of the Bad Quarto on the received text of *Romeo and Juliet*' in *Sh. Quarterly*, iv. i. (Jan. 1953); Hudson = ed. of Sh. by H. N. Hudson, 1856; J. = ed. of Sh. by Samuel Johnson, 1765; J.C.M. = J. C. Maxwell (private communications); J.E.C. = ed. by J. E. Crofts (*Warwick Sh.*), 1936; Jonson = *Works of Ben Jonson*, ed. by C. H. Herford and Percy Simpson, 11 vols., 1925–52; Kökeritz = *Sh.'s Pronunciation*, by H. Kökeritz, Yale, 1953; K. = ed. by G. L. Kittredge, 1939; Linthicum = *Costume in the Drama of Shakespeare and his Contemporaries*, by M. C. Linthicum, 1936; Lyly = *Works of John Lyly*, ed. by R. W. Bond;

3 vols., 1902; Madden = *The Diary of Master William Silence*, by D. H. Madden (2nd ed. 1907); Mal. = James Boswell's Variorum ed. of *Malone's Sh.*, 21 vols., 1821; *M.L.N. = Modern Language Notes*; *M.L.R. = The Modern Language Review*; *MSH = The Manuscript of Sh.'s 'Hamlet'*, by J. D. Wilson, 1934; *M.S.R. =* Malone Society Reprint; Nares = *Glossary* by R. Nares (new ed.), 1859; Nashe = *Works of Thomas Nashe*, ed. R. B. McKerrow, 5 vols., 1904–8; *N. and Q. = Notes and Queries*; On. = *A Sh. Glossary*, by C. T. Onions, 1911; Painter = 'The Goodly Hystory of the true and constant Loue betweene *Rhomeo and Julietta*' from *The Palace of Pleasure*, by William Painter, 1567 [cited from P. A. Daniel's reprint, New Sh. Soc., 1875]; Pope = ed. of Sh. by Alexander Pope, 1725; *R.E.S. = Review of English Studies*; Rowe = ed. of Sh. by Nicholas Rowe, 1709; Schmidt = *Sh.-Lexicon*, by Alexander Schmidt, 1902; Sh. Ass. Fac. = Shakespeare Association Facsimile; *Sh. Eng. = Shakespeare's England*, 2 vols., 1917; *Sh. Surv. = Shakespeare Survey*, 1948– , ed. by Allardyce Nicoll; Silver = *Paradoxes of Defence* by George Silver, 1599, ed. by J. Dover Wilson (Sh. Ass. Facs. 6), 1933; Steev. = ed. of J.'s Sh. by George Steevens, 1773; *Stud. in Bib.* = article by G. I. Duthie in *Studies in Bibliography* (Univ. of Virginia), iv, 1951; Theob. = ed. by Lewis Theobald, 1733; Tilley = *A Dictionary of the Proverbs in England in the Sixteenth and Seventeenth Centuries*, by M. P. Tilley (Univ. of Michigan), 1950; *T.L.S. = The Times Literary Supplement*; Warb. = ed. of Sh. by William Warburton, 1747; Welsford = *The Court Masque*, by Enid Welsford, 1922.

Names of the Characters. From Brooke Sh. takes the names Escalus, Paris, Montague, Capulet ('Capilet' or 'Capel' in Brooke), Mercutio, Tybalt, Lawrence, John, Juliet. Brooke generally has 'Romeus' but once

'Romeo' (l. 252), the form in Da Porto, Bandello, and others (Boaistuau and Painter have 'Rhomeo'). Brooke's Mercutio (in Da Porto 'Marcuccio Guercio' or Squint-Eyed) is merely a rather aggressive youth at the Capulet's dance who seizes Juliet's right hand in an icy grip while Romeo held her left in his warm one (ll. 253–63, 289–308). The name Benvolio originates with Sh., though the character had previously appeared in Bandello, Boaistuau, and Brooke. In Brooke, as in Bandello and Boaistuau, Peter is Romeo's man, who procures the ladder of cords (813) and accompanies him to the graveyard (2589 ff.) though he is not so named in Brooke in the first passage. Da Porto makes him a Capulet servant who acts as go-between for Juliet with Rom. Sh. calls him Balthasar (v. note 5. 3. 21 S.D.). The name Angelica (4. 4. 5) is Sh.'s invention, as are the characters and names of Sampson, Gregory, and Abraham.

Acts and Scenes. No division in the Qq; and none in the Ff. except for an initial 'Actus Primus. Scæna Prima.' Various editorial divisions from Rowe on. We follow *Camb.*, the modern standard; but 1. 5., 2. 2., 4. 4., and 4. 5. are not really new scenes.

Punctuation. The punctuation in Sh.'s draft is likely to have been very scanty; and, if our theory of the copy be sound, that was supplemented and/or corrupted by the copyist and the compositor in turn. At times we have found it advantageous to restore a piece of punctuation which had been altered in some later reprint. But in general we have followed the lead of the *Cambridge Shakespeare*.

Stage-directions. See Greg, *Editorial Problem*, pp. 162–4. The Q2 S.D.s bear out the contention that Q2 depends on foul papers. There are imprecisions such as 'Enter three or foure Citizens with Clubs or partysons' (1. 1. 71). Characters are referred to by diverse titles—e.g. 'Enter Capulets Wife and Nurse' (1. 3 head) over against 'Enter Lady of the house and Nurse' (4. 4 head), etc. At 3. 1. 33 a mute Petruchio enters (v. 1. 5. 131). On 'Enter Will Kemp' (4. 5. 99) see pp. 115, 209. In places the Q2 directions are defective or erroneous, and some necessary directions are lacking. The Q1 directions are characteristic of reporting, being frequently descriptive—e.g. 'Enter Iuliet somewhat fast, and embraceth Romeo' (2. 6. 16), 'Tibalt vnder Romeos arme thrusts Mercutio, in and flyes' (3. 1. 89), 'Enter Nurse wringing her hands, with the ladder of cordes in her lap' (3. 2. 31), etc. Greg (*op. cit.* p. 164) notes that 'in Q1 the directions grow proportionately more extensive as the play proceeds—perhaps the result of the reporter relying more on description as his recollection of the words was less.... Whoever wrote the Q1 directions had an intimate knowledge of the play and of the traditional stage business, such as the book-keeper would acquire; moreover he gives the impression of being concerned with production as well as description.' In this respect, then, Q1 is of definite use to editors and producers.

PROLOGUE

(Printed as a whole from a corrected page of Q1; cf. p. 115.)

S.D. (Dyce). Sp.-hdg. (Q2, above line 1). See G. 'chorus'.

8. *Doth* Eliz. 'plur.' Cf. Franz §156.

14. *here* i.e. in the author's work. *our* i.e. the actors'.

S.D. (Capell) Q2 om.

1. 1

S.D. *Loc.* (Capell). *Entry* (Q2) transposing 'with...Bucklers,' and 'of...Capulet.'

1. *carry coals* v. G. 3. *an* (edd.) Q2 'and'. So passim.

3–5. *choler, collar* (Q1) Q2 'choller' twice.

4–5. *draw...collar* i.e. keep clear of the halter. Cf. Tilley, C 513, N 69.

8. *Montague* Q2 'Mountague'. So passim.

14. *weakest...wall.* Cf. Tilley, W 185.

16. *weaker vessels* Cf. I Peter iii. 7, and Tilley, W 655.

19–20. *i.e.* the maids are not involved.

22. *cruel* (Q4) Q2 'ciuil'—minim misprint (v. p. 115).

24. *maids?* (Q1) Q2 'maids.'

27. *They...feel it*='It is they that feel it that must take it in sense (feeling)' (G.S.).

in (Q1) Q2 om.

30–1. *'Tis well...poor John* Sampson has just claimed to be a valiant man, as warrior and in a carnal sense. It is a good thing you are not a female (v. G. 'fish'), says Gregory; if you were, you would not give your male associates much satisfaction.

31–2. *comes two of* (Q1) Q2 'comes of' For compositor's omissions v. pp. 115–16.

32. S.D. Combines 'Enter two other seruing men.' (Q2) and 'Abraham and another' (Daniel). Cf. the Q2 sp.-hdgs. at 44, etc. No indication that 'another' is Balthasar, as Rowe conj. Mal. notes that the Montagues and Capulets were prob. distinguished on the stage by 'tokens' in their hats, and cites Gascoigne's *Devise for a Masque for the right honourable Viscount Mountacute* (1575) to this effect. Cf. p. 83, Gascoigne, *Posies*, ed. J. W. Cunliffe, 1907.

36. *Fear me not*=Have no fears for me. But Gregory picks the words up in their literal sense.

37. *thee!* Q2 'thee.'

40–1. *take...list* Cf. Tilley, T 27.

42. *bite my thumb* Cf. G. 'bite.'

54. *as you* sc. serve.

56. *Well* Implies a denial with prudent ambiguity. S.D. 'Enter Benuolio.' (Q2)+the rest (G.I.D.) The servants are Caps.; Ben. a Mont.; and the 'kinsman' (l. 58) is Tyb.

62. *washing* (Q2) Synonym for 'swashing' (Q4) v. G. May be a dig at Gregory, who is a menial. Laundresses beat or 'battled' the clothes in washing (cf. 'batler', *A.Y.L.* 2. 4. 48). O.E.D. ('washing'¹) cites *Plaine Percevall* (*c.* 1590), ed. 1860, p. 33: 'A washing blow of this is as good as a Laundresse...it can wipe a fellow over the thumbs'; and Golding's *Ovid's Met.* v. 252, 'Did with a long sharp arming sworde a washing blow him giue'. S.D. (Q2).

63–4. S.D. (G.I.D.) *Part...do* (as Capell). Prose in Q2.   64. S.D. Q2 'Enter Tibalt.'.

65. *heartless hinds* (*a*) cowardly menials, (*b*) 'deer without a stag to protect them' (J.E.C.). Ben. should engage a worthier adversary.

71. S.D. (i) 'They fight.' (Q1); (ii) 'Enter...fray. Then' (Capell). The text indicates that 'the fighting of the original six becomes a general brawl' (G.S.); (iii) 'enter...partisans,' (Q2); (iv) 'and an Officer' from Q2 sp.-hdg. 'Offi.' (l. 72).

73. S.D. (Q2) See G. 'gown'.

74. *long sword* v. G. An old-fashioned weapon, 'useless against a skilled rapierman' (J.E.C.).

75. sp.-hdg. Q2 'Wife.'   77 S.D. (Q2).

78. Q2 has 'Capulet, hold'.

79. sp.-hdg. Q2 'M. Wife. 2.' S.D. (Q2) 'Escalus' (Camb. < Brooke) Q2 'Eskales'.

88. *an airy word* i.e. some trivial insult or other. Cf. Brooke, 37, 'first hatchd of trifling stryfe'.

91. *Verona's* Q2 'Neronas'. In the comp.'s type-case the N box is just above the V.

94. *Cankered...peace* i.e. rusty from disuse.

96. *forfeit*=either 'penalty' or 'violation'; if the latter, 'pay'=pay for.

101. *Freetown* Q2 'Free-towne'. The name of 'Capilet's' castle in Brooke. 'Villa Franca' in the Italian story.

judgement-place No hyphen in Qq.

102. S.D. (after Hudson). Q2 'Exeunt.'.

115. sp.-hdg. Q2 'Wife.'.

117–18. Cf. 2. 2. 2–3.

119. *drave* (Q3+most edd.) Q2 'driue' Q1 'drew'. Yet Q2 may be correct, since 'drive' as pret. occurs in *Bonduca*, 1. 1. 114 (M.S.R.) and *F. Queene*, 1. ix. 38, 5; v. xi. 5, 8 [J.C.M.].

120. *sycamore* (Q5, Ff.) Q2 'Syramour'.

121. *city's side* (Q1+most edd.) Q2 'Citie fide'. But cf. 5. 3. 186.

126. *where...found* i.e. solitude.

127. *Being...self* A reductio ad absurdum of the aversion to company typical of the melancholy man, or, as here, of a normal young man indulging in a fashion-able mood.

128. *Pursued...his*=either 'indulged my own inclination for solitude by not pursuing Rom. who had a similar inclination' (G.I.D.), or 'followed the lead of my own fancy for solitude by refraining from any attempt to learn from him the cause of his fancy for the same' (K.) or 'followed my own inclination to solitude without owing any prompting to his inclination' (Deighton). Theob., following Thirlby, emended 'his' to 'him'.

129. *who* i.e. him who.

132. *Adding...sighs* Cf. 2. 3. 73, n.

138. *windows* = shutters, v. G.

140. *portentous* (F 2) Q 2 'portendous'.

145. *other friends* i.e. other people who are friends of mine.

146. *his* (Q 3) Q 2 'is'? Omitted letter (v. p. 115 *fin.*) *counsellor* v. G.

147. *I will...true* Bracketed in Q 2.
true sc. to his own best interests.

150. *As is the bud* etc. Rom.'s sorrow is destroying him within, as the unseen canker-worm destroys the rosebud.

152. *sun* (Theob.) Q 2 'same'. Prob. 'sunne' misread.

154. S.D. (Q 2).

158. S.D. (after Capell). Q 2 'Exeunt.'

164–6. *love?* (Q 5) Q 2 'loue.' *Out*—(Rowe) Q 2 'Out.'

love? (Q 5) Q 2 'loue.'

170–1. *Alas...will* Seems reminiscent of Brooke's 129–30:

Remoue the veale of loue that keepes thine eyes so blynde,
That thou ne canst the ready path of thy forefathers fynde.

170. *muffled* Cf. 1. 4. 4.

171. *see...will* i.e. see clearly enough to shoot his arrows accurately, so as to make mortals fall in love as he wishes. Contrast 2. 1. 33.

174. *more with love* Because he, a Mont., loves a Cap. Hence ll. 175–80. 'Every sonneteer characterized love by contrarieties' (Farmer).

176. *create* (Q 1) Q 2 'created' is impossibly harsh after 'hate' in l. 175, and metrically awkward. The collator or compositor perh. normalized unconsciously [J.D.W.].

178. *well-seeming* (Q 4, F 2), Q 2 'welseeing'— omitted letter. Q 1 'best seeming'.

180. *is not what it is* Cf. *Macb.* 1. 3. 141–2.

181. *feel no love in this* sc. in return.

184. *love's transgression* i.e. the way love overruns the limits.

188. *to too* (Q1) Q2 'too too'.

189. *made* (Q2) Q1 (+many edd.) 'raisde', poss. right. (E.g. 'made' may be a miscorr. of misp. 'raie'. Cf. 5. 3. 299, n.)

190. *Being...eyes* i.e. when a lover's troubles are cleared away, his love becomes a joyous thing.

191. *lovers'* (most edd.<Q1 'a louers') Q2 'louing'—perhaps an ex. of the comp.'s carelessness with word-endings (cf. p. 116, *init.*); 'louers' tears' is necessary to balance 'lovers' eyes' in l. 190 [J.D.W.] G.I.D. finds Q2 possible.

196–7. *I have lost myself* etc. Perh. reflects the advice 'become thyne owne' given to the love-lorn Romeus in Brooke (l. 112). Cf. G. 'lost'. For sentiments like this, expressing mental and spiritual confusion, cf. *Ado*, 4. 1. 68–70; *Troil.* 5. 2. 146. [G.I.D.] J.D.W. prefers Q1 'left' to Q2 'lost', and Daniel reads it: Rom. catches up Ben.'s 'leave'.

198. *that*=she whom.

199. *groan* Rom. professes to misunderstand 'sadness' (v. G.).

199–200. *Groan...who?* (as Hanmer). One line in Q2.

201. *Bid...make* (Q1) Q2 omits 'Bid' and reads 'makes'. All edd. follow Q1.

202. *A word* (Q2) Many read 'Ah, word' (Mal.< Q1); and 'Ah' is often spelt 'A' in Sh. Yet Q2 gives good sense. The 'word', as l. 203 shows, is 'sadness'. To ask Rom., 'sad' because 'sick' with love, to speak 'in sadness' (='seriously') is tactless.

206. *mark...hit* Indelicate quibble; cf. 2. 1. 33.

207. *in that hit you miss*=i.e. that shot went wide.

209–10. *And...armed, From* (Q2) Q1 'And...
arm'd: Gainst'. A.W., noting that if the pointing be
omitted after 'arm'd' Q1 gives much the better reading
of l. 210, and that 'And' in l. 209 may well be a common error, proposes for ll. 208–10:

With Cupid's arrow, she hath Dian's wit!
For, in strong proof of chastity well armed
'Gainst Love's weak childish bow, she lives unharmed.

210. *childish* Cupid was a child.
unharmed (Q1+most edd.) Q2 'vncharmd'.
212. *eyes* i.e. Rom's darting love-glances at her.
213. *Nor ope her lap...gold* i.e. she is so inflexible
that not even great bribery could ever move her. But
there is an indelicate ref. to Danaë. 'Saint-seducing' is
cynical. Cf. G. 'saint'.
214. *rich in beauty, only poor* (Q1) Q2 'rich, in
bewtie onely poore,'.
215. *with...store* Cf. G. 'store' and *Son*. 4. 13–14:

Thy unused beauty must be tombed with thee,
Which, uséd, lives th'executor to be.

217. *She hath* i.e. she has rejected him, because of
her vows, not simply because he is a member of an
enemy family.
makes (Q4, F2) Q2 'make'. Cf. *Son*. 1. 12 'mak'st
waste in niggarding'.
219. *Cuts...posterity* As no one but she is truly
beautiful, by refusing to marry and produce children,
who will be beautiful like her, she makes waste the
whole future. Cf. *Tw. Nt*. 1. 5. 245–7, and *Son*. 3
and 11.
220. *wisely too fair*=too prudently virtuous; cf.
Gent. 4. 2. 5–6 'too fair, too true, too holy, | To be
corrupted' etc., and G 'fair' (viii).
221. *To merit bliss*=to earn heaven.

227–8. *'Tis...more* (as Pope). One line in Q2. Cf. Brooke, 1767–8 (of Rom. in exile):

When he doth heare abrode the praise of ladies blowne
Within his thought he scorneth them and doth preferre his
    owne.

229–35. *These happy masks* etc. G.S. notes:

Half-masks of black were commonly worn by persons of quality when appearing in public. The point of the passage may be put thus: 'Just as black masks remind us (by contrary) of the beauties they hide; just as a blinded man never forgets the beauties that once he saw; so any surpassingly beautiful lady will merely remind me of the one who surpasses even that surpassing beauty.'

233. *mistress* i.e. other than Rom.'s own.

234–5. *a note...fair* i.e. her inferior beauty provokes comment which is like the marginal note of some (renaissance) poet, citing the source in Ovid or Virgil of his inferior verse [J.D.W.].

235. *who...fair* i.e. Rom.'s own lady.

237. *pay that doctrine* pay you your deserts by that lesson.

or else..debt Cf. Tilley, D 165.

S.D. Q2 'Exeunt.'

I. 2

Loc. (J.D.W.) Capell+most edd. 'A street'. No change necessary. Sc. 1 takes place in the morning; Cap. and Mont. are ordered (1. 1. 101) to present themselves at Freetown in the afternoon; they have now done so, and been required 'to furnish securities not to pursue their feud' (K.). Scc. 1 and 2 would of course be played continuously in Sh.'s theatre.

Entry 'Enter...CLOWN' (Q2); we add the rest.

6. *my suit* Paris and his suit are not mentioned in Brooke until after Rom.'s banishment (1857–86).

7. *But...o'er*=Only to repeat.

8. *a stranger* = a new-comer.

9. *fourteen* In Brooke she is a 'wily wench' of sixteen; in Painter almost eighteen. Jul.'s age, astonishing to us moderns, was prob. not so then. It is Marina's in *Pericles* and almost that of Miranda in *The Tempest*. Cf. also Porter's *Two Angry Women of Abington* (Mal. Soc. Rep. ll. 656 ff.) where fifteen is the right age for 'prittie maides' to marry.

13. *marred* Echoes proverb 'marrying is marring' (Tilley, M 701).

14. *Earth...she* At 3. 5. 165 he speaks as if Jul. had been an only child. Such minor inconsistencies are not uncommon in Sh.

Earth (Q2) Q4 (+most edd.) 'The earth'. But Q2 strikes a more solemn note.

15. *She is* (Q1+most edd.) Q2 'Shees'. Cf. p. 115–

16. *the...my earth* A difficulty. With Schmidt, Onions and Herford 'earth' = landed property; with Mal. it = body (cf. 2. 1. 2; *Son*. 146. 1); with Ulrici it = world, life; others think the word corrupt. 'Hopeful' = inspiring hope (cf. the exp. 'young hopeful').

18. *And, she agreed,* (Daniel) Q2 'And she agreed,'. Q3 and Ff. read 'agree', and Capell+many edd., accepting this, read 'An' for 'And' (= 'if').

25. *stars* i.e. ladies, who, however, being mortal, are 'earth-treading'.

dark heaven The feast is to be held at night.

26. *young men* (Q1, 2) Poss. a common error. J. conj. 'yeomen' to accord with l. 27. Cf. the misp. at 5. 3. 3 and n. there.

27. *well-apparelled* sc. with foliage.

29. *female* (Q1) Q2 'fennell'. Misreading poss. either way. Hoppe reads 'fennel', which 'was supposed to arouse the passions' (v. Nares), and glosses 'fennel buds' as 'love-inspiring girls'. Nares's evidence seems slender and Hoppe's gloss far-fetched.

32. *on more* (Q4) Q2 'one more'.

32–3. *Which...none* The syntax is confused, and Cap. quibbles on the prov.: 'One is as good as none' (Tilley, O 52), cf. *Son.* 136. 7–8: 'Among a number one is reckoned none; / Then in the number let me pass untold'. We paraphrase: 'Among which ladies, on "closer" view, mine may hold her own, although among a number one is reckoned none.' See G. 'stand', 'reckoning'.

34. S.D. (after Staunton) *trudge* v. G.

36. S.D. (after Mal.).

37. S.D. Q2 'Exit.'   38. S.D. (J.D.W.).

38–9. *written here! It* (most edd.<Q1 'written here',) Q2 'written. Here it'.

39–41. *It is written...nets* Parodies *Euphues* (Lyly, i. 180). 'The Shoemaker must not go aboue his latchet, nor the hedger meddle with anything but his bill. It is vnsemely for the Paynter to feather a shaft, or the Thatcher to handle the pensill.' [Tilley, C 480].

44. *I...learned. In* Q2 '(I...learned) in'.

44–5. *In good time!* Because, being gentry, they can read.

45. S.D. (Q2) From this entry (6 ll. from the top of sig. B 3ʳ in Q 1) down to 1. 3. 36 (3 ll. from the top of sig. B 4ᵛ) Q 2 was, we think, printed from Q 1, slightly corrected between ll. 44 and 57 but after that un-altered. Cf. pp. 113–15 and below l. 58 n.

46–7. *one .fire...anguish,* Alluding to the prov. notion that 'fire cools fire / Within the scorchéd veins of one new burned' (*K. John*, 3. 1. 277–8). Cf. Tilley, F 277. Brooke's prov. is 'And as out of a planke a nayle a nayle doth driue' (207), which Sh. uses in *Two Gent.* 2. 4. 191.

47. *another's anguish* = the anguish caused by another pain. Also prov.; cf. Tilley G 446.

48. *by backward turning* sc. by moving in another direction.

51. *poison* Cf. Brooke, 219, 'loves sweete impoy-sonde'.

52–3 *Your plantain leaf* etc. Cf. *L.L.L.* 3. 1. 69ff. K. explains:

Ben. has been prescribing a cure for hopeless love. Rom. parodies him by prescribing for a trivial wound: 'If I had a broken shin, I should know how to cure it; but hopeless love is something for which neither you nor I can prescribe the remedy'.

52, 53. *Your* Indefinite.

55–7. *Not mad* etc. Speaking figuratively of the tortures of unhappy love, Rom. describes literally the treatment accorded to madmen in Sh.'s time.

57. *and—God-den* Q2 'and Godden'. Dash and hyphen are Rowe's.

58 to 1. 3. 36 *God gi' god-den...eleven years* Identical in the Qq. v. p. 113 and n. above, l. 45 S.D.

58. *God gi' god-den* Q2 Q1 'Godgigoden'. v. G. 'God-den'.

60. *without book* To learn 'without book' was to learn 'by heart' (cf. 1. 4. 7; *Tw. Nt.* 1. 3. 27), or 'by ear', which is the sense the Clo. intends.

61. *see* Emphatic.

63. *Ye say* etc. Clo. understands that he knows neither letters nor language, i.e. that he cannot read. S.D. (after Collier).

64. S.D. (J.), Qq 1, 2 'He reads the Letter.' It is not a letter; the Q1 reporter calls it so. See l. 45 S.D. n., and p. 116, n. 3.

65–73. *Signior...Helena* Prose in Qq 1, 2; verse Dyce, ed. 2 (Capell conj.).

65, 68, 72. *Signior* Qq 1, 2 'Seigneur'. Sh. may have used the more appropriate Ital. form. See l. 45 S.D. n.

66. *Anselmo* (Dyce, ed. 2; Capell conj.). Q1 Q2 'Anselme'. Bandello and Painter call Friar John (5. 2) 'Anselme'. Cf. p. 116, n. 3.

67. *Vitruvio* (F3) Qq 1, 2 'Vtruuio'. Cf. p. 116, n. 3.

71. *and* (Q1) Q2 om.

75. *Up.* Dowden (reading 'Up—') comments: 'I believe that Rom. eagerly interrupts the Serv., who would have said "Up to our house"'. Rom.'s eagerness is accounted for by the mention of Rosaline (l. 71).

76–7. *Whither...house* (Theob.<Warb.) Q2 '*Ro.* Whither to supper? | *Ser.* To our house.' From Q1 (v. l. 45 S.D. n.). In view of Rom.'s eagerness Warb.'s conj. is clearly right. See l. 75, n.

80. *thee* (Q1) Q2 'you'. Q1 gives the normal address to servants.

84. S.D. Qq om.   88. *unattainted* v. G. and 1. 2. 50.

92. *fires* (Pope) Q1 'fire', Q2 'fier'. A common error. The sing. form spoils the rhyme (see p. 116, n. 3 and Greg., *Aspects*, 177).

93–4. *these* = these eyes of mine.

often drowned sc. in tears, on account of his love for Rosaline.

could never die i.e. despite his rejection by her, his love has remained firm.

heretics Because leading him to worship false deities.

95. *love!* (F2) Qq 1, 2 'loue,'.

98–9. *Herself...weighed* Rom.'s eyeballs are the two pans of a scale; both in l. 98 holding an image of Ros., while in l. 99 her image is balanced against that of another.

102. *seems* sc. to you.

104. *of mine own* = of my own lady, who will be there. S.D. Qq. om.

I. 3

S.D. *Loc.* (after Capell 'A room in Capulet's house').

Entry (Q 2) The Q 2 sp.-hdg. for Lady Cap in this sc. is 'Wife.' up to l. 50, where it changes to 'Old La.', and then again at l. 105 to 'Mo.'. Q 1 has 'Wife' or its contraction throughout. The Q 2 change at l. 50 may be due to the collator passing from Q 1 to dependence on the foul papers. See p. 113, and 1. 2. 45 S.D. n.

2 ff. *Now*, etc. Cf. Tilley, N 335, 'A nurse's tongue is privileged to talk', and Brooke, 652–60 (Nurse to Romeus):

And how she gaue her sucke in youth she leaueth not to tell.
A prety babe (quod she) it was when it was yong:
Lord how it could full pretely haue prated with it tong.
A thousand times and more I laid her on my lappe,
And clapt her on the buttocke soft and kist where I did
    clappe.
And gladder then was I of such a kisse forsooth:
Then I had been to haue a kisse of some olde lechers
    mouth.
And thus of Iuliets youth began this prating noorse,
And of her present state to make a tedious long discoorse.

The Nurse's speeches are set as prose and in italics throughout the sc. in both Qq. See *Sh. Survey* (1955).

4. *God forbid!* Apologizing for 'lady-bird' (v. G.). S.D. (Q 2).

10. *thou's* = thou shalt.

18. *shall* (Q 1) Q 2 'stal'.

24. *the earthquake* See p. xvi.

30. *bear a brain* Prov.; cf. Tilley, B 596.

34. *'Shake'*...*dove-house* i.e. the shaking of the dove-cot bade me bestir myself; v. G. 'shake' [A.W.]. J.E.C. cites Peele, *Old Wives Tale* (M.S.R. 801), 'Bounce quoth the guns' (= Bang went the guns).

34–5. *'twas...bid* Cf. Golding's *Ovid*, ii. 502:
'It was no neede to bid him chaufe'.

53. *it*. The old genitive.

59. *say I* Quibble on 'say "ay"'; cf. 45, 49, 52, 58.

66. *stands* Plur. *dispositions* (Q2) Most edd. read
'disposition' (F.); but v. quotations in O.E.D. 7.

67–8. *honour* (twice) Q1 'honor', Q2 'houre'.
Q2 makes sense in 67, but none in 68, and is
doubtless a minim-misreading.

69. *sucked...teat* Cf. Tilley, E 198. 'He sucked
evil from the teat'; *Tit.* 2. 3. 145; *R. III*, 2. 2. 30.

72. *mothers*. *By* (F.) Q2 'mothers by'.

73–4. *much...maid* Jul. is nearly fourteen; when she
was born Lady Cap. was much the same age. Thus Lady
Cap. is inferentially only about twenty-eight years old;
but she is married to an elderly man (cf. e.g. 1. 1. 75,
1. 5. 32) and acc. to Sh.'s sp.-hdgs. an 'Old La.' (v.
head-note).

77. *world—* (F4) Q2 'world.'
a man of wax v. G. 'wax'. But ironical also with
Sh.; Paris is never anything more. Cf. 3. 3. 126.

82–95. *Read o'er...no less* Cf. Brooke, 1893–5,

> the person of the man...
> With curious wordes she payntes before her daughters'
> eyes.

Cf. also G. M. Hopkins to C. Patmore, 24 Oct.
1887:

Is there anything in *Endymion* worse than the passage in
R. and J. about the County Paris as a book of love that
must be bound and I can't tell what? It has some kind of
fantastic beauty, like an arabesque, but in the main it is
nonsense.

85. *content* For the quibble, combining the two
metaphors ('married', l. 84, 'volume', l. 86) v. G.

86. *what obscured* sc. passion.

88. *unbound*   89. *cover* Two quibbles, v. G.

90. *The fish...sea* A 'philosophical' saw. A.W. notes that Chaucer (*Hous of Fame*, 747–60) gives 'fish dwelling in floode and see' as an example of how everything 'hath his propre mansioun'. The meaning perhaps is: Just as the fish needs the sea to live in, so a handsome man needs the embraces of a wife in order to live a full life. Cf. G. 'pride'. [G.I.D.]

92. *That book...story* The pages and the cover share the glory, i.e. are partners in evoking widespread esteem. Thus each benefits from connection with the other. [G.I.D.]

96. *bigger women grow*=women grow bigger. So Q2. Most edd. read 'bigger! Women grow', or 'bigger: women grow' (F.).

98. *I'll look...move*='I'll look at him with favour if what I see prompt me to love him' (K.).

100. *it* (Q1) Q2 om. S.D. (F.) Q2 'Enter Seruing.', Q1 'Enter Clowne.'.

103. *cursed* Because she should be helping in the pantry.

106. S.D. Q2 'Exeunt.'.

I. 4

This sc. begins 4 ll. from the top of C 1ʳ in Q1, which page might easily after correction have served as copy for Q2.

S.D. *Loc.* (G.I.D.; cf. l. 33). *Entry* (Q2) The 'masquers' (Q2 'maskers') implies disguise; for Romeo's v. 1. 5. 97, n. The young men, masked and in the customary 'disguises', are about to gate-crash the Capulet ball. In Sh.'s time such intrusions were regarded as a compliment (cf. 1. 5. 17, 121). Enid Welsford, *The Court Masque*, p. 102, distinguishes between this type of 'impromptu social' masking and the formal masquerade which reached its fullest English development at the Stuart court. Both were of Italian origin, though much influenced by the traditional English 'mummery'. The masquers might send a 'trunchman' or 'presenter' ahead to deliver a formal speech (v. *Timon*, 1. 2. 124 ff.); or they might enter with him (v. *L.L.L.* 5. 2. 158 ff., where the convention is treated comically). And the speech might convey a greeting to the host, a compliment to the ladies, or an 'apology' for intruding. The masquers then invited ladies of the house-party to a dance, followed by flirtation. Cf. also *Much Ado*, 2. 1. 76 S.D. n., *Hen. VIII*, 1. 4. 63 ff., and E. K. Chambers, *Med. Stage*, i. ch. xvii, *Eliz. Stage*, i. 152–4.

3. *The date* etc.=Such rigmaroles are out of date.

4. *Cupid* The masquers' trunchman or presenter, was traditionally a boy, and often a Cupid. Cf. Welsford, pp. 31, 150, 151; Chambers, *Eliz. Stage*, i, 190–1.   *hoodwinked* v. G. and cf. 1. 1. 170.

5. *Tartar's...bow* Sh. calls it so to distinguish it from the English bow; actually Cupid's lip-shaped bow was a Grecian one. Cf. Smith: *Dict. of Ant.* 'arcus'.

7–8. *Nor...entrance* (Q1). Q2 om. See p. 115, *fin.* Cf. *L.L.L.* 5. 2. 158 ff.   *without-book* recited by heart; cf. 1. 2. 60, n.   *entrance* Trisyllabic.

9. *by what* sc. standards.   10. *measure* v. G.

11. *Give me a torch* The torchbearers, attendants at all masquing, looked on, but did not participate either in the dance or the love-making. Cf. l. 38.

19–21. *I am...woe* Note the quibbling 'sore—soar' and 'bound—bound'.

23–4. *And to...thing* Q2 heads this 'Horatio.'—presumably Sh.'s slip.   *to sink in*=to get sunk in (cf. ll. 41–2).   *should you*=you would.

28. *Prick...pricking* Quibbles. v. G.   *for*=(a) in return for, (b) for the purpose of.

30. *A visor for a visor!* Implying that the face is as ugly as the mask. Cf. the prov. 'A well-favoured visor

will hide an ill-favoured face (Tilley, V 92). Cf. G.
'visor' and 1. 5. 56.

31. *quote* (Q3) Q2 'cote'—the older sp. v. G.

32. S.D. (J.)—at l. 29.

34. *betake*... i.e. dance.

36. *rushes* The common Eliz. floor-covering. They
are 'senseless', so that to 'tickle' them is waste of time.

37. *proverbed* etc. Cf. Tilley, C 51 'A good candle-
holder proves a good gamester' [John Crow, *Sh. Quart.*
iii. 266]. Such is Rom.'s excuse.

39. *The game...done* Cf. Tilley, P 399, 'When
play is best, it is time to leave'; and Ben.'s words at
1. 5. 119. Rom. means: the night's entertainment will
never be better than now (and will prob. be worse), so
I am finished with it. Cf. ll. 106 ff. and 1. 5. 120.
done (Q1) Q2 'dum'—perh. minim-misreading.

40. *dun's the mouse* A quibble on 'done', but lit. = the
mouse is dark-coloured, i.e. not easy to see at night;
hence a prov. way of saying 'Be quiet and unseen (as
a mouse)'; hence again the constable's watchword.
Cf. *Ado*, 3. 3. 34–8; Tilley, D 644; Dekker, *P. Grissill*,
1. 2. 5

41. *Dun...mire* Alluding to another prov. expr.
'Dun in the mire' = stick-in-the-mud; where 'Dun' = a
horse. Cf. Tilley, D 642, 643. Horses often got stuck
in the mud of Eliz. roads.

41–2. *mire, Or save-your-reverence love* From Q2
'mire Or saue you reuerence loue', with 'you' corrected to 'your' (F.). Most edd. read 'mire Of this
sir-reverence loue' (<Q1). But Q2+F. is more like
Mer., since it implies that Rom.'s ridiculous love is
something muckier than mire; v. G. 'Save-your-
reverence'.

43. *burn daylight* = waste time (lit. burn torches or
candles by day). Rom takes the lit. sense, and objects,
it being night.

44. *Nay, that's not so* So begins sig. C1ᵛ in Q1, which prob. after correction served with sig. C2ʳ as copy for Q2. See p. 115.   *delay* (Q2) Capell 'delay;'

45. *our lights* i.e. our torches.   *like lights* (J.) Q1 'like Lampes', Q2 'lights lights'—a comp.'s dittograph; cf. p. 116. Mer., piqued by Rom.'s glumness, retorts with a laboriously exact explanation. Greg (*Aspects*, pp. 179–80), accepting Capell's 'delay;' (l. 44), proposes 'light lamps'.

46–7. *Take...wits* i.e. don't take me too literally, but think of my meaning; for 'the things I mean are five times as sensible as the things I say' (J.E.C.).

46. *judgement* Q2 'indgement'.

50. *I dreamt...to-night* Barker (p. 7) writes: 'The Queen Mab speech...is as much and as little to be dramatically justified as a song in an opera is'. But it enables Sh. to register the effect of foreboding in Rom.'s dream without telling us what the dream was. For when Mer. has ended we no longer expect Rom. to give details; and yet have been prepared for the even vaguer 'misgiving' in ll. 106–11 [J.C.M.]. Cf. 5. 1. 1, n.

53. *O then...with you* Q1 follows this with '*Ben.* Queene Mab whats she?' which many edd. adopt, unnecessarily. *Queen Mab* Nothing is now known of this fairy beyond the present passage; but cf. l. 54, n. It is even doubtful whether 'Queen' should not be 'quean', since 'midwife' and 'queen' go oddly together. She seems to be a sort of incubus. Cf. O.E.D. 'mab'=slattern, a woman of loose character. Jonson's Mab in *A Satyre*, 1603 (Jonson, vii. 121 ff.), a kind of female Puck, and Drayton.'s in *Nimphidia*, 1627, both draw upon Sh.'s.

54–91. *She is...bodes.* Q2 here presents two anomalies: (*a*) though the rest of the dialogue in the sc.

is correctly printed as verse, these 38 ll., occupying the lower portion of sig. C2^r, appear as 26 ll. of prose; (*b*) ll. 59–61 ('Her chariot...makers') occur after l. 69; thus, as Lettsom notes, making Mer. preposterously describe the parts (ll. 62–9) before mentioning the coach itself. The explanation looks simple: Q2 was at this point being set up from Sh.'s foul papers, and he had added an afterthought or afterthoughts which the compositor at first overlooked but was later forced to crowd into a page already set up as verse, in order to save himself redistributing his type. But this would imply a solicitude for the accuracy of the text on Creede's part for which there is little evidence else-where in Q2, and assume that he was both lucky enough to disover the omission and lucky enough to be able to accommodate the missing matter in the space available. It involves too a further and more insuperable difficulty. Since 26 from 38 leaves 12, Sh.'s hypo-thetical addition(s) must have totalled a dozen lines, neither more nor less. Now, if the speech be examined there seem to be two alternative pairs of passages, and two only, which might have been additions, i.e. which can be omitted without serious injury to the context, viz. (i) the obviously misplaced ll. 59–61, together with ll. 77–81 ('Sometime...benefice'), which look like an afterthought, since 'courtier's nose' is repeti-tious after 'courtier's knees' (l. 72); or (ii) ll. 77–81 as before, together with ll. 62–9 ('Her waggon-spokes', etc.) which are a more likely addition than ll. 59–61, since the whole would naturally occur to Sh. before the parts. Neither alternative, however, fits the case. For (i) amounts to 7 ll. only, which is 5 too few, and (ii) to 13 ll., which is 1 too many. Actually, indeed, the position of both cases would be worse, if the conjecture of 'counsellor's nose' for the apparent repetition 'cour-tier's nose' be accepted (v. note *ad loc.*). If, on the other hand, we suppose that Q2 was here, as elsewhere, set up from a corrected copy of Q1, no grave difficulties arise. Indeed, the misplacement of ll. 59–61 finds an obvious explanation in the fact that they are omitted in Q1 and would therefore have been the collator's marginal addition to that text. As for the prose lining, if one corrects Mer.'s verse in Q1 so as to bring it into accordance with Q2, it becomes clear that the Q2 compositor, baffled by the problem of lineation, would almost inevitably decide that the easiest and quickest solution was to set up the bulk of the speech as prose.

54. *midwife* Steev. notes:

The fairies' midwife does not mean the midwife to the fairies, but that she was the person among the fairies whose department it was to deliver the fancies of sleeping men of their dreams, those 'children of an idle brain'.

56. *alderman* (Q2) Q1 'Burgomaster'.

57. *atomi* (Q1) Q2 'ottamie'.

59–61. *Her chariot...coachmakers* After l. 69 in Q2. See ll. 54–91, n., Daniel p. 105, and Dyce's *Sh.* (2nd ed.) note *ad loc.*

60. *joiner squirrel* 'So called from his chisel-like teeth. The "old grub" is the kind of insect *larva* that bores holes in nuts' (G.S.).

61. *Time out of mind* Actually coaches were an innovation in Sh.'s day. Cf. *Sh. Eng.* i. 204–5.

o'mind (Capell) Q2 'amind'.

62. *waggon-spokes* Cf. 'waggoner' (l. 67), but 'chariot' (l. 59). 'Chariot' and 'waggon' might be interchangeable words (cf. *F. Queene* i. ii. 29 with ii. ix. 10); yet the transition is very abrupt, and 'waggon' goes ill with 'gallops' (l. 70).

64–6. *Her traces...of film* (Q2) It is difficult to visualize moonbeams as collars round the necks of tiny coach-horses, but the framework of the common spider's-web might suggest the shape of a horse's collar. Thus the orig. Sh. MS. may have run:

> her traces of the moonshines watry beams,
> her collors of the smallest spider web,...

and the comp. or collaborator, misled by 'of the' in both lines, may have transposed the latter halves [G.I.D.].

66. *film* (F 2) Q 1 'filmes', Q 2 'Philome'.

69. 'It was supposed...that when maidens were idle, worms bred in their fingers' (Nares). cf. O.E.D. 'idle' 4. d. *maid* (Q 1) Q 2 'man' (prob. misreading).

72. *O'er* (Q 1) Q 2 'On'. Cf. 'O'er' in ll. 73, 74 and *MSH*, p. 107 (r : minim).

76. *breaths* Q 1 'breathes', Q 2 'breath'. *sweet-meats* Such 'kissing-comfits' (*M.W.W.* 5. 5. 20) are not unknown to-day.

77. *courtier's* After 'courtier's knees' (l. 72) this is suspect. Moreover 'smelling out a suit' suggests a legal officer of some kind (A.W.); and Q 1 has 'Lawers'. Collier proposed 'counsellor', i.e. counsellor-at-law, the old term for barrister. Cf. O.E.D. 3 and *Meas.* I. 2. 103 'good counsellors lack no clients'.

78. *smelling out a suit* K., accepting 'courtier's' explains:

discovering some person who has a petition to the king. For a fat fee the courtier will undertake to gain the royal favour for the petitioner.

81. *Then dreams he* (Q 1) Q 2 'then he dreams'. There seems no reason why Sh. should have departed from the order in ll. 78 and 83, while 'he dreams' is metrically awkward.

84. *Spanish blades* Q 1 'countermines'. Spain, particularly Toledo, was famous for its swords.

85. *healths...deep* Cf. *2 H. IV*, 5. 3. 56, 'I'll pledge you a mile to th'bottom'.   *fathom* Q 1, Q 2 'fadome'.

87. *prayer* i.e. to ward off evil.

90–1. *bakes...bodes* The matted hair of unclean persons was attributed to elves, who if it were disentangled might be provoked to further malice. Cf. *Lear*, 2. 3. 10, 'Elf all my hair in knots'. Elves and fairies hated 'sluts and sluttery' (*M.W.W.* 5. 5. 46).

90. *elf-locks* (Q1), Q2 'Elklocks'—prob. a literal error; cf. p. 115, *ad. fin.*

93. *bear* (*a*) weight of a man, (*b*) children.

95. *she—* (F2) Q2 'she.'.

100. *inconstant...wind* Proverbial, v. Tilley, W 412.

102. *angered* sc. at finding her cold to his advances. *puffs away* suggests scorn (v. O.E.D. *puff* vb. 2), as well as violence.

103. *his side* (Q2) Edd. freq. read 'his face' (Q1). Veering away from the north the wind first turns its side towards the south before facing right round. An anon. conj., 'aside' (apud *Camb.*) is attractive but unnecessary. *dew-dropping* rainy (but suggesting warmth and fertility).

108. *his*=its.

111. *vile forfeit* sc. his worthless life.

112–13. *But...sail* Cf. Brooke ll. 799–800:

In stormy wind and waue, in daunger to be lost:
Thy stearles ship (O Romeus) hath been long while betost.

113. *sail* (Q1) Q2 'sute' (misreading).

114. S.D. (J.D.W.) Q2 'They march about the Stage, and Seruingmen come forth with Napkins'. 'Marching about', a stage-convention to signify a change of locality (v. Chambers, *Eliz. Stage*, iii. 99–100 and cf. *ibid.* pp. 38, 117, n. 5.), was also the time-honoured opening movement of a masque (cf. Welsford, pp. 58 ff., 155 ff.). After this Q2 has 'Enter Romeo.'—mistakenly, for Rom. has not gone out, and

there was no pause or change of sc. on Sh.'s stage. But since we are supposed to pass from the street into Cap.'s hall, a change of locality, first marked by Hanmer, is necessary in a reader's text.

1. 5

S.D. *Loc.* (Theob.)   *Entry* (J.D.W.<Q2 entries cited at 1. 4. 114, n.; 1. 5. 26.)

1–16. Q2 heads these six speeches *Ser.*, 1., *Ser.*, 2., *Ser.*, 3. respectively.

1–5. As verse in Q2; 1–2 as prose first in Pope, 3–5 first in Q3.

2. *He* ... i.e. he thinks himself too good to ... Plate was beginning to supersede wooden trenchers etc. in Sh.'s time, v. *Sh.'s Eng.* ii. 119–20.

3. *good manners* = decent behaviour.

6. *joined-stools* (Rowe) Q2 'ioynstooles'. Elsewh. in Sh. 'ioynd' or 'ioynt'.

9. *Nell*— Q2 'Nell,'. Theob. 'Nell.'.

14–16. As prose first in Pope. As verse in Q2 ('boyes, | Be').

15–16. *the* ... *all* Cf. Tilley, L 395. 'A proverb, used as an encouragement to cheerfulness and a merry life' (K.). 'The longer liver' is Death. S.D. Q2 'Exeunt. | Enter all the guests and gentlewomen to the Maskers.'.

17. sp.-hdg. Q2 'I. Capu.' So at ll. 35, 40.

18. *walk a bout* (Capell) Q1 'haue about', Q2 'walke about'. Cf. 2. 5. 51, *Ado*, 2. 1. 77–8, n., and *Dekker's Plague Pamphlets*, ed. F. P. Wilson, p. 231 (notes) 'have about with'. Here prob. refers to a round dance of some kind.

24. *A whispering tale* Cf. Webster, *Duch. of Malfi*, I. I. 373–4:

> A visor and a mask are whispering rooms
> That were never built for goodness.
>
> [Welsford, p. 136.]

27. *A hall!* i.e. clear the floor! S.D. after l. 26 in Q2.

28. *turn...up* The servs. have cleared the tables but have not yet removed the boards from the trestles and stacked both away. The ball involves both main and inner stages.

30. *Ah, sirrah,* etc. He hugs himself. 'In passages of soliloquy "ah sirrah" is app. addressed by the speaker to himself. *A.Y.L.* 4. 3. 165, *2 Hen. IV*, 5. 3. 17' (Onions). Cf. l. 126.

32. *past our dancing days* A prov. exp.; cf. Tilley, D 118.

42. S.D. (Camb.).

42–4. *What...bright* Cf. Brooke, 246: 'With torche in hand a comly knight did fetch her foorth to daunce'.

45–6. *she hangs...rich jewel* Cf. *Euphues*, 'a fair pearle in a Murrian's eare' (Lyly, ii. 89), and *Son.* 27. 11:

> Which, like a jewel hung in ghastly night,
> Makes black night beauteous and her old face new.

night (edd.) Q2 'night:'

55. S.D. (after Collier, ed. 2).

58. *stock and honour*=honourable stock. Hendiadys.

64. *it?* (Ff., Q5) Q2 'it.'.

77. *goodman boy*='Master Malapert'. Cf. *Lear*, 2. 2. 48 and G. To grace someone with a courtesy title belonging to a lower rank than oneself was a delicate form of insult. Cf. *Ric. III*, I. I. 66, n.

81. *be the man* i.e. play the man—though you are

nothing but a 'saucy (v. G.) boy'. Cf. Tilley, T 188 'You are ipse'.

84. *I know what* = I know what I am talking about. 'A reminder to Tyb. that Cap., being head of the family, could "scathe" him in various ways, esp. in purse' (G.S.).

85. *time* sc. to put you in your place.   *time*— Q2 '*time*,'.

86. *Well said* = Bravo! (to the dancers).   *hearts!* —*You* Q2 'hearts, you'.

87–8. Q2 'Be quiet, or more light, more light for shame,| Ile make you quiet (what) chearely my hearts.'. Q5 '...or (more light, more light for shame)...'.

89. *Patience perforce* Prov. exp. Cf. Tilley, P 111.

90. *different* v. G.   *greeting* sc. of each other.

91–2. *shall, Now seeming sweet, convert* Q2 'shall | Now seeming sweet, conuert'. Lettsom's conj. is attractive—'shall | Now-seeming sweet convert'. S.D. Q2 'Exit.'.

93–106. *If I...take* The sonnet-form of this first exchange gives it a dream-like effect.

93. S.D. (after Capell).

94. *shrine* i.e. her body is the habitation of a divine spirit.

sin Q2; Q1 'sinne'. (J. D. W. ed. i. conj. 'pain'. Warb.+ most edd. read 'fine' which, A. W. points out, makes an ugly jingle with 'shrine' and seems too secular in associations for the conceit of a pilgrim at the shrine, which demands a word suggesting penance and/or atonement for the sacrilege of the hand, which the original text fully suggests.

95. *ready* (Q1) Q2 'did readie', inferior in both netre and sense. The 'did' was prob. added inadvertently by the collator or the comp.

97. *pilgrim* Jul. catches up Rom.'s conceit. Some think that Rom. is attired as a pilgrim or palmer for the masquerade. The supposition, though not necessary to explain the conceit, finds support in the fact that 'romeo' is It. for 'pilgrim' or 'palmer'. *wrong* sc. in accusing it of profaning the shrine.

98. *Which* i.e. Rom.'s hand. *in this* i.e. in touching mine.

99. *saints* Ref. to images of saints in shrines.

100. *palm to palm* Cf. Brooke, 267, 'Then she with tender hand his tender palme hath prest'.

103–4. *do, They pray: grant thou* (White; see Furness). Q2 'do, They pray (grant thou)'. Rom. means 'my lips pray that lips be allowed to do what hands do, namely kiss'.

105. *move* v. G. 106. *move not*=stand still.

107. S.D. (Rowe). In Sh.'s England one kissed a lady when meeting or taking leave. But Barker (page 53 n.), supposing 'that the kiss of greeting (which Erasmus found so pleasant) was a kiss on the cheek', notes that 'Romeo kisses Juliet on the lips'. He also suggests (p. 8 n.) that 'the company drift up towards the inner stage' so that 'the two find themselves alone'.

110. S.D. (Capell). *You kiss by th' book* i.e. You make a ritual of kissing. 112. *bachelor* v. G.

118. *dear* v. G. *debt* v. G. Cf. Brooke, 325; 'Thus hath his foe in choyse to geue him lyfe or death'.

119. *Away...best* Cf. 1. 4. 39, n.

122. S.D. None in Q2. Q1 'They whisper in his eare.', which no doubt reflects contemporary stage practice. 'Maskers excuse themselves with a bow' (Capell).

125. *More torches* i.e. 'to escort the maskers to the gate' (K.). The masquers' torches are burned out, or nearly so. S.D. (G.I.D.).

126. *Ah, sirrah* See n. on l. 30.

127. S.D. (after Mal.) None in Q2. Q1 '*Exeunt*.'.

130. *What's...out of door?* Cf. Brooke, 347 'What twayne are those (quoth she) which prease vnto the doore', and the rest of the dialogue with the Nurse.

131. *Petruchio* Cf. 3. 1. 33, n.

132. *there* (Q1) Q2 'here'.

140—1. *Prodigious...enemy* Cf. Brooke, 357, 'What hap haue I quoth she, to loue my fathers foe?'. *Prodigious* i.e. like a deformed or monstrous child.

142. *this, what's this?* (Q1) Q2 'tis? whats tis.'.

143. S.D. (Q2).   144. S.D. Q2 'Exeunt'.

2. Prologue

S.D. and sp.-hdg. (edd.) Q2 simply 'Chorus'. 'The use of this Chorus is not easily discovered' (J.). Barker (pp. 32—3) suggests it was written to cover the removal of stools, etc., required in 1. 5. It reads as if hastily composed. Q1 omits.

3. *groaned for* This second 'for' is superfluous; Rowe's conj. 'sore' is attractive.

4. *matched* (Q3) Q2 'match'.

6. *Alike* i.e. Both.

7. *complain* Cf. 'groaned for' (l. 3).

8. *love's sweet bait...hooks* Cf. Brooke, 388, 'As oft the poysond hooke is hid, wrapt in the pleasant bayte'.

14. *extremities* sc. their desperate situation. Cf. Tilley, D 357.

S.D. (edd.).

2.1

S.D. *Loc.* The editorial scenes 2.1 and 2.2 are headed by Camb. 'A lane by the wall of Capulet's Orchard' and 'Capulet's Orchard'. Our S.D. combines these. Painter (p. 104), but not Brooke, speaks of Rom. walking 'alone up and downe' a 'little streat' or 'narrow Lane' outside Capulet's 'gardein'. For 'orchard' v. 2.1.30, 34; 2.2.108. The whole was played continuously in Sh.'s theatre; but how? Barker (p. 10) holds that the audience had to imagine the 'wall' and that Rom. hid 'somewhere about the stage'; Chambers (*E. Stage*, iii. 98) thinks Rom. 'must have a wall to leap'. *Entry* 'Enter—alone' (Q2). This S.D. heads sig C4ᵛ in Q1, which from here down to the end of D1ᵛ (2.2.56) after correction served, we think, as copy for Q2; cf. pp. 113–14, and *Sh. Survey* (1955).

2. *Turn back...out* In the old 'philosophy' (i.e. science), man's body was 'earth' (cf. 1.2.14; 3.2.59; Gen. ii. 7; and *Merch.* 5.1.65, 'this muddy vesture of decay'); earth was a 'heavy' element (hence 'dull' = heavy, with a quibble on 'melancholy'); on Earth all motion was downwards by attraction to its centre, which was also the centre of the geocentric universe; finally the heart was the centre of the microcosm, Man. Thus, since Juliet has his heart, Romeo's motion must be towards her. Cf. Brooke, 829 'Approaching nere the place from whence his hart had life'. S.D. i. (< Mal.) ii. 'Enter...Mercutio' (Q2) + J.D.W.

3. *cousin Romeo* (Q1) Q2 'Cofen Romeo, Romeo' —prob. a dittograph; cf. p. 116.

3–4. *He...bed.* One line in Q2.

6. *Call...too* As in Q1 and all edd. Q2 continues 'Nay...too.' (in a separate line) to Ben., with sp.-hdg. 'Mer.' at 7. What follows is a piece of satire

on the conventional melancholy Eliz. lover; and refers,
of course, to Rom.'s first love.

7. *Romeo, humours...lover* 'In conjuring up
a spirit different names were recited, with the idea that
the right name would cause the spirit to appear and
speak' (K.). Q1 reads 'Romeo, madman, humours,
passion, liuer'. Noting that this order 'emphasizes the
descent from man to his complaints', Greg is attracted
by 'the reading "liuer",...the seat of the disease of
love' (*Aspects*, p. 147). The words, 'liuer' and 'louer'
are easily misread for each other.

8–10. *Appear...'dove'* Jibes at the conventional
melancholy lover.

9. *one* (Q1) Q2 'on'.

10. *Cry...'dove'* (<Q1) Q2 'Crie but ay me,
prouaunt, but loue and day'—a misreading of the words
in MS. See Greg, *Aspects*, p. 181, and *Sh. Survey*
(1955).

11. *my gossip* i.e. that loose-tongued old woman.
gossip (Q1), Q2 'goship'—perh. a copy-spelling; cf.
O.E.D. 'gossip'.

12. *heir* (Q1 'heire') Q2 'her'.

13. *Abraham* (Q2; Q1) Many edd. (after Upton
and Steev.) read 'Adam', supposing a ref. to Adam Bell,
the notable archer (v. *Ado*, 1. 1. 244). But the sly
rogue Cupid, with nothing but a scarf about his loins,
is like the 'abraham' men, who wandered half-naked
about the world begging and stealing (cf. *Lear*,
2. 3. 9–20; N.B. 'Blanket my loins'). [Hosley, p. 18,
n. 21, also sees an allusion to 'Abraham men' but
glosses it 'beggarly, hypocritical']. K. finds the name
apt to one who 'hath been five thousand years a boy
(*L.L.L.* 5. 2. 11).

trim (Q1) Q2 'true'—a minim-misreading.
Greg notes (*Aspects*, p. 181): 'The original reading
must be "trim", as in the ballad—"The blinded boy

that shootes so trim"'. Sh. alludes to this ballad of *King Cophetua* (printed in R. Johnson's *Crowne Garland of goulden roses*, 1612, and *Percy's Reliques*) four times elsewhere (*L.L.L.* 1. 2. 106–7, 4. 1. 64–6; *R. II.* 5. 3. 80; *2 H. IV*, 5. 3. 104).

16. *ape* A term of endearment, = 'poor fellow' (Herford). Cf. *2 H. IV*, G.

dead i.e. for love. A performing ape was 'trained to "play dead"' (Strunk, *M.L.N.* xxxii, 215 ff.).

19–20. *By her fine…lie* Cf. Palingenius, *Zodiacus Vitae* (tr. B. Googe, 1576), p. 45 'What should I here commende her thighes, or places that there be?' [J. E. Hoskins, *Sh.'s Derived Imagery*, 1953.] Contrib. by J.C.M.

21. *in thy likeness* Pretending Rom. is dead (cf. l. 16), Mer. invokes his ghost.

24–6. *To raise…down* Conjurer's jargon, quibbling indelicately; v. G. 'circle', 'stand', 'lay'.

27–8. *My…name* One line in Q2.

33. sp.-hdg. Q2 'Mar.'   *hit the mark* Another quibble, as is 'medlars' (l. 36). From l. 33 to 2. 2. 56 ('enemy to thee')=sig. D1 of Q1, which was copy for Q2 after correction. Cf. 2. 2. 38–43, n.

38. *open-arse and* (J.D.W.) Q2 'open or' Q1 'open *Et caetera*' (=pudenda; cf. *2 H. IV*, 2. 4. 180). Most edd. follow Q1. But Mer. is more precise: (i) he talks of medlars, and 'medlar' is 'open-ers' in Chaucer (*Reeve's Prol.* 17) and still 'open-arse' in dialect (v. O.E.D. and D.D.), while 'ers' or 'ars' might easily be misread 'ore' in Sh.'s hand, and then transcribed or set up 'or'; (ii) he speaks of the fruits as complementary not alternative so that 'and' not 'or' is required. But once the scribe or compositor had accepted 'or' the 'and' would naturally be deleted as superfluous. G.I.D. concurs, having already with the help of R. D. Gibbs conj. 'arse', as also (since this note

was in draft) have Hosley (p. 21) and Kökeritz (p. 137), though none indicate 'or' as the seat of the corruption.

poperin pear v. G. A common variety in Eliz. orchards; here an allusion to the *membrum virile*, prob. owing to its shape. Tourneur, *Atheist's Tragedy*, 4. 1, has a passage quibbling at length on 'medlar' and 'poperin pear' in the same equivocal senses.

41–2. *Go…found* As in Pope (<Q1). Q2 div. 'here | That'.

S.D. Q2 'Exit.' For the sc.-division v. 2. 1. *Loc.* (head).

2. 2

1. S.D. (after Rowe, at l. 3). None in the Qq or Ff.

3. *Juliet is the sun* Cf. 3. 2. 17 'thou day in night' and Brooke, 1726, 'For eche of them to other is as to the world the sunne'.

5. *sick and pale* (Q1, Q2) Poss. 'sick' is here a Q1 anticipation of Q2 'sick and green' (l. 8) where Q1 reads 'pale and greene'. Did Sh. write 'wan and pale'? Cf. *Err.* 4. 4. 107; *Tit.* 2. 3. 90 [A.W.]; and p. 116, n. 3.

6. *her maid* Because virgins were the nymphs of Diana, the virgin goddess of the moon.

8. *sick and green* A ref. to 'green-sickness', i.e. 'an anaemic disease which mostly affects young women about the age of puberty and gives a pale or greenish tinge to the complexion' (O.E.D.).

9. *fools* (*a*) i.e. to remain unmarried, (*b*) a poss. quibble on fool = court jester, whose motley would include green.

10–11. *It is…were* As in J.; one line in Q2. 'It is my lady' was poss. a 'first shot' which Sh. intended to cancel. In line 11 we can hardly help recalling 2. 1. 37, where 'O that she were' (overheard by Rom.) is used of a very different conception of love.

16. *do* Q1 'doe', Q2 'to'.

17. *their spheres* i.e. the concentric tubes which, containing the various heavenly bodies, were supposed to rotate around the static earth acc. to the astronomy of Ptolemy (2nd cent. A.D.), an astronomy generally accepted till superseded by that of Copernicus (died 1543) in the seventeenth century.

20. *eyes* (Q 1) Q 2 'eye'. Cf. 'eyes' (l. 18).

23. *see...hand* Cf. Brooke, 518, 'In windowe on her leaning arme her weary hed doth rest'.

29. *white-upturnéd* (Theob.'s hyphen) i.e. 'so that the whites show clearly'.

31. *lazy-passing* (Collier, Hoppe) Q 2 'lazie puffing', Q 1 'lasie pacing'. Most edd. accept Q 1 'pacing', but that implies taking steps, which is absurd with 'clouds' and 'sails'. Macbeth's 'cherubim horsed | Upon the sightless couriers of the air' refers to winds in hurricane and is no parallel. Even less can Q 2 'puffing' claim support from the angry puffing of the wind in 1. 4. 102 above. 'Puffing' on the other hand is an easy *a* : *u* misreading of 'passing' which accords with the rest of the image and of which 'pacing' (Q 1) may indeed be a sixteenth century spelling, or homophonic substitution. This note, which withdraws from the position taken in *Stud. in Bib.* (iv. 24–6), is partly indebted to J.C.M.

38–9. *'Tis but...Montague* = Your family name is of no importance. Even if you were not a Montague, you would still be yourself; and it is you I love.

38–43. *'Tis but...call a rose* (A.W.). The Qq texts run:

Q 1   *Iul*: Tis but thy name that is mine enemie.
        Whats *Mountague*? It is nor hand nor foote,
        Nor arme, nor face, nor any other part.
        Whats in a name? That which we call a Rose,
        By any other name.... [etc.]
Q 2   *Iu*: Tis but thy name that is my enemie.

> Thou art thy selfe, though not a *Mountague*,
> Whats *Mountague*? it is nor hand nor foote,
> Nor arme nor face, ô be some other name
> Belonging to a man.
> Whats in a name that which we call a rose,
> By any other word.... [etc.]

Clearly Q 2 here derives from a corrected passage of Q 1 in which the collator's marginal additions from the foul papers have somehow got misplaced (cf. p. 115). Malone and most subs. edd. read:

> *Jul.* 'Tis but thy name that is my enemy;
> Thou art thyself, though not a Montague.
> 40 ' What's Montague? it is nor hand, nor foot,
> Nor arm, nor face, nor any other part
> Belonging to a man. O, be some other name!
> What's in a name? that which we call a rose
> By any other name... [etc.]

giving an extra metrical foot in l. 42 and an awkward repetition of 'other' in ll. 41–2. A.W. omits the second 'other', which she takes to be an actor's anticipation of 'any other name' (l. 44), and rearranges. See *Sh. Survey* (1955).

39. *art* (Q 2). J.C.M. proposes 'wert', which J.D.W. finds attractive.

44. *name* (Q 1 + all edd.) Q 2 'word'—a not difficult minim + *e* : *d* misreading of 'name', which seems required by the idiom: one calls a person or thing by its 'name' not by its 'word' [J.D.W.]. G.I.D. finds 'word' possible and supposes the Q 1 reporter simply repeated 'name' from l. 43. N.B. Since Q 2 was here being printed from the corrected Q 1, if Sh. wrote 'name' the corrector must have misread it as 'word' and substituted it for 'name' which he deleted. Cf. p. 115.

45. *were* (Q 1) Q 2 'wene'.   46. *owes* v. G.

53-4. *By...am.* As in F; one line in Q 2.

55. *saint* This recalls Romeo the pilgrim (1. 5. 101) [Delius].

64–5. Closely follows Brooke, 491–2.

66. *With...walls* Cf. Brooke, 830 'So light he wox, he lept the wall'. Note too the contrast with 1.4. 19–22.

69. *stop* (Q 2). Cf. *L.L.L.* 1. 1. 70; *Oth.* 5. 2. 264. Q 1 and most edd. 'let' (='obstacle').

75. *night's cloak* Cf. 3. 2. 14 and Brooke, 457, 'But when on earth the night her mantel blacke hath spred'.

76. *but*=unless.   80. *prompt* (Q 1) Q 2 'promp'.

83. *that vast...sea* Cf. 'the furthest inch of Asia' (*Ado*, 2. 1. 248); and *Son.* 44. 5–6.

washed Q 1 'washt', Q 2 'washeth'.

84. *adventure* 'i.e. like a Merchant Adventurer' (J.E.C.).

92–3. *false. At lovers' perjuries They* Q 1 'false: | At Louers periuries they'. Q 2 'false at louers periuries. | They'. A notion found in Ovid, *Ars Amatoria*, i. 633, and Tibullus, iii, 6, 49–50; but proverbial in Sh.'s day; cf. *O.D.P.* p. 328 and Tilley, J 82. Malone cites *Alcida. Greene's Metamorphosis* (Grosart's *Greene*, ix. 80) 'Jupiter laughs at the periurie of louers.' Other lines, quoted by Douce and many edd., which purport to be from a trans. of the *Ars Amatoria* by Marlowe, are later, and belong to Thos. Heywood (v. *T.L.S.* corr. 11. 12. 24; 16. 7. 25).

95. *think'st* (Q 5+edd.) Q 2 'thinkest'.

99. *haviour* (Q 1) Q 2 'behauior'—prob. compositor's expansion.

101. *more* (Q 1) Q 2 om. Metrically necessary. *cunning* (Q 1) which Pope and most edd. adopt. Q 2 'coying' would be tautological (cf. 'strange'), and goes oddly along with 'have'; perh. a misreading of 'conyng', badly written.

104. *true-love* Q2 'truloue'. Most edd. read 'true love's' (<Q1). For the adj. 'true-love' cf. *Gent.* 2. 7. 46; *R. II*, 5. 1. 10, etc.

106. *Which* Antecedent 'yielding'.

107. *vow* (Q2) Many edd. read 'sweare' (Q1).

108. *tops*— (Rowe). Qq 'tops.'.

110. *circled* (Q1) Q2 'circle' (? misreading of 'circld'). *orb*=sphere. See l. 17 n.

115. *love*— (F2). Q1 'loue', Q2 'loue.'.

116. *swear. thee*, Q2 'sweare,' 'thee:'.

119–2. 3. 17. Here a corrected leaf (D3^{r,v}) of Q1 prob. formed copy for Q2. Cf. p. 115 and *Sh. Survey* (1955).

119–20. *Too like...'It lightens'*. The same thought in *M.N.D.* 1. 1. 145–8. Cf. Brooke, 209 'This sodain kindléd fyre' etc.

125–7. *O wilt...for mine* Cf. Brooke, 563–4 'els fauour found he none | That night, at lady Iuliets hand, saue pleasant woordes alone'.

131. *frank*=generous.

132. *the thing I have* sc. her love for him.

136. S.D. (Rowe<F. 'calls within').

137. *nurse!*— (Mal.) Q2 'nurse,'.

138. S.D. (edd.) Rowe 'Exit.' Qq, Ff om.

141. S.D. (after Rowe 'Re-enter Juliet, above.') None in Qq.

143–4. *If that...marriage*. Cf. Brooke, 535–6 'But if your thought be chaste...If wedlock be the end and marke which your desire hath found...'.

146. *rite* (F3) Q2 'right'—a Sh. spelling.

148. *And...world* Cf. Brooke, 540 'And following you where so you goe, my fathers house forsake'.

149, 151. Capell's arrangement. Q2 prints 'Madam.', without sp.-hdg, in right-hand margins, where the words prob. stood in Sh.'s MS. Cf. Greg, *Ed. Prob.* p. 61 n. 2 and below 5. 3. 71, n.

150. *anon.*— (edd.) Q2 'anon:'.

151. *thee—...come—* Q2 'thee (by and by I come) Madam.'

152. *suit* (Q5+most edd.; Q4 'sute') Q2 'strife'. Cf. Brooke, 543–4 'and now your Iuliet you be seekes | To cease your sute' [cited by Delius, 1872 and Camb. note v]. Sh. follows Brooke very closely in this scene. Cf. notes above.

154. *soul—* (after Theob.) Q2 'soule.'. S.D. Qq om. Ff. '*Exit.*'.

156. *Love...love* Cf. 'Love is the loadstone of love' (Tilley, L514).

157. *toward* i.e. as boys go toward... S.D. (after Capell).

158. *Hist...hist!* Prob. the soft call, whistle or chirrup, a falconer uttered to 'draw' a hawk 'along'. Not found in contemp. books on falconry, but seems intended by Milton in *Il Penseroso* (l. 55) 'And the mute Silence hist along', where Silence is imaged as a bird. Simon Latham (*Second Book of Faulconry*, 1658, ch. xii. pp. 39–40) bids the falconer use the voice 'softly...especially with your tongue in whistling and chirping'; and gives two reasons for this: (1) that it teaches the hawk to keep close at hand, and (2) that it enables one to go fowling secretly (i.e to poach!). Secrecy, as l. 160 shows, was Jul.'s need. G. Markham, *Country Contentments*, 1675, bk. 1, ch. v, p. 30 under 'Of Luring Hawks' also speaks of 'chirping your lips together'.

159. *tassel-gentel* v. G. and l. 167, n. A 'tribute paid by Jul. to her lover's nobility of nature' (Madden, p. 151). Cf. *The Book of Hawking (ad fin.)* of *The Book of St Albans* (1486): 'Ther is a Fawken gentill, and a Tercel gentill, and theys be for a prynce' [cited O.E.D. 'tercel-gentle'].

160. *Bondage* Alludes to the strict control kept upon

unmarried girls in an Eliz. household. Cf. l. 158, n. *ad fin.*

hoarse (Q 1, Q 2). J.D.W. thinks this a common error (v. p. 116, n. 3), a memorial anticipation of 'hoarse' (l. 162), where it = 'hoarse with shouting', the last meaning required here. Daniel's conj. 'husht' fits the context. Cf. *Merch.* 1. 3. 120, 'in a bondman's key with bated breath and whisp'ring humbleness'. G.I.D., who accepts 'hoarse', interprets it 'unable to speak loud'.

161–2. *Else...than mine* Alludes to the story of the nymph Echo, in Ovid's *Metam.* iii (ll. 443–500, Golding's trans.), who fruitlessly pursued Narcissus with her echoing cries until she hid herself for shame 'in dennes and hollow caves' and finally pined away until nothing but her voice was left. *mine* (Q 1) Q 2 om.

163. *my 'Romeo'* (< Q 2 'my Romeo') Q 1 'my Romeo's name'—which most edd. read, and J.D.W. inclines to think correct.

167. *My niëss!* (J.D.W.) Q 2 'My Neece', Q 1 'Madame', Q 4 'My Deere', F 2 'My sweete'. Most edd. read 'My dear!' The Q 2 'Neece' is a natural misinterpretation of 'niesse' (or 'nyas', the older variant of 'eyas' in *Ham* 2. 2. 342). Jonson spells it 'niaise' and explains (*Devil is an Ass*, 1. vi. 18 marg.; cf. Simpson, x, 230) 'a young Hawke tane crying out of the nest'. Thus 'niëss' is apt both to young Jul. calling from her bedroom window; and as Rom.'s reply to 'falcon-gentle'. But unlike a 'tassel-gentle', which, being wild-caught, had learnt to fly, a 'niëss' has never flown; and the falconer has only to climb to the aerie and the lovely little creature will be his. Greene, who has the word three or four times in his prose, spells it 'niesse' and applies it fig. to an inexperienced girl; e.g. *Tullies Loue* (Grosart, vii. 167)

'If shee be so ramage let hir flye, and seeke for a Niesse that may prooue more gentle'. See also Cotgrave 'niais'. Finally, cf. 1. 2. 8 'My child is yet a stranger in the world'.

What (Q2) Q1 'At what'—which most edd. read, unnecessarily.

o'clock (edd.) Q1, Q2 'a clocke'.

169. *year* (Q2) Most edd. read 'years' (Q1). For 'year' as pl. v. Franz, §190.

172. *forget, to* (Q3) Q1, Q2 'forget to'.   *to*=in order to; so also in l. 173.

173. *Rememb'ring* 'I' (l. 172) is the subject.

175. *Forgetting* 'I' is again the subject.

178. *her* (Q1) Q2 'his'. The 'wanton' could be of either sex, but 'her' is more apt to the context, while Q2's 'his' might be caught from 'his' in l. 179. [J.D.W.] G.I.D. prefers 'his'.

180. *silk* (Q1) Q2 'silken'—prob. comp.'s unconscious expansion (cf. p. 116). The thread is tied to the bird's leg.   181. *his*=its.

184. *Parting...sorrow* Prov.; cf. Tilley, P 82. One line in Q1. Div. 'night. | Parting' in Q2.

186–7. *Sleep dwell...to rest.* Q1+most edd. give to Rom. Q2 gives l. 186 to *Iu.* and l. 187 to *Ro.* Despite Hosley (pp. 27–8) Q1 is undoubtedly correct: each lover has a farewell couplet in parting, while ll. 186, 187 clearly belong to the same speaker. As the next note shows Sh.'s MS. or the collator's copy was very confused at this point [Partly indebted to A.W.] Cf. Clifford Leech, *Sh. Quart.* v. 94–5.

187. S.D. None in Qq.

187–8. Between these ll. Q2 has [version A]:

The grey eyde morne smiles on the frowning night,
Checkring the Easterne Clouds with streaks of light,
And darknesse fleckted like a drunkard reeles,
From forth daies pathway, made by *Tytans* wheeles.

and then repeats them at the beg. of 2. 3 as ll. 1–4 of the
Friar's speech, thus [Version B]:   [night,

    Fri. The grey-eyed morne smiles on the frowning
    Checking the Easterne clowdes with streaks of light:
    And fleckeld darknesse like a drunkard reeles,
    From forth daies path, and *Titans* burning wheeles:

Note: (i) Version A, though printed as part of
Romeo's speech, cannot be his, since it describes his
'blessed blessed night' (2. 2. 139) as 'frowning' and
'like a drunkard'. (ii) Yet Sh. must have written it,
since if we allow 'fleckted' to be a misprint or misreading of 'flecked' or 'fleckled', the second a diminutive
of the first, then 'flecked (=blotchy) like a drunkard'
is an image very much in his manner, while the last
line is not only good sixteenth cent. astronomy, but
probably an echo from his well-thumbed Golding
(v. note 2. 3. 4). (iii) On the other hand, Version B
cannot be one of his 'first shots', because 'From
forth...Titan's wheels' makes nonsense in the last
line, as Steev. long ago noticed. Where then does it
come from? The opening of 2. 3. runs in Q 1:

                                [night,
    Frier: The gray ey'd morne smiles on the frowning
    Checkring the Easterne clouds with streakes of light,
    And flecked darkenes like a drunkard reeles,
    From forth daies path, and *Titans* fierie wheeles:

Version B, we suggest, is merely a rather careless reprint
of this.   It contains three misprints, 'checking',
'fleckeld' and 'burning', which last was obviously
'caught' from 'burning eie' in the line below. But
the rest is identical. In short the collator was to blame:
he copied out from the MS. the beginning of the Friar's
speech into the margin of Q 1, but omitted either to
indicate where it should be inserted or to delete the
Q 1 version, so that the Q 2 compositor had to make the
best of yet another of his messes.

188–9. *Hence will I...tell* Cf. Brooke 557–60:
To morow eke betimes, before the sunne arise:
To fryer Lawrence will I wende, to learne his sage aduise.
He is my gostly syre, and oft he hath me taught
What I should doe in things of wayght, when I his ayde
  haue sought.

188. *my ghostly sire's close cell* (J.D.W.; conj. by
Delius in 1872). Q2 'my ghostly Friers close cell'.
Q1 'my Ghostly fathers Cell'—which all edd. read.
As 'my ghostly father' recurs at 2. 3. 45 the Q1
reading looks like a reporter's anticipation, while the
proposed emendation of Q2, which assumes a misreading of 'siers' (cf. 'sier' *Son.* 8. 11) as 'friers', is
supported, as Delius notes, by Brooke's 'gostly syre'
(v. previous note) and 'Lawrence secret cell' (l. 1264).
'Ghostly friar' is absurd.

2. 3

S.D. *Loc.* (Mal.). *Entry* (Q2).
1–4. *The...wheels* taken from 2.2.in Q2 (v.p. 161).
3. *darkness fleckéd like a drunkard* cf. 2. 2. 187–8 n.,
and G. 'flecked'. *fleckéd* (Q1; 2. 3. 3.) Q2 (2. 2.)
'fleckted'.
4. *day's pathway...wheels* i.e. diurnal track of the sun
through the sky. Cf. Golding's *Ovid*, ii. 172–5 (Phoebus
to Phaeton), 'A brode byway cut out a skew...Keepe
on this way: my Charyot rakes thou plainely shalt espie'.
7. *ours* i.e. it belongs to his fraternity.
8. *With baleful weeds* etc. He is a Franciscan and
'represented as a doctor and a medical botanist'
(*Sh. Eng.* i, 415). Thus Sh. prepares us for Jul.'s
potion [Farmer, v. Furness]. Cf. Tilley, E 32, 'The
Earth that yields food yields poison also', and E 31.
9–10. *The earth...womb* The earth receives dead
things into it, and, partly with their help, produces new
vegetation. Cf. *Ant.* 1. 1. 35–6; *Son.* 19. 2.

11–12. *And from...find*—And we find the various offspring of her womb (i.e. plants) sucking at her kindly bosom.

13. *many virtues* Q2 'many, vertues'.

15. *O mickle* etc. Cf. Brooke (2109–11):

What force the stones, the plants, and metals haue to
    woorke,
And diuers other thinges that in the bowels of earth do
    loorke,
With care I haue sought out, with payne I did them proue.

Spoken by the Friar as he gives Juliet her potion.
powerful grace 'efficacious virtue' (J.).

18–81. Comprises leaf D4 (r. and v.) of Q1, from a corrected copy of which Q2 may have been printed. The same prob. applies to E1 (r. and v.), i.e. 2. 3. 81 to 2. 4. 65. Cf. p. 115.

17. *For nought so vile* etc. Cf. Tilley, N 327.

18. *to the earth*='to the inhabitants of the earth' (Mal.).

19–20. *Nor aught...abuse* Cf. Tilley, N 317, and Brooke, 573–4:

For iustly of no arte can men condemne the vse,
But right and reasons lore cry out agaynst the lewd abuse.

aught Q2 'ought'.

20. *Revolts...birth*=is false to its proper nature.

stumbling on abuse=and so falls into corruption. Perhaps Sh. has in mind immoderate indulgence in food or drink.

22. *And vice* etc.='a quality that is in itself a fault may, under some circumstances, result in a good action' (K.).   *sometime* (Q2); Capell and most edd. read 'sometime's' (<Q1 'sometimes'). But 'is' can be understood.

S.D. Q2 'Enter Romeo.' Pope and most edd. place

this at l. 30, overlooking the 'dramatic touch that makes the victim of poison enter when poison is the subject of discourse' (G.S.).

24. *Poison* etc. Punc. as in Q2. Prob.='poison hath residence and healing hath power'.

25. *For this* etc. i.e. the rind of this flower strengthens with its smell ('that part') every portion of the body of the person who smells it.

smelt, with that part cheers Q2 'smelt with that part, cheares'.

26. *stays* (Q2 'staies'). Q1 (+most edd.) 'slaies'. But 'to bring the heart to a stand-still, and with it all the senses' is surely far better than 'to slay the heart, and with it all the senses' (Mommsen); the more so that it prepares us for Jul.'s potion.

28. *herbs*—Q2 'hearbes,'. *grace and rude will* A constant thought with Sh. Cf. *Caes.* 2. 1. 65–8.

30. *death* Primarily spiritual death, of course. *that plant*=the man.

31. *Benedicite* v. G. 38. *golden sleep* Cf. *1 H. IV*, 2. 3. 43; *R. III*, 4. 1. 84.

40. *with some* (Q2) Q1 and most edd. 'by some'. Cf. Schmidt, 1382*b*.

50–1. *me...Both* Q2 'me: | Thats by me wounded both,'.

52. *holy physic* i.e. the healing power of marriage.

54. *foe* i.e. Jul. 65. A Franciscan speaks.

70. *sallow* i.e. pale with grief.

72. *season* v. G. *that of it doth not taste* i.e. that no longer tastes of love. Salt preserved meat in the winter and so kept its flavour.

73. *The sun...clears* It was a stock notion that the sighs of lovers added 'to clouds more clouds' (1. 1. 132). Cf. *Tit.* 3. 1. 212.

74. *ring yet* (Q1+most edd.) Q2 'ringing yet'— prob. a dittograph; cf. p. 116, *init.*

75–6. *Lo...not washed off yet* Cf. Brooke, 2557–8:

Wherfore when he his face hath washt with water cleene,
Lest that the staynes of dryed teares might on his cheekes be
    seene.

80. *may* = are allowed to.

82–2. 4. 98. *For doting...a sail!* For this passage
sigs E 1ʳ,ᵛ and E 2ʳ of Q 1 would form a convenient
copy for Q 2 with very little correction. Cf. p. 115.

85. *chide me not. Her I love now,* Q 2 'chide me not,
her I loue now.' Q 1 'chide not, she whom I loue now'.

88. *did read...spell* i.e. he was like a child pretending to read from a book, but really reciting phrases
learnt by heart. Cf. Tilley, R 38.

that (Q 2, Dowden), Q 1 (and Pope, Camb., etc.)
'and'. The antecedent of 'that' is 'love'. Cf. Greg,
Aspects, p. 146.

90. *In one respect* = 'in virtue of one consideration'
(Herford).

91–2. *For...love* Echoes Brooke, 427–8 [Juliet
loqu.].

For so perchaunce this new aliance may procure
Vnto our houses such a peace as euer shall endure.

93. *I...haste* = I have urgent need of speed.
94. S.D. Q 2 'Exeunt.'

2. 4

S.D. *Loc.* Capell and most edd. 'A street'. 'We are
again in the open street or square of the first scene in
the play—a full-stage scene' (G.S.). *Entry* (Q 2).

1–7. Except for ll. 4–5 Q 2 prints this as prose.
Steev + most edd. re-line as verse and we agree,
pace Hosley, p. 24.

1. *devil* (F 3) Q 2 'deule'—a Sh. spelling.
should = can.

6. *kinsman* (Q1) Q2 'kisman'. Cf. p. 116.

9. *answer it*=accept the challenge. Mer. pretends
to misunderstand, jocularly casting aspersions on the
state to which love-sadness has reduced Rom.'s valour.

11–12. *Nay he* etc. i.e. he will show [lit. render an
account to] the sender how he can fight when challenged. Cf. G. 'dare', and *2 H. VI*, 3. 2. 203.

14. *run* (Q2) Q1+most edd. 'shot'; but three
weapons are implied, dagger ('stabbed'), sword ('run
through') and bow ('butt-shaft').

15–16. *pin...cleft*, v. G. 'pin', and *L.L.L.*
4. 1. 135. For the jest in 'butt-shaft' v. G.

18. Q2 assigns to '*Ro.*' (!); Q1 to '*Ben.*'.

19. *Prince of Cats* The cat in *Reynard the Fox* is
called Tibert. Cf. Nashe (McKerrow, iii. 51)
'Tibault...Prince of Cattes'.

20. *captain of compliments* 'complete master of all
the laws of ceremony' (J.) *He fights* (Q2) Q1 reads
'Catso; he fights—' in which the bawdy exclamation
(<It. 'cazzo'=membrum virile) is apt both to speaker
and context.

20–6. *He fights...hai!* Mer. ridicules the Italian
duello, fought with thrusting rapiers, becoming very
fashionable in London about 1590, to the disgust of
all honest adherents of the English sword with its
cutting edge. N.B. 'duellist' is first recorded from this
passage in O.E.D. and 'duello' from *L.L.L.* 1. 2. 172.
See *Sh. Eng.* ii. 389 ff. and J.D.W.'s Introd. to Silver,
who wrote to prove 'the true grounds of Fight to be
in the short auncient weapons'.

20–1. *as...pricksong*='with careful attention to
accuracy, as when one sings a tune from written or
printed music—not from memory or "by the ear"'
(K.).

21. *time* etc. 'Time' refers to the motion of the
feet; 'distance' to that which a fencer should keep

between himself and his opponent; and 'proportion' to rhythm. Cf. Castle, pp. 8–9, 11.

21–3. *he rests...bosom* i.e. he will make two feints, with the briefest poss. pause between each, and then, on the third beat, he will strike. *rests* (Q3) Q2 'rests, Q1 'rests me', read by Mal.+most edd.

23. *butcher...button* The earliest Italian fencing master in London, Signior Rocco, boasted he could 'hit anie Englishman with a thrust vpon anie button'; and 'this was much spoken of' (Silver, p. 65; cf. p. 16). First cited by Staunton.

duellist Cf. ll. 20–26, n. Q2 'dualist' (2).

23–5. *The very...cause!* No comma in Q2, Q1, or F, though all edd. read one after 'house' except J.E.C., who rightly explains the exp. as an affected way of saying 'the finest school of instruction in the punctilio of the challenge' (J.D.W.). Touchstone (*A.Y.L.* 5.4. 50 ff.) jestingly recounts seven causes for taking up quarrels among gentlemen, and *The Booke of Honor and Armes*, 1590 (? by Sir Wm. Segar) reduces the 'causes' to two mortal insults or accusations (cited *L.L.L.* 1. 2. 170, n.).

25–6. *passado...hai!* v. G. Terms of the duello describing the three passes in ll. 20–1. Mer. no doubt suits the action to the word. All his speeches, in fact, involve lively action and much change of voice.

hai (Grant White) Q2 'Hay'.

28–9. *affecting fantasticoes* 'affected coxcombs' (Herford). *new tuners of accent* Every generation of fops has them! Mer. illustrates the latest 'tune' in what follows.

29. *fantasticoes* (Q1) Q2 'phantacies'.

31. *grandsire* (Q2, Q1 'graundsir') And then he suddenly changes his key and addresses Ben. as if they were a couple of old fashioned greybeards.

33. *pardon-me's* Q1 'pardon mees' Q2 'pardons mees'—poss. final 'e' of 'pardone' misread as final 's'

(cf. confusion of 's' and 'e' suggested at 2. 1. 38, n.).
No need to translate the exp. (with Theob.) 'par-
donnez-mois' or (with Camb. < Q4) 'perdona-mi's':
Sh.'s fops are English.

33–5. *who...bones!* i.e. who are such sticklers for
the latest fad that they object to sit upon an honest
bench without a cushion under their poor bones.
'Grandsire' Mer. mocks at the courtiers who wince at
the hard seats in the Presence Chamber at Whitehall.
In *A Treatise on Playe* (*c.* 1597), first pub. 1769, the
foppish Sir John Harington complains of 'the great
plank forms' at court, and the 'waynscot stooles so hard
that, since great breeches were layd asyde, men can
skant indewr to sitt on'; and pleads for 'easye quilted
and lyned forms and stools for the lords and ladyes'
instead (*Nugae Antiquae*, ed. 1804, i. 202). J.E.C.
cites.   35. S.D. (Q2).

36–45. *Here comes* etc. See *Sh. Survey* (1955).

37. *Without his roe* i.e. without his deer (dear).
Also a herring without its roe, or 'shotten herring'
(*1 H. IV*, 2. 4. 126; cf. *Troil* 5. 1. 68), stood for an
emaciated person, a spunkless good-for-nothing.

38. *fishified!* become cold and bloodless. *Now is he
for* Cf. 'I am for' (*L.L.L.* 1.2.177). *Petrarch* (Q1) Q2
'Petrach'—a poss. spelling (cf. Chaucer's 'Petrak'),
but prob. comp.'s omission.

40–1. *marry...her!*. Is Mer. meant to be laughing
at Rom.'s rhymes or pretending that Rom. explains
why Laura is more famous than Ros.?

41. *gipsy* v. Introd. p. xi to *Ant. and Cleo.*

42. *gray* The colour then most admired in eyes.
Cf. *V.A.* l. 140.

43–4. *bon jour* (< Q1) Q2 'Bonieur'.

slop v. G. 'Having been up all night, he is still in his
masquing-clothes: loose-fitting French slops and
dancing-pumps' (l. 60) (J.E.C.).

48. *Can…conceive?* Have you no understanding at all?

50–1. *strain courtesy.* Cf. Lyly, *Bombie*, 3. 3. 34 (ed. Bond).

52–3. *such a case,…hams* 'What Mer.'s indecent tongue means…cannot be doubtful' (Ulrici).

54. *curtsy* Q 2 'cursie'. The point, such as it is, lies in the fact that 'courtesy' and 'curtsy' were virtually the same word.

55. *kindly* = (*a*) aptly, (*b*) graciously.

56. *most courteous* Ironical.

57. *pink* v. G. for quibbles.

58. *flower?* (Q 1) Q 2 'flower.'.

60. *my pump…flowered* 'A pump was a single-soled, low shoe, which fitted the foot closely without ties', and was for indoor use. In 'flowered' Rom. refers, not to 'shoe-roses' which came in a little later (v. *Ham.* 3. 2. 276), but to his pumps being 'pinked' i.e. punctured in a pattern, as was then the fashion, and poss. decked with soil from Cap.'s orchard (cf. ll. 43–4, n.). For 'pump', 'pink', etc. v. Linthicum, pp. 253–5, etc.

61. *Sure wit!* Oh, infallible wit! *wit! Follow* Q 2 'wit follow'.

63–4. *solely singular* v. G.

66. *singleness* v. G.

67. *Come between us* Mer. begs his second in the duel to intervene.

69. *Switch and spurs!* = Keep it up! v. G. *a match* = a win. *Switch* (Pope) Q 1, Q 2 'swits'—the old sp.

71. *our wits* (Q 2) Q 1 (+many edd.) 'thy wits'.

wild-goose chase A steeplechase of the follow-my-leader type. v. G.

73–4. *Was…goose?* = Did that 'goose' come home to you?

75–6. *Thou . . . goose*=You were never anything but a goose when in my company.

77. *bite . . . by the ear* Lit.=‘caress fondly’ (O.E.D. ‘bite’ 16); but Mer. would bite hard.

78. *good goose, bite not* Prov. cf. Tilley, G 349.

79. *sweeting* v. G.

80. *sharp sauce*= (*a*) keen retort (cf. *A.Y.L.* 3. 5. 69 ‘sauce her with bitter words’), (*b*) piquant relish.

81. *And is . . . goose*=And isn’t apple-sauce the right thing with a tasty goose? Cf. the prov. ‘Sweet meat must have sour sauce’ (Tilley, M 839). *sweet* also refers to his ‘sweet’ (i.e. dear) friend.

82–3. *O . . . broad!* i.e. you can make your little wit go a very long way; v. G. ‘cheveril’.

85. *broad* v. G.

97. S.D. (J.D.W.)—placed as in F1. Q1, 2 ‘Enter Nurse and her man.’, placed after ‘geare’ (l. 98) in which Capell and most mod. edd. agree. We have no doubt that Q2 (prob. <Q1) is wrong and that ‘goodly gear’ like ‘sail’ refers, not as some suppose to Mer.’s bawdy, but to the Nurse’s voluminous garments and ship-like motion, aping the deportment of a fine lady. [Hosley also places after l. 97.]

99. *a shirt and a smock*=a man and a woman.

103–4. *for . . . face* Cf. 1. 4. 30, n.

106. *good-den* Mer. corrects her. As she started out at 9 a.m. (emphasized by Sh., v. 2. 2. 168, 2. 5. 1–11), we may infer she had spent the three hours dressing herself to meet Rom.

110. *What a man* i.e. what kind of a man.

111–12. *God . . . to mar.* Cf. Tilley, G 188, ‘God has done his part’; M 48, ‘To make or mar’.

118. *the youngest* because the only one. *worse* Said instead of ‘better’ for fun. The Nurse takes it seriously and Mer. comments ironically.

122. *confidence* She means ‘confidential conference’.

124. *indite* Jestingly for 'invite'; cf. Hostess (*2 H. IV*, 2. 1. 27).

125. *So ho!* =What ho! Lit. the hunter's cry on sighting a quarry; hence 'found', 'hare'.

126. *What*, Q2 'What' The comma (conj. by Allan Carr) points the hunting allusion. Cf. G. 'find'.

127–8. *a hare...spent* Ref. to the Nurse, who is elderly and physically unattractive.   *hare* Called 'bawd' in North Midland dial. (Cf. D.D. and O.E.D. 'bawd').   *lenten pie* v. G.

128. S.D. From Q1, which doubtless here reflects contemporary stage practice.

129–34. As two lines in Q2. For the quibbles in 'hare', 'hoar', 'meat', v. G.

133. *too much for a score* =not good enough for one to be reasonably expected to pay for it.

138. S.D. 'singing' conj. Farmer, adopted by Dyce.

'*lady...lady*' 'The Ballad of Constant Susanna' contains the lines: 'Susanna she was callde by name | A woman fair and vertuous | Lady lady: | Why should we not of her learn thus | To live godly.' Mer. could give this with great point. Cf. *Tw. Nt.* 2. 3. 83–4, n.

S.D. (after Q1) Q2 'Exeunt.'

141. *ropery* Q2 'roperie' Q1 'roperipe'. The two words mean much the same thing: v. G.

149. *skains-mates* (Q2, Q1 'skaines mates'). Unexplained; poss. a common error (v. p. 116, n. 3). But if 'skenes-mates' (<'skene'=dagger) be intended, that (as Mal. noted) would='cut-throat companions', a not unapt description of e.g. Doll Tearsheet, who threatens to thrust a knife into Pistol's 'mouldy chaps' (*2 H. IV*. 2. 4. 124).

S.D. <Q1 'She turnes to Peter her man.'

150–2. *at his pleasure* etc. Indelicate quibbling; v. G. 'use', 'tool' and cf. 1. 1. 27 ff.

159. *in* = into.

163. *weak* Blunder for 'wicked' [Singer].

165. *mistress.* Q2 'Mistresse,'.　*thee*— (F2) Q2 'thee.'.

169. *dost* Q2 'dooest'.　*me!* Q2 'me?'.

171–2. For 'protest' = declare love, v. *M.W.W.* 3. 5. 69.

173–4. As in Delius and Camb. One line in Q2.

174–6. *come to shrift...married* Cf. Brooke, 633–4:

> if Iuliet come to shrift,
> She shalbe shriued and maried.

176. *Here is...pains* In Brooke (667) he gives her 'vi. crownes of gold'.

182. *tackled stair* v. G. Rope-ladders being used on ships, we are naturally led on to nautical metaphors.

183. *topgallant* v. G. The lofty 'platform on the mast from which [the topgallant sail] was handled' (*Sh. Eng.* i. 157) and which was reached by the shrouds or rope-ladder.

186. *mistress* Trisyllabic.

187. *Now God...thee* Cf. Brooke, 635 'gods blessing haue your hart'.

189–90. Lined as by Rowe. As prose in Q2.

hear (F1) Q2 'here'.

one i.e. a third party. Prov. cf. *Titus*, 4. 2. 144, and Tilley, T 257.

191. *I* (F2) Q2 om.　*my man's...steel*, Cf. Brooke, 809–11.

193. *when...thing* Cf. Brooke, 653–4:

> A prety babe (quod she) it was when it was yong:
> Lord how it could full pretely haue prated with it tong.

thing— (Rowe) Q2 'thing.' See 1. 3. 25–45 for what might have followed, had discretion allowed.

194–5. *lay knife aboard* 'i.e. establish his claim. The diner at an ordinary brought his own knife with him and used it not only to mark his place but also to secure his helping' (J.E.C.). But quibbling on the nautical 'lay aboard'=attack (cf. *2 H. VI*, 4. 1. 25).

199. *rosemary* The bridegroom wore a bunch of it at the wedding (*Sh. Eng.* ii. 147). But v. 4. 5. 79.

200. *a letter* i.e. the same letter.

202. *Ah* (edd.) Q2 'A' A common Sh. spelling.
dog-name; (Hoppe, 'dog-name.') Q2 'dog, name'. Edd. freq. read 'dog's name;' from Q3 ('dogs-name.'). Cf. Persius, *Sat.* i. 109: 'Sonat hic de nare canina littera'; Jonson, *Eng. Gram.* 'R is the Dogs Letter, and hirreth in the sound'; and *Summer's Last Will* (Nashe, iii. 254, 658): 'They arre and barke at night'. *R is for the—No;* (Ritson and edd.) Q2 'R. is for the no,'. P. Williams (*N. and Q.* cxcv. 181–2) suggests that the word she does not say is 'arse'.

203. *begins with some other letter* She cannot spell. The initial letter of 'rosemary' and 'Romeo' does not sound like 'ar', so she thinks they must begin with some other letter.

204. *sententious* She means 'sentence', 'sentences' or even 'sententias'. *you* quibbling on 'yew'.

207. *times.* [Romeo goes] *Peter*! (after Dyce). Q2 'times *Peter*.'

209. *Before and apace*=go before me, and quickly too. Q1 'Peter, take my fanne, and goe before.' S.D. Q1 'Ex. omnes.' Q2 'Exit.'.

2. 5

S.D. *Loc.* (Globe); cf. 'gate' (20).

1–10. *nine...till twelve* For the cause of the delay v. 2. 4. 106, n.

5. *glides* (Q2) Plur. Cf. Franz, §679.

7. *draw Love* i.e. pull the chariot of Venus.

9. *highmost hill* In Golding's *Ovid* (ii. 84–7; *Met.* ii. 63–6) Phoebus warns Phaeton: 'the morning way Lyes steepe vpright, so that the steedes...haue much adoe to climb against the Hyll.' Cf. *Son.* 7. 5 'the steep-up heavenly hill'.

11. *three* (Q3) Q2 'there'.

13. *be swift* (anon. Camb.) Q2 'be as swift'— poss. compositor's anticipation.

15. *And...me*=And his words would bandy the Nurse back to me.

15–16. *And his...dead* As in Rowe. Q2 prints in one line and prefixes it with sp.-hdg. '*M*' (elsewh. =Lady Cap.; v. pp. 112–13). Camb. (Note vii) conj. that ll. 15–17 are an interpolation. If so the '*M*' may be a misreading of '*Iu.*', and the lines an afterthought by Sh.

16. *many feign* Q2 'many fain'. J. conj. 'marry, feign' and Grant White 'marry, fare', which last J.D.W. and A.W. find attractive.

17. S.D. (Theob.) Q2 'Enter Nurse.'.

20. S.D. None in Q2.

the gate=the side-door of the stage.

21. *look'st* (Q4 and edd.) Q2 'lookest'. ·

26. *jaunce* Q2 'iaunce', Q1 'iaunt'. Cf. G. At *R. II,* 5. 5. 94 'jauncing'=prancing.

have I (Q2) sc. 'I am having' Q1 (+most edd.) 'haue I had'. Poss. Sh. wrote 'had I'.

39–40. *man...Though* Q2 'man: *Romeo,* no not he though'. She is being arch.

41–2. *a body* (Q2) Q1 'a baudie' F2 'a bawdy'.

not to be talked on=not worth talking about.

45. *serve God* 'A phrase signifying: "well, enough of that subject"' (G.S., but citing no authority).

47. *What...marriage* Cf. Brooke, 684: 'But of our mariage say at once, what aunswer haue you brought?'

50. *o' t'other* Q2 'a tother'.

51. *about* Poss. 'a bout' (=a trapesing); cf. 1. 5. 18, n.

55–7. As prose in Camb. (Walker conj.). As if verse in Q2.

57. *virtuous—Where* Q2 'vertuous, where'.

58–9. Lined as by Rowe. As two lines in Q2, ending 'she be?' and 'repliest:'

60–1. All inverted commas editorial.

62. *Marry...trow!* =Hoity-toity, indeed!

68. *hie* (Q5) Q2 'high' *Lawrence*' Q2 'Lawrence'.

71. ='Any sudden news always makes your cheeks scarlet in a second' (K.). Hanmer conj. 'straitway at my news'—looking forward to ll. 72–6.

74. *a bird's nest* i.e. Jul.'s room. Cf. 2. 2. 167, n., and G. 'bird'.

75. *in* =for.

77. *Go; I'll* (Camb.) Q1 'Go ile'.

2. 6

S.D. *Loc.* (Capell). The inner stage represents the interior of the cell. The sc. presumably takes place on the main stage, and at the end (see l. 35) the actors enter the cell. The inner-stage curtains may be closed throughout the sc.; or, if they are open, the Friar closes them at l. 37.

1. *smile* i.e. may they smile.

4. *the exchange of joy* =the mutual joy.

9. *violent...ends* Prov.: cf. Tilley, B 262, N 321.

11–13. *The sweetest...appetite.* Cf. Tilley, H 560. *in* =through, on account of.

14. *long love doth so* Ref. to the prov. 'Love me little love me long' Tilley, L 559.

15. *Too swift* etc. Cf. 2. 3. 95. S.D. (Q2) Q1 'Enter Iuliet somewhat fast, and embraceth Romeo'.

The first part of this doubtless preserves contemporary stage usage, but the embracing should wait for the Friar's hint in l. 21.

16. *so light a foot* She is buoyed up by love.

17. *the everlasting flint* 'The moralising Friar thinks of the hardness and sharpness of the path of life' (Dowden).

21. *confessor* Accent on first syllable.

22–3. *Romeo...much* It was the custom to return a lady's greeting with a kiss (cf. 1. 5. 107, S.D.). The Friar bids Rom. do this for him; and then 'Juliet says she will have to greet him too because the payment on behalf of the Friar has been altogether excessive' (J.E.C.). We add a S.D. accordingly.

25. *and that*=and if.   *more* sc. than mine.

27. *music's* Q3 'musickes', Q2 'musicke'. Rom. is thinking of the music of her speaking voice.

28–9. *both Receive in either*=each of us receives from the other.

30–1. 'When a person has a full conception of his happiness, all language is too poor to express the truth; he is satisfied to *feel* the joy and does not pride himself on adorning it with words' (K.).

31. *his*=its.

32. *count their worth*=reckon up (and exactly state) the amount of their possessions.

34. *sum up sum of half my* Capell conj. 'sum up half my sum of'.

37. S.D. (F2) None in Q2. Q1 'Exeunt omnes.'.

3. 1

S.D. *Loc.* (Capell)   *Entry* Q2 [adding 'their' to make 'men' clear].

2. *Capels are* (Q1+J.E.C.), Q2 'Capels', Q4+ most edd. 'Capulets'.

3–4. *Lining Rowe's.* As prose in Q2. The change from Ben.'s gentle jog-trot verse to Mer.'s swift prose brings out the difference in their temperaments. Cf. Clifford Leech, *Sh. Quart.* v. 94.

5 ff. *Thou art* etc. Mer. retorts to Ben.'s attempt to keep the peace by making him out a fire-eater like himself. His words not inaptly describe 'the quarrelsome habits of empty-headed young men of those days' (Egerton Castle, *Schools and Masters of Fence*, ed. ii, p. 78).

5. *these* (Q2). Many edd. read 'those' (Q1) and J.D.W. prefers it, in view of 'these' in l. 4.

6. *me*   8. *him* Ethical datives.

10. *Am I* A slight emphasis on 'I'.

12. *moved* provoked.   *moody* = irascible, angry.

14. *to* (Pope) Qq1, 2 'too'.   15. *such* sc. as you.

16. *Thou?* Q2 'thou,'.

22. *as full...meat* Prov. exp.; cf. Tilley, K 149.

23. *egg* i.e. a rotten egg.

27–8. *new doublet...Easter* Gallants blossomed out at Easter, and perh. tailors advertised their spring fashions by wearing them in person before that. Cf. O.E.D. ('lenten' B 2) 'of clothing, etc.; mournful-looking, dismal'—citing 'lenten suit' from Beau. and Fletcher, *Honest Man's Fortune*, 4. 1.

28. *his new shoes* i.e. the new shoes supplied by him.

29. *riband* The usual shoe-lace; cf. Linthicum, p. 283.

31–2. *any...quarter* = my life would not be worth $1\frac{1}{4}$ hours' purchase.

33. *fee-simple?* (F) Q2 'fee-simple,'. *O simple!* = O, what a poor joke!   S.D. Q2 'Enter Tybalt, Petruchio, and others.' In initial S.D.s Sh. often names a character for whom he finds no use later; cf. Chambers, *Wm. Sh.* i. 231. But see 1. 5. 131.

34. *comes* (Q2) A good Eliz. plur.; cf. Franz, §679.

38. *us?* (Q3) Q2 'vs,'.

39. *a word...blow* Prov. exp.; cf. Tilley, W 763.

44, 45, 48. v. G. 'consort'.

44. *consort'st* (F.) Q2 'consortest'. *Romeo*— (Rowe) Q2 '*Romeo.*' Tyb. is no doubt about to ask Mer. where Rom. is likely to be.

45–6. *minstrels* hired fiddlers. Minstrels were considered menials. Cf. 4. 5. 114–15, and Elyot, *Governour* Bk. 1, ch. vii (*ad fin.*) 'a common servant or minstrel'.

47. *fiddlestick* i.e. his sword.

51. *And* (Capell) Q2 (+many edd.) 'Or'. But 'And' gives better sense, and 'Or' was easily caught from l. 52.   *reason coldly*=discuss calmly.

52. *depart* part.

55 ff. The fight on 18 Sept. 1589 between Marlowe and Bradley, in which Thomas Watson intervening to part them slew Bradley, bears some resemblance to what follows. See Eccles, *Chr. Marlowe in London*, 1934, pp. 9–10, 35–6.

55. *my man*=the man I am looking for.

56. *livery* As if 'man' in l. 51='servant'. Cf. l. 57 'he'll be your follower'=(*a*) 'he will pursue you there, to fight with you', (*b*) 'he will be your attendant'.   58. *man*=i.e. a man indeed.

59. *love* (Q2) Icily polite. Q1 (+many edd.) 'hate'. 'An offer or grant of *love* can be expected, but not of *hate*' (Delius).

62–3. *excuse...To*=absolve me from feeling the anger appropriate to....

63. *none*— Q2 'none.'.

67. *injured* (Q3) Q2 'iniuried'.

68–9. *devise...love:* Q2 'deuise:...loue,'.

73. *Alla...away*='The Italianate   thrust-tech-

nique carries the day.' A hint that Rom. dare not stand up against the new-fashioned rapier (cf. l. 72, 'vile submission' and 2. 4. 20–26, nn.)

Alla stoccata (Knight+Camb. etc.)   Q2 '*Alla stucatho*', Q1 '*Allastockado*'. It seems best to modernize in view of the uncertainty as to exact form. H. E. Cain (*Sh. Assoc. Bulletin*, Jan. 1942) proposes 'Allo steccato', which he interprets 'To the field or lists'. But this misses the point. Sh. uses 'stoccado' as a term of fence in *M.W.W.* 2. 1. 201, of which 'stucatho' is an admissable phonetic, and therefore spelling, variant. S.D. (Capell).

74. *rat-catcher* i.e. cat. Cf. 2. 4. 18, n.

76–9. *Good King of Cats* etc. 'Being a cat, I suppose you have nine lives. One of them I mean to take; and then, according as you treat me well or ill, I'll spare your eight other lives or thrash you until you have lost them all' (K.). Cf. Tilley, C 154.

78. *dry-beat* Hyphen Rowe's.

79–80. *pluck...ears* Suggests a reluctant sword.

82. S.D. 'Drawing' (Rowe).   84. S.D. (Capell).

89. S.D. (Q1). Q2 'Away Tybalt.'. Cf. *Tw. Nt.* 3. 4. 277, 'He gives me the stuck in' [J.E.C.].

90. *o*' Q2 'a'.   *both your* (Dyce+most mod. edd.) Q2 'both'. Q2 prints the speech as verse, 'your' is needed for the metre, and is the sort of word Q2 omits [J.D.W.] G.I.D. would follow Q2.

93. S.D. (after Capell).

95–6. *wide as...door* Cf. Tilley, B 93, 'As broad as a barn door'.

97. *a grave man* Grave for the first and last time!

98 *for* v. G.   99. *cat* Cf. l. 76.

101. *by the book of arithmetic* Cf. 2. 4. 20–1, n.

106. *worms' meat* Cf. Tilley, M 253, 'A man is nothing but worms' meat' (from St Bernard).

I have it (as Dyce). Begins next line in Q2.

107. *soundly too. Your* Rowe 'soundly too—your'
Q2 'soundly, to your'   *houses!* (Hanmer), Q2
'houses.'.   S.D. Q2 'Exit.'

111. *slander* See ll. 59–60.

114. *temper* v. G. for the quibble.   S.D. Q2
'Enter Benuolio.'

115. *Mercutio's* (F2+most edd.) Q2 'Mercutio
is'—comp.'s expansion. Cf. p. 116.

117. *scorn the earth* Alludes to Mer.'s scoffing
spirit.

118. *on moe days doth depend*=hangs threateningly
over more days to come.

119. *begins the* (Q5) Q2 'begins, the'.
S.D. (Capell) Q1 'Enter Tybalt.' Q2 om.

121. *Again!* (J.D.W.<Capell 'Again?') Q2 'He
gan'. Perhaps the collator or comp. took 'a' of 'again'
for colloquial 'he' and normalized it. Cf. p. 116; note
two poss. normalizations in 'quoth he' (1. 3. 42) and in
the servant's speech (1. 5. 1–2). Q1+edd. 'Aliue'.
Hoppe conj. 'He gay'.   *slain?* (F1) Q2 'slaine,'.

122. *respective lenity*=considerations of mercy.

123. *fire-eyed* (Pope<Q1), Q2 'fier end'. See p. 117
and cf. *1 H. IV*, 4. 1. 114, 'the fire-eyed maid'
(=Bellona). The Furies of course came from Hell.

130. S.D. (Q2).   132. *up* v. G.; again in l. 138.
135. *Fortune's fool* v. G. 'fool'.   S.D. (Q2).
139. S.D. (Q2).   141. *all* (Q1, F). Q2 'all:'.
144. *kinsman* (Q1) Q2 'kisman'. Q2 has this also
in ll. 147, 175, 2. 4. 6. Cf. p. 116.

145–6. *child...spilled* A rhyme in Eliz. English.
(Kökeritz, p. 418).

146. *O prince! O husband?* O, (Capell, Dyce, etc.).
Q2 (+Camb. etc.) 'O Prince, O Cozcn, husband, O'.
The 'Cozen' was prob. caught from l. 145; its removal
perfects the metre.

154–5. *displeasure. All this—utter̀d...bowed*—
Q2 'displeasure all this vtrered,...bowed'.

157–8. Ben. omits the fact that Mer. had forced
Tyb to fight him (72 ff.).

160–1. *with one hand...with the other* If not
metaphorical, this suggests that they fought with
daggers in their left hands and rapiers in their right.
See *What Happens in 'Hamlet'*, p. 279.

164. *Hold...part* Cf. Brooke, 999, 'Part frendes
(sayd he) part frendes, helpe, frendes to part the fray'.

165. *agile* (Q1) Q2 'aged' Prob. misreading.

166. *rushes* i.e. he rushes.

171. *And to 't...lightning* Cf. Brooke, 1031,
'Euen as two thunderboltes' etc.

172–3. *slain,...fly:* Q2 'slaine:...flie,'.

175. *the Montague* i.e. Romeo.

176. *false* 'The charge of falsehood...though
produced at hazard, is very just' (J.). Cf. ll. 157–8, n.

182. *his*=Mer.'s.   *owe?* (Q3) Q2 'owe.'.

183. *Not Romeo prince*, etc. Q4 (+most edd.)
assigns to '*Mon.*'; Q2 to *Capu.*—which G.I.D.
supports, noting that Cap. at 1. 2. 2–3 and 1. 5. 64 ff.
shows a desire to be pacific; and here apparently, as in
1. 5, wants to prevent trouble, and thinks Tyb. blameworthy. J.D.W. finds it dramatically incredible that
Cap. should contradict his wife on such a matter before
the Prince.

187. *hearts'* (Q2) Cf. *1 H. VI*, 3. 1. 26, 'From
envious malice of thy swelling heart'. Camb. (+many
edd.) read 'hate's' (<Q1 'hates'), which is attractive.
The two words are easily interchanged by printer or
reporter. Cf. 3. 2. 73 (Q1 'hate', Q2 'heart', where
Q2 is certainly correct), and *R. III*, 2. 2. 117, n.

188. *my blood*=Mercutio, a blood-relative.

lie a-bleeding Prov. exp.; cf. Tilley, A 159.

190. *the loss of mine*=my loss.

191. *I* (Q1 + all edd.) Q2 'It'.

194. *he is* (Q2) Theob. (+ most edd.) 'He's'. As 'hour' is dissyllabic and Q2 is prone to expansion J.D.W. thinks 'he's' is prob. right. G.I.D. dissents.

196. *but murders* i.e. only encourages further murders.

S.D. Q2 *'Exit.'*.

3. 2

S.D. *Loc.* 'An Apartment in Capulet's House' (Rowe), 'Capulet's orchard' (Camb. + most mod. edd.). Yet no indication of an outdoor sc.; a natural place for Jul. to await the Nurse is her own room. *Entry* (Q2).

1. *Gallop apace* Cf. Marlowe, *Ed. II*, 4. 3. 45

> Gallop apace, bright Phoebus, through the sky.

T. W. Baldwin, *Sh.'s Five-Act Structure*, pp. 765 ff. connects these lines with Brooke's 821–6, in which the lovers find the day's interval between the wedding at the Friar's cell and its consummation so tedious that were

> The sunne bond to theyr will, if they the heauens might gyde:
> Black shade of night and doubled darke should straight all ouer hyde;

and with ll. 919–20 in which, at the end of the night, on the contrary

> The hastines of Phoebus steeds in great despyte they blame.

fiery-footed Cf. Golding's *Ovid* ii, 491 [*Met.* ii. 392] 'firiefooted' (of the horses of the sun). We owe this parallel to Dr Percy Simpson.

2. *lodging* v. G. In the west.

waggoner Golding's word for Phaëton (ii. 394).

3–4. *Phaëton...immediately* Cf. *3 H. VI*, 1. 4. 34

'made an evening at the noontide prick'. *Phaëton* (Q1)
Q2 'Phaetan'.

5. *curtain* sc. of darkness. *love-performing* i.e. for
the fulfilment or enacting of love.

6. *runaways'* (Delius) Q2 'runnawayes'. Not in
Q1. One of the best known cruxes in Sh.; Furness has
28 pages on it. If plur., interpreted by Delius etc.
as 'vagabonds at night'—a gloss unsupported by
O.E.D. ('runaways' in *R. III*, 5. 3. 316=deserters),
and 'prosaic' (Herford) at best. If sing., taken as
referring to Phoebus (Warb. and Dowden), though
Jul. (ll. 1–2) implies that he does not run away; to
Cupid (Halpin); to Juliet herself (Massey); to Night
with 'eyes'=stars (Steev., cf. *Merch.* 2. 6. 47 'For the
close night doth play the runaway'). Among emendations are 'Renomyes'=Renommés (Mason), 'ru-
moures'=rumour's (Heath, etc.), 'unawares' (Jackson)
'rude day's' (Dyce), 'envious' or 'curious' (Clarke).
J.D.W. proposes *'cunningest'*, a word which suggests
scandal-mongering curiosity (cf. l. 7 'untalked-of' and
Schlegel's trans., 'Damit das Auge der Neubegier sich
schliess'), and like 'runnawayes' begins with ten to
a dozen minim-letters followed by 'gest' instead of
'yes'. *wink*=pay no heed v. G.

8–9. *Lovers…beauties* Cf. Marlowe, *Hero*, i.
191, 'dark night is Cupid's day' [Mal.]; ii. 240–2,
'Rich jewels in the dark are soonest spied' etc.; and
318–22. For beauty as light cf. 5. 3. 85–6.

amorous rites Also found in *Hero*, ii. 64. *rites* (F4)
Q2 'rights'.

9. *By* (Q4) Q2 'And by'. The 'And' makes bad
metre and bad sense.

11. *sober-suited* Hyphen from F4. Cf. Milton, *Il
Pens*. 32–3.

14. *Hood…unmanned…bating* Terms of falconry
(v. G.), applied to the agitation of her blood.

15. *strange* i.e. untamed, shy.   *grown* (Rowe + most edd.). Q2 'grow'. G.I.D. thinks Q2 possible with 'And' understood at the beginning of l. 16; J.D.W. dissents.

19. *snow upon* (Q4; G.I.D. and A.W.), Q2 'new snow vpon'. Most edd. read 'new snow on' (<F2); The 'new' is Sh.'s false start (v. p. 113). One cannot have *old* snow on a raven's back!

21. *he* (Q4 + most edd.). Q2 'I'. It is the glorious dead who become stars acc. to the time-honoured classical notion (cf. *1 H. VI*, I. I. 55–6 and the end of Jonson's lines to Sh. in F1), while Rom. must die before he can be cut up into little stars [J.D.W.]. G.I.D. prefers 'I' and thinks Jul. implies 'after I am dead let no single woman enjoy him: let him be an inspiration to the whole world'. J.D.W. interprets: 'if, gentle Night, you will give him to me now, you may have him when he is dead to make stars of.'

26–8. 'The metaphor is quickly changed. First Jul. has herself bought a house but not taken possession; then she is herself the thing sold but not yet enjoyed' (Houghton).

31. *nurse*, Q2 'Nurse.'. S.D. (Q2) Q1 'Enter Nurse wringing her hands, with the ladder of cordes in her lap.' An acrobatic feat!

34. *The cords* Lined as by Hanmer. Prefixed to l. 35 in Q2.   35. S.D. (after Capell).

42. *it? Romeo!* (Camb.) Q2 'it Romeo?'.

45. *Hath...himself?* Her deduction from the Nurse's last words.

45, 47, 50. *ay* Q2 'I'. Always printed so in sixteenth century.

47. *death-darting* (Q3) Q2 'death arting'.

49. *those eyes* i.e. Rom.'s. 'Eyes' carries on the punning.

shut (Capell). sc. in death. Q2 'shot'.   *makes* An Eliz. plural.

51. *Brief sounds* (F4) Q2 'Briefe, sounds,'. *of my* (F+most edd.). Q2 'my'. G.I.D. finds the Q2 metre very effective, the line beginning with two isolated strong accents. J.D.W. dissents.

53. (*God...mark!*) As in K. Q2 'God... marke,' v. G. 'mark'.

here She points to her bosom.

56. *swounded* (Q1) Q2 'sounded'.

57. *bankrout* v. G.   *break* a quibble on 'break' =go bankrupt.

at once=at one stroke, once for all; v. G. 'once'.

59. *Vile earth* Her own body. *resign* sc. yourself.

60. *one* (Q4) Q2 'on'.   *bier* (Rowe<Q4) Q2 'beare'.

66. *dearest...dearer lord* (Q2) Q1 (+many edd.) 'deare loude [=dear-loved]...dearest'. 'Dearer' topping 'dearest' is more effective.

72, 73. sp.-hdgs. From Q1. Q2 continues l. 72 to Jul and gives l. 73 to Nur.

73. *serpent...flowering* Cf. ll. 81–2; *Macb.* 1. 5. 64–5; Genesis iii. 1–6.

76. *Dove-feathered* (Theob., subs.) Q2 'Rauenous douefeathered'. 'Rauenous' is a poss. compositor's slip (cf. 'raven', 'ravening', in the same line); but more prob. Sh.'s. false start. See p. 113.

79. *damnéd* (Q4) Q2 'dimme' (misreading of 'damnd').

85–7. *There's...dissemblers.* Lined by Capell, after Pope. Two ll. in Q2, div. 'men, | All'. She applies the saw, 'there is no faith in man' (Tilley, F34) to the male sex only.

87. *All forsworn...dissemblers* 'With the emphasis three times on *all*, and *forsworn* pronounced as a trisyllable, the line reads well enough' (Dowden).

90. *Blistered...tongue* Cf. Tilley, R84, 'Report has a blister on her tongue'.

98–9. *what tongue...mangled it* Cf. Brooke, 1144–5 'wroth with her selfe,...gan say. | Ah cruell murthering tong' etc.

101. *would...husband* Knowing Tyb.'s temperament, she may conjecture this; but Sh. prob. stretches a point for the sake of antithesis.

104. *joy* sc. that Rom. has survived.

116. *sour...fellowship* Cf. Tilley, C 571.

120. *modern* v. G.   *lamentation* Objective. *moved?* (edd.) Q 2 'moued,'.

121–2. *But...banishèd! To* Punct. ours. Q 2 'But with...death, | Romeo is banished: to'. Mod. edd. punct. variously.

121. *rearward* Military metaphor—quibbling on 'rear-word', which Hudson read (<Collier conj.).

126. *that word's death*=the death involved in that word.

128. *corse* (Q 4) Q 2 'course'.

129–3. 3. 26 ('law') Q 2 may here be printed from a corrected copy of sig. F 4ʳ in Q 1.

135. *maiden-widowèd* Rowe's hyphen.

143. S.D. Q 2 'Exit.'.

3. 3

S.D. *Loc.* (Capell)+'with...back' (J.D.W.).   *Entry* (Q 1). Q 2 'Enter Frier and Romeo.'.

3. S.D. (Q 1)+'from...study' (J.D.W.).

6–7. *Too...company!* Carries on the implied metaphor in 'acquaintance'.

10. *vanished* (Q 2, Q 1 'vanisht'). K. sees a jingle with 'banishment', glosses 'was breathed', and comments: 'The phrase suggests that words are breath and have no permanent existence.' This seems far-fetched. We suspect a common error (cf. 3. 2. 129–3. 3. 26, n.), i.e. a substitute in the reporter's memory (? by attrac-

tion with 'banisht') for a more difficult or unusual word, possibly 'vantaged' (J.D.W.). Cf. *Son.* 88. 12; *F.Q.* 1. iv. 49. 4; and p. 116, n. 3.

15. *Hence* (Q1+most edd.). Q2 'Here'—which is far less forcible and is an easy minim error for 'hence'. Note that Rom. repeats it in l. 19, as if stung by it. G.I.D. assents with doubts.

19. *is banished* (Q1, subs.) Q2 'is banisht'.

20. *world's exile* = exile from the world.

20, 21. '*banishèd*' (Q2, without inverted commas). 'Edd. who adopt "banishment" (in l. 21) from Q1... sacrifice...a perfectly Sh. inaccuracy of speech, originating in Rom.'s passion' (Delius).

22–3. *Thou...golden...smilest...me* i.e. you slay me with euphemisms. Cf. Erasmus, *Adagia*, 450 f.: 'De pulcro ligno vel strangulare' [Tilley, G 19].

26. *rushed* (Q1, Q2 'rusht'). Poss. a common error i.e. a Q1 error for 'thrust', uncorrected by the Q2 collator. Cf. p. 116, n. 3.

30–2. *every cat...may look on her* Cf. 'A cat may look at a king' (Tilley, C 141).

34. *courtship* v. G.

38. *Who* Antecedent 'lips'.

39. *Still blush* i.e. her lips are always red.   *their own kisses* i.e. the 'kisses' that one lip gives the other when they are closed.

40–4. *This may...I am banishèd*. The obvious duplication and/or confusion in these lines has been dealt with in various ways by different critics. Camb. and most mod. edd. omit 43 and rearrange the rest in this order: 42, 40, 44, 41; reading, however, 'but' for 'when' in l. 40. J.D.W. conj. that ll. 42–4 were Sh.'s first shot, for which he later substituted ll. 33–9 ('But Romeo...kisses sin'); writing these seven new lines in the margin or on a slip, and forgetting to delete the three old ones. The context gains if these three are left out, while nothing is lost but l. 44, which is distinctly weak. G.I.D. concurs. F. omits ll. 43–4.

45. *sharp-ground* Hyphen from F 4.

50. *confessor* Accent on first syllable.

51. *absolver* (Q 1) Q 2 'obsoluer'. Cf. 3. 5. 233, n. Hyphen from F.

53. *Thou* (Q 1 + most edd.) Q 2 'Then'. *a little speak* (Q 2) Many edd. read 'but speake a word' (Q 1); but this involves an awkward repetition of 'word' (cf. l. 52) [G. White].

56. *philosophy* For which the Franciscans were famous; e.g. Duns Scotus, William of Ockham, Roger Bacon. Cf. Brooke, 567–8:

> Not as the most was he, a grosse vnlearned foole:
> But doctor of diuinitie proceded he in schoole.

58. *Yet 'banishèd'?* = 'Still that fatal word' (K.). *Hang up* i.e. on the wall, like armour (cf. l. 55)— which was falling into disuse *c.* 1590 (v. *Sh. Eng.* i. 127–8).

60. *Displant a town* i.e. Verona, where Jul. is, to wherever Rom. shall go.

62. *madmen* (Q 1) Q 2 'mad man'.

63. *wise men...eyes* The prov. was 'Discreet women have neither eyes nor ears' (Tilley, W 683).

66–144. *Wert thou...thy love* Q 2 may well here be printed from a corrected copy of sig. G 1ʳ·ᵛ in Q 1.

69. As one line in Q 1. As two in Q 2, div. 'speake, | Then'.

mightst...mightst (Q 1) Q 2 'mightest...mightst'. *tear thy hair* Cf. Brooke, 1291, 'his golden locks he tare'.

71–81. S.D.'s (J.D.W.) translating: l. 71, 'Enter Nurse, and knocke' (Q 2); l. 74, 'They knocke' (Q 2); l. 76, 'Slud knock' (Q 2); l. 78, 'Knocke' (Q 2); l. 80, 'without' (Rowe); l. 81, 'Enter Nurse' (Q 2, at l. 79).

73–4. *groans...infold me* Cf. 2. 3. 73, n.

75–8. Punc. virtually Camb.'s. Q2 mostly uses commas.

76. S.D. Q2 'Slud knock'. Is 'Slud' a corruption of 'Loud', or (perhaps) of an actor's name, e.g. 'Slye'?

78. *simpleness*=folly (in not rising).

80. *errand* (Q4) Q2 'errant'—a variant spelling.

82–118. *O holy...life lives* Q1 (G1ʳ,ᵛ) is very close to Q2 in this passage. Cf. p. 115.

83. *Where is my* (Q1+most edd.). Q2 'Wheres my'—one of the few erroneous contractions in Q2, perhaps comp.'s anticipation of 'wheres' later in the line.

84. As one line in Q1. As two in Q2, div. 'ground, | With'.

86–7. *O...predicament!* Given to Friar by Steev. (<conj. Farmer) and many edd. Q2, Q1 continue to Nurse. But 'predicament' was a medieval philosophical term, only recently applied to personal situations (v. O.E.D.), and therefore outside the Nurse's range, though specially apt to the Friar; cf. l. 56, n. A common error; cf. ll. 82–118, n. and p. 116, n. 3.

90–1. *For Juliet's sake*, etc. O=a groan; but with a *double entendre*; cf. G. 'circle (b)'; *Cymb.* 2. 5. 17.

92. S.D. (Dyce ed. ii<Q1 'He rises').

94. *not she* (Q2) Some edd. read 'she not' (Q1). *old* v. G.

98. *concealed lady*=secret wife (v. G. 'lady'). Accented on 'con'.

cancelled=made null and void by Tyb.'s death and Rom.'s banishment [G.I.D.]. A legal term; cf. *Lucr.* 26; *1 H. IV*, 3. 2. 157; *R. III.* 4. 4. 77; *Macb.* 3. 2. 49.

101. *on...cries* v. G. 'cry'. Cf. *A.Y.L.* 2. 7. 70. Rom. understands correctly—cf. ll. 102–5.

102–3. *As...gun*, Lined as by Rowe. One line in Qq 1, 2.

108. *mansion* An ironical comparison with 3. 2. 26 suggests itself. S.D. (Q1) None in Q2.

109–13. *Art thou...both!* As Mal. notes, Sh. here closely follows Brooke, 1353–8:

Art thou quoth he a man? thy shape saith, so thou art:
Thy crying and thy weping eyes, denote a womans hart.
For manly reason is quite from of thy mynd outchased,
And in her stead affections lewd, and fansies highly
    placed.
So that I stoode in doute this howre (at the least)
If thou a man, or woman wert, or els a brutish beast.

Then follows a sermon on the wisdom of fortitude, the first 23 ll. of which furnished Sh. with material for Margaret's speech in *3 H. VI*, 5. 4. 1–38.

110. *denote* (Q1) Q2 'deuote'.

111. *unreasonable...beast* Cf. *Ham.* 1. 2. 150.

113. *And* (Q2) Some edd. read 'Or' (Q1).

114. *amazed* v. G.   *order* i.e. the Franciscan.

117. *lives* (F4; cf. Q1 'that liues in thee'). Q2 'lies'—perh. an omitted letter.

119. *Why rail'st* etc. Brooke (1325 ff.) tells us that Rom. rails against 'nature', 'the time and place of [his] byrth', 'the starres aboue', and 'all the world' (1347). And though Sh.'s Rom. has not expressly done this, K. notes that 'in effect he does rail on his birth in ll. 104–8; on heaven's mercy (note the Friar's comment in l. 24): and on earth—the whole world except Verona—in ll. 17, 18'. And Sh. is closer to Brooke in l. 119 than to his own version.   *rail'st* (F1) Q1 'raylest'.

120–1. *Heaven and earth meet* etc. Cf. Gen. ii. 7; man is both dust and immortal spirit. By suicide a man loses not only bodily life but all hope of eternal bliss.

122. *sham'st* (F1) Q2 'shamest'.

123. *like a usurer*—who takes 'a breed for barren metal' (*Merch.* 1. 3. 131); instead of using the talents

God had given him, as a gentleman, a lover, and a man of intellect should.

129. *Killing* = because you kill.

131. *Misshapen* = ill-directed (with a quibble on 'shape', ll. 122 ff.).

132-3. *Like powder* etc. v. G. 'flask'.

133. *set afire* i.e. becomes a flaming passion.

134. *defence* v. G.

136. *wast...dead* = wished to be dead.

143. *misbehaved* (Q1) Q2 'mishaued'.

144. *pouts upon* (Q4) Q2 'puts vp', Q1 'frownst vpon'. Many edd. adopt 'pout'st upon' (Q5); but 'pouts' is a common Shn. 2nd pers. sg., and involves the minimum change in Q2.

fortune = good fortune.

148. *till the watch be set* And the gates shut.

151. *friends* v. G.   162. S.D. (Q1) Q2 om.

163. *Here, sir, a ring* (Q2) Q1 'Heere is a Ring Sir'. Daniel conj. 'Here, sir's a ring'.

164. S.D. (Q1) Q2 om.

166. *here...state* = 'the whole of your fortune depends on this' (J.), i.e. on obeying the following injunctions.

168. *disguised* (Q3) Q2 'disguise'.

172. *thy* This change from 'your' (ll. 166, 169) marks the affectionate hand-grasp.

174. *so brief* = thus hastily.

3. 4

S.D. *Loc.* (Rowe). *Entry* (Q2).

4. *Well...die.* Cf. 3. 3. 92.

8. *no times* (Q2; G.I.D.) Q1 (+most edd.) 'no time'. J.D.W. thinks Q2 'times' prob. a compositor's error, repeating the plur. earlier in the line, and prefers 'no time' for style: the change of number *points* the

change in meaning. The line contains a kind of double pun; 'woe'—'woo' being the second.

11. *mewed...heaviness*=shut up with grief [G.I.D.]. Cf. G. 'mew'.

S.D. (after Q1) Q2 om.   13. *be* (Q1) Q2 'me'.

16. *ear* (J.D.W.) Cf. *Ant.* 3. 6. 58–9 'acquainted My grievèd ear'. Q2 'here'—prob.<copy-spelling 'yeere'; cf. *2 H. IV*, 1. 2. 190, n.   *son* For this (usual) anticipation, cf. 4. 1. 2, 'father'.

17, 20, 21. Rowe's dashes.

19. *ha, ha*=h'm, h'm (G.S.) Cf. G.

20. *O'...O'* (Capell) Q2 'A...a'.

23. *We'll* (all edd.<Q1 'Weele') Q2 'Well,'. J.D.W. takes 'But...Thursday?' (l. 28) as casting back to l. 22 'do you like this haste?'; believes ll. 22–8 spoken to Paris; and so prefers 'we'll'. G.I.D. prefers Q2 'Well' and thinks the whole speech (ll. 19 ff.) spoken to Lady Cap. down to l. 28, when (at 'But') Cap. turns to Paris. The dialogue reflects Brooke, 2255–75, in which Cap. proposes a 'costly feast' and Paris deprecates it (cf. 4. 4. 6, n.).

29. *O'* (Capell) Q2 'a'.

33. *Light*... Called to a servant.

34–5. *Afore...Good night* Arranged as Dyce. Q2 prints 'Afore...by and by' in one line. Poss. Sh. wrote the whole in one line at the foot of a page. Cf. the foot of p. 3 in his Addition to *Sir Thomas More*.

'tis (Dyce) Q2 'it is'.

3. 5

S.D. *Loc.* (J.D.W.) *Entry* (J.D.W.) Q2 'Enter Romeo and Juliet aloft'. Q1 'Enter Romeo and Iuliet at the window.'

1–59. Comprises all but the last two lines of sig. G3r,v in Q1, which after correction may have been copy for Q2; cf. pp. 113–15.

1. *not yet near day* etc. Cf. Brooke, 1703–14, which ends

As yet he saw no day, ne could he call it night,
With equal force decreasing darke fought with increasing
   light.

7. *severing* A quibble: (*a*) the streaks of light seem to split up the clouds; (*b*) dawn, with its red-streaked clouds, is parting the lovers.

9. *candles* The stars. Cf. *Macb*. 2. 1. 5, 'Their candles are all out'. *jocund* (F4) Q2 'iocand'.

13. *exhaled* (Hosley, p. 20, n. 27) Q2 'exhale' Q1 'exhales'. Q2 (<Q1), omits 's'. Most edd. accept Q1; but since Juliet denies that the sun has yet risen, it cannot be now exhaling. Cf. p. 116, n. 3.

19. *the* (Q1) Q2 'the the'. Cf. p. 116.
morning's eye i.e. the sun at peep of day.

29. *sweet* Emphatic.   *division* Musical term, apt to the lark; v. G.

31. *changed eyes* (Rowe, ed. ii) Qq, 1, 2 'change eyes' —a common error (cf. p. 116 n. 3). The toad's eyes being more beautiful than the lark's, it was 'a common saying among the people that the toad and the lark had changed eyes' (J.), i.e. at some past date, not that like the Graiae they swopped them at will. [J.D.W.] G.I.D. agrees 'reluctantly', since it makes the pattern in ll. 31–2 differ from that in ll. 29–30. [Hosley p. 20, n. 27 conj. 'changed'.]

33. *affray* v. G.

34. *Hunting thee hence* etc. An allusion to the custom of awakening the newly married with the blowing of horns. Cf. G. 'hunt's-up'.

36. *More light…woes* Cf. Brooke, 1725 'Then hath these louers day an end, their night begonne'.

S.D. (Q1; at l. 59) Q2 'Enter Madame and Nurse.'. See p. 123.

38. *Nurse?* (Theob.) Q 2 'Nurse.'.

40. S.D. (J.D.W.) None in Qq. Cf. l. 68, n.

42. S.D. (after Q 1 'He goeth downe.') Q 2 om. Rowe has 'Romeo comes down by the Ladder into the Garden.'

43. *friend*=sweet-heart, v. G. The line is a chiasmus. Most edd. read '...so? My lord, my love, my friend!' (Q 1).

45. *For in a minute* etc. Cf. Brooke, 747 'Eche minute seemde an howre, and euery howre a day'.

52–3. *all these...to come* Cf. Tilley, R 73, 'The remembrance of past sorrow is joyful.'

our times (Q 2) Q 1 'the time'. Poss. 'our time'.

54. *O God* etc. This speech, which begins sig. H 3^v in Q 2, is given the sp.-hdg. '*Ro.*' though its catchword on H 3^r is '*Iu. O*'.

55. *thee, now* (Pope) Q 2 'thee now.'.

so low (Q 2). Many edd. read 'below' (Q 1).

57. *look'st* (Q 1) Q 2 'lookest'.

59. *Dry...blood* Acc. to the old physiology, in times of sorrow the blood flowed back to the heart (cf. *Caes.* 2. 1. 289, n. and Tilley, S 656).

S.D. Q 2 'Exit.'.

61. *what dost thou with*=what concern have you with.

62. *renowned* (<Q 1) Q 2 'renowmd'—a common Eliz. form.

64. S.D. (after Capell 'within') Q 2 'Enter Mother.' For her sp.-hdgs. see p. 113.

65. S.D. suggested by Adams (p. 274).

66. *Is she...early?* i.e. 'Is she not laid down in her bed at so late an hour as this? or rather is she risen from bed at so early an hour of the morn' (Mal.). For 'not' Daniel conj. 'yet'.

67. S.D. (i) (J.D.W.); (ii) (Capell). For Q2's v. l. 64 S.D. n.

68. *Why* etc. This sharp question and Jul.'s excuse are natural, if the door is locked.

74–7. In 'loss' and 'friend' Jul. refers ostensibly to Tyb., covertly to Rom. *feeling* v. G.

82. *pardon him* (Q4+most edd.) Q2 'padon' She speaks of course ambiguously, but wishes her mother to understand:—'May God pardon the wretched murderer—I do, as a good Christian should: and yet I am grieved by the murderer as I am grieved by the other man' (G.I.D.).

83.='No man grieves my heart as he does by his absence'. For the colloq. 'like he' v. Franz §287c. Abbott, §206. But poss. a compositor's slip; no parallel elsewh. in Sh.

85. *from*=away from. *reach* She really means 'embrace'.

90. *unaccustomed* v. G. Sinister.

94. *till…him—dead—* (Pope) Q2 'till…him. Dead'. Q1 'Till…him, dead'. Jul. intends to leave it doubtful whether 'dead' relates to Rom. or to her 'poor heart'. 97. *temper* v. G.

99. *sleep* (*a*) in my arms, (*b*) in death.

101. *To wreak…cousin* This line (not in Q1) is a foot short, prob. through comp.'s omission. F2 reads 'Cozin, Tybalt'; Lettsom conj. 'ever bore'; and there are other conjectures.

105. *needy* (Q2) Q1 'needful'. 'Needy'= poverty-stricken, destitute (of joy) (G.I.D.).

106. *I beseech* (Q4) Q2 'beseech'.

110. *expects* (Q2) For this 2nd sing. form v. Franz, §152.

126. sp.-hdg. Q2 '*Ca.*' up to 160 where it changes to '*Fa.*' See p. 123.

air (Q4+most edd.) Q2 'earth' (line not in Q1). Mal. thought Q2 poss., because 'philosophically [i.e. scientifically] true', and cited *Lucr.* 1226 'the earth doth weep, the sun being set'. But 'weep' is not 'drizzle', and 'drizzling', like 'rain' (l. 128), always implies 'falling' elsewh. in Sh., while the image in *Lucr.* compares dew with tears resting, not falling, upon the face of the earth (cf. *M.N.D.* 3. 1. 190). Thus Q 2 'earth' must be a misprint, e.g. for 'air', 'heaven', or 'sky'. Poss. 'eire' misread 'erd'. [J.D.W.] G.I.D. concurs.

128–9. Lined as in Q 4. As one line in Q 2.

128. *rains downright* Ref. to Jul.'s tears.

129–30. *How now...body* A close parallel with *Titus*, 3. 1. 222–30 (v. note there).

129. *conduit* Cf. G. and *Titus*, 2. 4. 30, 'As from a conduit with three issuing spouts'. Brooke uses 'conduit' for weeping twice.

130. *showering?...body* (Q 5) Q 2 'showring... body?'.

131. *counterfeits a* (F 1, 'counterfaits a') Q 2 'countefaits. A'. For the form of the vb., v. l. 110, n.

133. *is*, F 4 'is', Q 2 'is:'.

138. *our*=my. The pompous old man speaks like a monarch. Note 'delivered' and 'decree'.

139. *gives* (Q 3) Q 2 'giue'.

140. *I would...grave* Cf. *Arcadia* (1590) I, st. 5, p. 33, 'assured her mother, she would first be bedded in her grave, than wedded to Demagorus'.

142. *How?* (Q 5) Q 2 'How'.

145. *bride* (Q 2) In Sh.'s time 'bride' is poss. for a man (v. O.E.D. 'bride', sb.¹ 2), but archaic, and thus odd in coll. speech. J.D.W. thinks 'bridegroom' (Q 3 + most edd.) prob. the true reading.

149. *How, how! how, how!* (Capell) Q 2 'How, how, howhow'.

chop-logic (Q 1 + most edd.) Q 2 'chopt-lodgick'. G.S., taking 'chopt-logic' for the argument, and 'chop-logic' for the arguer, suggests that Cap. means

'How now, Miss Argument'. But (i) the two forms
would be indistinguishable on the stage; and (ii) O.E.D.
lends no support to such a difference in meaning, and
treats 'chopt-logic' as a mere sp. of 'chop-logic',
giving no instance of the sp. but this. J.D.W. thinks it
a misprint; G.I.D. is impressed by G.S.'s note.

150–1. Lettsom conj. '"Proud" and yet "not
proud", and I thank you not: | And yet "I thank
you".'—which is attractive.

151. *proud',...you?* (G.I.D.) Q2 'proud mistresse minion you?' Edd. freq. read '"proud": mistress
minion, you,' (Q5, subs.). *mistress* Trisyllabic.

153. *fettle* v. G. Freq.=groom a horse (O.E.D. 1)
and, with 'fine joints', seems to do so here. Cf. [of
a woman] 'Our fily is fetled vnto the saddle', *Schole-
house of Women* (l. 571), c. 1560. [W. C. Hazlitt,
Early Pop. Poetry, iv. 127].

155. *drag...hurdle* As traitors were dragged to
the gallows.

156–7. *green-sickness...tallow-face* Hyphens from
F4. v. G. Jul.'s sufferings have made her pale.

157. *Fie...mad?* Prob. addressed to Jul. Both
parents turn upon her, and though the Nurse seems for
a time her ally, she deserts her in ll. 212 ff. [J.D.W.]
G.I.D. thinks the line may be addressed to Cap. and
cites l. 175, and 1. 1. 75.

158. S.D. (<Q1 'She kneeles downe.') Q2 om.
161. *o'* (Theob.) Q2 'a'.
164. *itch. Wife, we* (Camb.<Capell). Q2 'itch,
wife, we'.

170. *Wisdom?* (Q1) Q2 'wisdome,'.

171. *Prudence. Smatter* Q3 'Prudence, smatter',
Q2 'Prudence smatter,'. *gossips,* (Q1) Q2 'gossips'.

172. O *Godigoden!* Q1 gives to '*Cap*'. Q2 prints
'Father, ô Godigeden' as part of Nurse's speech, and
as if 'Father' were her exclamation (cf. 4. 4. 20, n.).

Cap.'s other speeches on this page of Q2 are prefixed
'*Fa*'. [Hosley attempts to defend Q2 (pp. 32–3)].

174. *a gossip's bowl* Cf. *M.N.D.* 2. 1. 47.

175. *You are too hot* Lady Cap. takes more care to
protect her old servant than her daughter. Cf. l. 157 n.
[J.D.W.]

176. *God's...play,* (G.I.D.) Q2 (in 2 ll.) 'Gods
bread, it makes me mad, | Day, night, houre, tide, time,
worke, play,'. 'Houre, tide, time,' is prob. a series of
Sh.'s 'first shots', i.e. rejected but undeleted experiments
in the foul papers. See p. 113, and *Sh. Survey* (1955).

177. *still my care hath been* Cf. Brooke, ll. 1962 ff.
'I with long and earnest sute' etc.

180. *trained* (most edd.<Q1 'trainde'). Q2
'liand'. Q3 'allied'. Capell conj. 'lianc'd'—which
might have been misread 'liand'; but 'trained' is
graphically close also [Hosley, p. 20, proposes 'limb'd'
(sp. 'limd' or 'limmd')].

184. *in...tender*=at the very moment when fortune tenders this wonderful offer.

187. *I'll pardon you*=I'll give you leave *to go*! Cf.
Gent. 3. 2. 98.

190. *Lay...heart*=lay it to heart.

194. *Nor...good*=Nor shall you inherit a penny
from me.

205–8. *My husband...earth?* G.S. paraphrases:
'My faith to my husband is registered in heaven; therefore I am not free [to marry anyone else], unless my
husband, having died, sends from heaven to release
me from my vow.'

212–13. *Faith...nothing* Lined as by Capell. One
line in Q2—poss. due to Sh. 'crowding' a little at the
foot of a page. Cf. 3. 4. 34–5, n.

220. *green* (Q2) Green eyes were considered
beautiful. Cf. *Two Noble Kinsmen*, 5. 1. 150, 'thy rare
green eye'.

233. *absolved* (Q3, subs.) 'obsolu'd'. Cf. 3.3.51, n.

235–4. 1. 96. *Ancient damnation* etc. Comprises sig. H2ʳ·ᵛ and H3ʳ of Q1 which may well have been used as copy for Q2 after slight alterations on H2 but heavier ones on H3ʳ. Cf. 4.1.49 ff. n., and pp. 113–16.

240. *shall be twain*=shall be unfriendly. Cf. Tilley, T 640.

242. S.D. Q2 'Exit.'.

4. 1

S.D. *Loc.* (Capell). Since at l. 17 Jul. comes 'toward' the cell, at the outset the Friar and Par. are prob. on the inner stage, the curtains being open, while Jul. enters on the main stage.

3.=And his haste will not be lessened by any reluctance on my part.

7. *talked* Q1 'talkt', Q2 'talke'.

8. *Venus...house* Besides the surface meaning there is an astrological quibble: 'Venus'=the planet; 'smiles not' does not shed a beneficent influence; 'house'=one of the twelve parts into which the old astronomy divided the heavens.

10. *do* (Q2) Q1, Q3 and many edd. 'doth'.

11. *marriage* Trisyllabic.

20. '*may be*' *must* Inverted commas ours. Q2 has a comma after 'be'. Cf. Tilley, M 1331, 'What must be must be'.

34. *to my face* (*a*) to myself directly (quibbling on l. 28), (*b*)=about my face.

36. Her hidden meaning is, 'Perhaps I *have* slandered it in calling it *my* face (l. 34), for it, like the rest of me, belongs to Rom.

38. *evening mass* 'Prob. due to [Sh.'s] ignorance or forgetfulness of the fact that mass was not (normally) celebrated in the evening', though the expression

appears to be a literal rendering of *missa vespertina* = vespers [O.E.D. 'mass' 2. c].

40. *entreat...alone* i.e. beg you to leave us alone at the time. O.E.D. ('entreat' 2. c) misquotes and misinterprets.

43. S.D. Q2 'Exit.'.

44. *shut the door* Par. exits, prob. by the door at the back of the inner stage, leaving it open.

45. *cure* (Q1 + most edd.) Q2 (+ G.S. and Hoppe) 'care'—an *a* : *u* misreading, we think. 'Past care' would = 'no longer to be worried about', which conflicts with 'past hope' and 'past help'. Cf. 4. 5. 65 [G.I.D.].

49–96. *On Thursday...no pulse* The corr. material in Q1 (H3^r) was prob. used as copy for Q2, though requiring a good deal of correction. The two texts contain a number of closely parallel ll., viz. 49–51, 61–5, 67–78, 81, 83, 86–7, 92, 94–5, with the common spellings 'vmpeere', 'coapst' and in 83:

With reekie shankes [Q2 shanks] and yealow chaples [Q2 chapels] sculls:.

54. *this knife* For the evidence that Eliz. ladies sometimes wore knives at their girdles, v. Cunnington, *Eng. Costume in 16th c.* p. 85.

55–67. *God joined* etc. Here Sh. closely follows Brooke, 2019–29.   57. *label* v. G.

59. *this* sc. knife (cf. 54).   *them both* i.e. hand and heart.

60. *long-experienced* (Pope) Q2 'long experienst'. *out...time* = from the experience of your long life.

62. *bloody* Either proleptic or = cruel.

63. *umpire* i.e. 'This knife shall decide the struggle between me and my distresses' (J.) v. G. In Brooke Juliet twice threatens to kill herself with 'bloody knife' (496, 1915).

64. *commission* Another legal term; v. G.

69–70. *Which...prevent* Cf. 2 Prol. 14, n.

72. *slay* (Q1) Q2 'stay'.

74. *chide* etc.=shame away this shame.

75. *That* Antecedent 'thou' (l. 73).   *it*=shame.

76. *And, if* Q2 'And if', which might='an if' or simply 'if'.

77–8. *O bid...tower* Mal. cites ll. 245–7 of *King Leir* (before 1594):

> Yea, for to doe you good, I would ascend
> The highest Turret in all Brittany,
> And from the top leape headlong to the ground.

Cf. also Brooke, 1603–4; Juliet threatens

> Hedlong to throw her selfe downe from the windowes haight,
> And so to breake her slender necke with all the bodies waight.

78. *any* (Q2) Q1 (+some edd.) 'yonder'.

79. *thievish ways*=roads infested by robbers.

81. *hide* (Q2) Some edd. read 'shut' (Q1).

83. *chapless* Q1 'chaples', Q2 'chapels'.

85. *lay* (J.D.W. < Q1 'Or lay me in tombe with one new dead'.) Q2 'hide'. Comp. repeats from l. 81. G.I.D. concurs.

his shroud (Q4) Q2 'his,'. The Q4 word is obviously required.

94. *distillèd* (Q1+most edd.). Q2 'distilling'. The Q2 rdg. (v. p. 116, *init.*) might be acceptable as='permeating the body' (cf. l. 95, 'through all thy veins'), were not the Friar obviously referring to the 'baleful weeds' and 'weak flower' of 2. 3. 8, 23. Cf. Brooke, cited 2. 3. 15, n.

96. *a cold...humour* i.e. a 'humour' (v. G.) that makes you cold and drowsy.

98. *breath* (Q3; cf. Q1 'No signe of breath') Q2 'breast'. Cf. pp. 115–16.

99. *fade* (Q3) Q2 'fade:'.

100. *To wanny* (Kellner, *Restoring Sh.*, §118, c.) Q2 'Too many' F1 'To many', Q4 'Too paly', Q5 (+most edd.) 'To paly'. The graphic outline of Q2's 'many' makes 'wany' in Sh.'s MS. certain.

windows v. G.; cf. l. 101.

102. *supple government* power or control of movement.

109–11. *as the manner...be borne* Cf. Brooke, 2523–5:

An other vse there is, that whosoeuer dyes,
Borne to their church with open face vpon the beere he lyes,
In wonted weede attyrde, not wrapt in winding sheete.

110. *In* (Q3) Q2 'Is'.   *uncovered* etc. Cf. *Ham.* 4. 5. 164, 'bare-faced on the bier'. After this line Q2 has 'Be borne to buriall in thy kindreds graue:'— prob. Sh.'s undeleted 'first shot'. See p. 113.

111. *shalt* (Q3) Q2 'shall'.

112. *Capulets* Sh. perh. wrote 'Capels'; cf. 5. 1. 18, 5. 3. 127.

115. *and he* (Q3) Q2 'an he'.

116. *waking* (Q3) Q2 'walking'. Cf. 4. 3. 49, n.

119. *inconstant toy* Brooke's words; v. G. 'toy'. *womanish dread* cf. Brooke's 'womanish fear'.

126. S.D. Q2 '*Exit*.'.

4. 2

S.D. *Loc.* (Rowe). Prob. a main stage sc. *Entry* (Camb.) Q2 'Enter Father Capulet, Mother, Nurse, and Seruing men, two or three.'.

1. S.D. (after Capell).

3–6. sp.-hdgs. (Mal.) Q2 'Ser.'.

6–7. *'tis...fingers:* Prov. (Tilley, C636). One who did not, 'had no faith in the excellence of his own viands' (K.).

9–10. Lined as by Pope. One line in Q2.

S.D. Q1 'Exit Seruingman.' Q2 om.

14. *a peevish...harlotry* Again at *1 H. IV*, 3. 1. 196.

21. S.D. (J.D.W.) Q1 'She kneeles downe'. Q2 om.

24. *this knot knit up* Cf. Brooke, 2276 'The wedlocke knot to knit soone vp'.

tomorrow morning i.e. Wednesday (cf. 4. 1. 90), the day before the Thursday on which Cap. had previously fixed the wedding. Jul. quickly and without comment accommodates herself to Cap.'s change of plan. Cf. 'not till Thursday' (l. 36) and 'tomorrow' (l. 37).

26. *becoméd* (F1) Q2 'becomd'. No other ex. in O.E.D.

29. *see, the* Q2 'see the'. The old brain creaks, like Polonius'.

31–2. *Now...to him* Cf. Brooke, 2249–50:

In all our common weale scarce one is to be founde
But is, for somme good torne, vnto this holy father bounde.

33–4. *into my closet...ornaments* Cf. Brooke, 2234–5:

Vnto my closet fare I now, to searche and to choose out
The brauest garmentes and the richest iewels there.

36. sp.-hdg. Q2 '*Mo.*' So also at l. 38.

37. sp.-hdg. Up to this point of the sc. Q2 heads Cap.'s speeches 'Ca.', 'Cap.' or 'Capu.'. Here and at l. 39 it has 'Fa.'. See p. 113, *init.* S.D. Q1 'Exeunt Nurse and Iuliet.'. Q2 'Exeunt.'.

45. *up him* (Q2) Edd. freq. read 'him up' (F1).

Cf. Franz, § 444; *Temp.* 3. 3. 56, 'to belch up you'; and 'deck up her' (l. 41 above).

46. *My heart...light* Tilley (L 277) cites 5. 3. 90.

47. S.D. Q2 '*Exit.*'.

4. 3

S.D. *Loc.* (Rowe)+'at...curtains' (J.D.W.).

1 ff. In this sc. Sh. follows Brooke closely, though with interesting departures.

5. S.D. Q2, Q1 'Enter Mother.'. Sp.-hdgs. at 6, 12, Q2 'Mo.', Q1 'Moth.'.

8. *behoveful* (F4) Q2 'behoofefull'.

12. *business* Trisyllabic.

13. S.D. Q2 'Exeunt.'.

15. *faint cold*=causing faintness and coldness.
thrills through= shivers through; cf. *Meas.* 3. 1. 122.

18. *Nurse!*— (Hanmer) Q2 'Nurse,'.

20. Lined as by Hanmer. Prefixed to l. 21 in Q2.

23. S.D. (<J. 'Laying down a Dagger'). For Q2 'lie thou there' Q1 reads 'Knife, lye thou there'; cf. 4. 1. 54, n.

29. After this Q1 has 'I will not entertaine so bad a thought', adopted by Steev. and some later edd.

36. *like*=likely.

37. *conceit of*=thought aroused by.

39. *As in a vault*=since I shall be in a vault....
receptacle v. G. Accented 'réceptácle'.

46. *So early* Cf. ll. 30–2.

47. *mandrakes'* (Mal.) Q2 'mandrakes'. v. G.

49. *O, if I wake* (Hanmer) Q2 'O if I walke', Q4 'Or if I wake', F2 'Or if I walke'. Cf. 4. 1. 116, n.

53. *rage* v. G.

57. *Stay* 'In her vision she imagines he is going to hurt Rom.' (Delius).

58. *Romeo...thee* (Q1+most edd.) Q2 'Romeo,

Romeo, Romeo, heeres drinke, I drinke to thee'. The
Q 1 line bears the authentic stamp. Some explain Q 2's
long unmetrical line as a frantic outburst. But Mozart
and Wagner do not throw music to the wind when
securing their great emotional effects: on the contrary.
And it is poss. to account for Q 2 as a corruption of the
line as correctly reported in Q 1. Thus: (i) it begins and
ends with the same words, (ii) 'Romeo, I come'
might be misread 'Romeo, Romeo', (iii) Dyce's conj:
that a marginal S.D. 'heere drinke' was mistaken as an
afterthought and fitted into the dialogue, would explain 'heeres drinke' [J.D.W.]. G.I.D. concurs.

'The sudden vision of Romeo in the vault, and
Tybalt vengefully seeking him out, drowns all consideration but the longing to join him there' (Herford).
She toasts Romeo to encourage him in the fight, as
the Queen toasts Hamlet in *Ham*. 5. 2. Cf. Brooke,
2399–400:

As she had frantike been, in hast the glasse she cought,
And vp she dranke the mixture quite, withouten farther
    thought.

S.D. (Q 1) None in Q 2.

4. 4

S.D. *Loc*. (Dyce). Prob. acted on the main stage.
Entry < Q 2 'Enter Lady of the house and Nurse.', and
Q 1 'Enter Nurse with hearbs, Mother.'.

2. S.D. (Q 2).

5. *Angelica* Is this the Nurse or his wife? Much
debated by edd. Prob. Nurse, as she replies.

6. *Spare not for cost* In Brooke, 2260 ff., Paris
bids Cap. 'spare so great a cost' Cf. 3. 4. 23, n.

11. *mouse-hunt* Cf. G. and Tilley C 136, 'Cat after
kind, good mouse hunt'.

12. S.D. (J.D.W.) Q 2 'Exit Lady and Nurse.'.

13. *A jealous...there?* One line in Q2; an alex-
andrine. *jealous hood* (Q2) F4+most edd. 'jealous-
hood' (glossed 'jealousy'). O.E.D. compares 'mad-
cap' and interprets 'hood' either 'as the type of a female
head' or 'as a disguise for a jealous spy'. S.D. Q2
prints after 'there'.

14. sp.-hdg. (Capell) Q2 'Fel.'

15. S.D. (after Camb.) No exit in Q2.
haste. Sirrah, Q5 'haste: sirrah', Q2 'haste sirra,'.

17. sp.-hdg. (Capell) Q2 'Fel.'. *I...logs*
Quibble: (*a*) I am good at finding logs, (*b*) I am a
loggerhead (i.e. blockhead).

20. *Thou* (Q1) Q2 'Twou'. S.D. (after Camb.).
Good faith (Q4+most edd.) Q2 'good father'—
prob. 'faith' misread as 'fath.' At first we took 'good
father' as a mild oath: cf. *1 H. IV,* 2. 4. 386, n. 'O, the
father'. But that parallel turns out to be a mare's nest,
derived from Schmidt, unsupported by O.E.D.;
Mist. Quick. merely alluding to Papa Henry as played
by Jack Falstaff. Cf. *supra* 3. 5. 172, n.

21. S.D. Q2 'Play Musicke.', after l. 20.

27. Separate line in F1. Appended to l. 26 in Q2.
S.D. None in Qq, where 4. 5. 1. follows on from 4. 4.
27 with no break or S.D. A common error; cf. p. 116.

4. 5

S.D. *Loc.* (Camb.<Theob.)+'the curtains...bed'
(J.D.W.). *Entry* (Hanmer).

4. *You take*=see you take.

6–7. *set up...but little* Nash has the same jest at
i. 384. 35 ff.

7. *God forgive me* sc. for that jest.

10. *take...bed*=find you still in bed; with
a quibble in 'take'.

11. *fright* With a poss. quibble on 'freight'.

Will it not be? = can nothing wake you? S.D. (after Capell, who has 'goes towards the Bed' at l. 9).

13. S.D. (after Capell).

15. *weraday* Q2 'wereaday'; v. G.

16. S.D. (edd.) Q1 'Enter Mother.', Q2 om.

17. sp.-hdg. Q2 '*Mo*.'. So (or '*M*') throughout the sc.

21. S.D. (edd.) Q2 'Enter Father.', Q1 'Enter Oldeman.'.

22. sp.-hdg. Q2 '*Fa*.'. So (or '*Fat*.') throughout the sc.

23. *dead, deceased:* Q2 'dead: deceast,'.

26. *blood...settled* Again *2 H. IV*, 4. 3. 101, *2 H. VI*, 3. 2. 160. See G. 'settled'.

32. *Ties...speak* Cf. Brooke, 2453–4, 'That he ne had the powre...to speake'. Mal. notes that Sh. here follows Brooke, forgetting that Cap. is to be 'clamourous in his grief'. But C.B.Y. plausibly suggests that Sh. deliberately introduced the contradiction in order to underline the ludicrous nature of these conventional lamentations and to get in a dig at Cap.

S.D. 'Enter...County' (Q2) + 'with Musicians' (Q4).

36. *wife. There* Q2 'wife, there'. F2 (+Camb.) 'wife: see, there' (cf. Q1 'see, where she lyes'). But the pause after 'wife' adds to the solemnity. Cf. 1. 2. 14, n.

37. *defloweréd* (<Steev. 1793) i.e. 4 syllables. Q2 'deflowred'. The expansion makes F2 'deflowred now', which many follow, unnecessary.

40. *all; life, living, all* (Collier). Q2 'all life liuing, all'.

41. *thought long* (Q3) Q2 'thought loue'—perh. 'lone' ('g' om.) miscorrected, v. G. 'think long'. Brooke (l. 2274) has the phrase.

45. = 'In his ceaseless, toilsome, progress from moment to moment'.

48. *catched* Capell conj. 'snatched'.

49 ff. *O woe!* etc. G. White suggests that in 'this speech of mock heroic woe' Sh. ridicules Jasper Heywood's trans. of Seneca. Cf. the exclamatory grief of Pyramus and Thisbe, *M.N.D.* 5. 1. [Dowden] and l. 32, n.

51. *behold* (Q3) Q2 'bedold'.

55, 59. The adjs. ref. to the speakers themselves.

56. *detestable* Accented détestáble.

58. *Not...death!*—'not "my life", as I have so often called you, but still in death my loved one' (Deighton).

65. *cure* (Theob.) Q2 'care'. Cf. 4. 1. 45, n.

66. *confusions. Heaven* (edd.) Q2 'confusions heauen'.

69. *Your part* = the body.

70. *his part* = the soul. Cf. G. 'part'.

72. *advanced* sc. socially, by marriage to Par.

75. *in this love* sc. for Jul., expressed by your copious lamentations.

76. *she is well* Cf. 5. 1. 17, and Tilley, H 347.

79. *rosemary* v. G. A symbol of lasting affectionate remembrance.

80–1. *as the custom...church* Cf. 4. 1. 109–11, n., and Brooke, 2523–5.

81. *All in* (J.D.W.). Q2 'And in'—comp. repeats 'and' from ll. 79, 80. Many edd. read 'In all' (Q1).

82. *fond* (F2) v. G. Q2 'some'. *nature* v. G.

83. *reason's merriment* i.e. it is ridiculous to weep for one who is in heavenly bliss. Cf. Feste's catechism, *Tw. Nt.* 1. 5. 60 ff.

84–90. *All things...contrary* A rewriting of Brooke, 2507–14.

88. *solemn* =appropriate to a ceremony, here a wedding.

94. *ill* sc. committed by you.

95. S.D. (after Q1) Q2 'Exeunt manet.'.

96. sp.hdg. '1 Musician'. We follow Capell (<Q1) in the attributions to this character. Q2 has a variety of hdgs.—'*Musi., Fid., Fidler., Minstrels, Minst., Minstrel. Min.*'. See p. 113, *init.*

put up...pipes =shut up; cf. G. 'pipe' and Tilley, P 345. The phrase occurs 4 times in Nashe, once, in connexion with 'silver sound' (v. l. 123, n.) and once spoken by Harvest in *Summer's Last Will* (iii. 263, 933), who leading out his chorus of Reapers says, 'We were as good euen put vp our pipes, and sing Merry, merry, for we shall get no money'—a close parallel.

99. *by my* (Q1) Q2 'my my'. Cf. p. 116, *init.*

the case...amended Cf. the prov. 'the case is altered', Tilley, C 111.

S.D. (<Q4) Q2 'Exit omnes. Enter Will Kemp.' Kemp is the name of the actor who plays 'Peter'. See p. 115. The 'Exit omnes' may be variously explained. (1) Sh. may have orig. intended the sc. to end here, adding ll. 100–44 later; or (2) the very feeble ll. 100–44 were not Sh.'s at all but added to the scene by some one else (perhaps Nashe, cf. parallels in ll. 96, 123, 130–1, 132, nn.) to give Kemp an extra piece of 'fat' [J.D.W.].

100–44. These ll., arranged as prose by Pope and subs. edd., are printed as very irregular verse in Q2, the comp. evidently following his copy and being at some pains to do so, including three turn-overs.

100. '*Heart's ease*'. A song current in Sh.'s day; the tune survives; the words are lost.

105. *full of woe* (Q4) Q2 'full:'. 'My heart is full of woe' is the burden of the first stanza of a popular

Ballad of Two Lovers. Prob. the foul papers gave enough to remind the prompter, or Kemp, what should be quoted. Cf. Greg, cited below, l. 126, n.

105. *merry dump* The words are comically incongruous; v. G. 'dump'.

114. *give you the minstrel*=call you good-for-nothing, cf. 3. 1. 45–6, n.

115. *serving-creature* Also used contemptuously.

117. *will carry no crotchets*=put up with no whims. Cf. G.

re fa Musical notes—respectively the second and fourth in the scale. Here used comically as verbs: 'I'll play a pretty tune on your head with my dagger' (Deighton), I'll beat you.

119. *you note us* 'You' and 'us' are emphatic. See G. 'note'.

120. sp.-hdg. Q2 '*2. M.*'.

122. *Then...wit!* Assigned as in Q4. Continued to previous speaker in Q2, which has sp.-hdg. 'Peter.' before 'I will dry-beat...'.

123. *iron wit* Cf. G.; Nashe, ii. 261. 24; and *R. III*, 4. 2. 28.

125–7, 140. Peter quotes from a poem entitled *In Commendation of Music,* by Richard Edwards, found in *The Paradise of Dainty Devices,* 1576.

125. *grief* (Q1+most edd.) Q2 'griefes'. Q1 agrees with *The Paradise.*

126. *And doleful...oppress* (Q1; Capell). The dramatist 'did not trouble to write more than the first and last lines' of a well-known stanza (Greg, *Ed. Prob.* p. 62, n. 2). Q1 is evidence that the missing line was spoken on the stage, while 'oppress' is needed to rhyme with 'redress' in l. 141.

127. *sound*— Q1 'sound,' Q2 'sound.'.

129. *Catling* This name, 'Rebeck' (132), and 'Soundpost' (135) are appropriate for musicians; v. G.

130–1. *silver...sweet sound* For this cf. Nashe, *Jack Wilton*, 1594 (ii. 222. 6 ff.):

This siluer-sounding tale made such sugred harmonie in his eares that...he could haue found in his hart to haue packt vp hys pipes and to haue gone to heauen without a bait.

132, 135. *Pretty* (Q1 'Pretie', 'Prettie') Q2 'Prates'. Almost cert. a misprint of 'pratie', a common 16th cent. sp. of 'pretty' found (as 'pratty') twice in Nashe's *Summer's Last Will* (iii. 237. 117; 239. 175) where the word, as here, is spoken by a Clown.

137–8. *singer...say* The singer sings—he cannot speak! As 'Soundpost' associates him with a stringed instrument, perhaps Pet. calls him the singer in order to be able to make this feeble joke.

139. *have no gold for sounding*=are not paid in gold for their music-making.

143. sp.-hdg. Q2 'M.2.'   *Jack!* i.e. Jack (v. G.) that he is!

144. S.D. Q2 'Exit.'.

5. 1

S.D. *Loc.* (edd.). *Entry* (Qq)

1–24. *If I...stars* The links here between the Qq suggest that a corrected I3ʳ of Q1 was used as copy for Q2. Cf. *Sh. Survey*, 1955.

1. *flattering truth* (Q2) Q1 'flattering Eye'. Many unnecessary emendations proposed. Truth= honesty. J. paraphrases: 'If I may only trust the honesty of sleep, which I know, however, not to be so nice as not often to practise flattery'. And 'flattering'= 'encouraging with hopeful representations', with no dominant idea of falsity. Rom. has foreboding dreams just before meeting Jul. (v. 1. 4. 50, n.) and joyful

dreams when about to hear of her death. Cf. 5. 3. 88–90, and Tilley, L 277.

3. *bosom's lord*=Love..   *his throne*=my heart. Cf. *Tw. Nt.* 1. 1. 36–8 and note.

8–9. *breathed...revived* Cf. *Hero & Leander*, ii. 3, 'He kissed her and breathed life into her lips'.

in=into.

11. S.D. (<Q 1 'Enter Balthasar his man booted.'). Q 2 'Enter Romeo's man.'.

15. *How...Juliet?* (Q 2 'How doth my Lady, Juliet?' 'We may assume that the compositor blundered through repeating part' of l. 14 (Greg, *Aspects*, p. 179).

24. *e'en* (Collier<Q 1 'euen') Q 2 'in'—prob. Sh.'s spelling; cf. *Ant.* (New Sh.), p. 124.

defy you (Pope+most edd<Q 1 'defie my') Q 2 'denie you'. Dowden writes: '"deny" may be right in the sense "disown, repudiate"....See 5. 3. 111.' To J.D.W. there is no choice. In 'defy' a tragic hero challenges the universe to do its worst; in 'deny' a philosopher 'repudiates' judicial astrology. 'Denie' may be one of Q 2's 'literals' (v. p. 116) or poss. a misreading of a copy-sp. 'deuy' (for 'defy'). G.I.D. concurs. Sh. found 'defy' in Brooke, who describing Rom.'s distraction at the news of banishment, writes: 'He cryed out (with open mouth) against the starres aboue' (1328) and 'He blamed all the world, and all he did defye' (1347).

25–6. *ink and paper...post-horses* All mentioned by Brooke (2604, 2612).

37 ff. *an apothecary* etc. Sh. elaborates Brooke's account of the shop, with its few boxes and the small show of wares in its window (2567–70).

41. *Sharp misery...bones* Mal. cites Sackville's *Induction* (on Misery; ll. 253–4): 'His face was leane ....And eke his hands consuméd to the bone.'

42–4. *tortoise...alligator...fishes* 'Such curiosities were regularly displayed in apothecaries' shops' (K.).

45–8. 'Boxes' and 'shew' both occur in Brooke's account of the apothecary's shop (2569–70) as does 'speeding gear' (l. 60; 2585).

47. *cakes of roses* v. G.

57. S.D. (Q1) Q2 om.

58. sp.-hdg. Q2 misprints '*Kom.*'.

60. *soon-speeding gear* Hyphen <F4. Cf. ll. 45–8, n.

62. *life-weary taker* (Q5) Q2 'life-wearie-taker'.

67. *any he*=any man.

69. *is in*=is indicated by.

70. *starveth*='are hungry.' (Dowden). Otway's emendation 'stareth', accepted by Rowe, is unnecessary.

71. *Contempt and beggary*=contemptible beggary. Hendiadys.

hangs upon thy back Ref. to his threadbare clothing.

74. *it*=the world's law.

76. *pay* (Q1+edd.) Q2 'pray'—a 'literal' misprint or minim misreading. Rom. is in no mood to 'pray' to anyone, and 'pay' is the inevitable Sh. complement of 'poverty'.

77. S.D. (<Collier).

84. *in flesh* v. G. 'flesh'. 84, 86. S.D.'s (J.D.W.).

5. 2

S.D. *Loc.* (edd.) *Entry* (Q1, Theob.) Q2 'Enter Frier Iohn to Frier Lawrence.', and then, after l. 1, 'Enter Lawrence.'. In all versions of the story but Brooke's and Sh.'s Friar John is called Friar Anselm.

1–13. *Holy...Romeo?* The links here between the Qq suggest that the lower half of Q1 of sig. I 4ʳ served as copy for Q2 after correction. Cf. *Sh. Survey*, 1955.

6. *associate me* Franciscans were enjoined to travel in couples, to be a check upon each other.

8. *searchers* v. G.

17. *fortune! By my brotherhood,* Q 2 'fortune, by my Brotherhood,'. Cf. Q 1 'Now, by my holy Order,| The letters were not nice,'.

27. *accidents* v. G.

5. 3

S.D. *Loc.* (Camb.) *Entry* (Camb.) Q 2 'Enter Paris and his Page.' Q 1 'Enter Countie Paris and his Page with flowers and sweete water.'.

1. *stand aloof* v. G. 'stand'.

3. *yond yew-trees* (Pope) Q 2 'yond young Trees', Q 1 'this Ew-tree', Q 2 'young' poss. a misreading of 'yeugh'—a 16th cent. sp. Cf. l. 137.

Lay thee all along=lie at full length.

4. *thine ear* (Q 1) Q 2 'thy eare' Before a vowel 'thine' is usual with Sh. except when the pron. is emphatic. Cf. Schmidt 'thine' [G.I.D. prefers Q 2].

8. *hear'st* (Rowe, ed. ii) Q 2 'heareſt'. Cf. p. 116 and l. 26, n.

11. S.D. (Capell) F 2 'Exit.' Q 1, Q 2 om. but Q 1 gives 'Paris strewes the Tomb with flowers.'.

12–17. *sweet...weep* The sestet of a sonnet. This charming but conventional mourning emphasizes by contrast the stark fierce passion of 5. 1. 24, 34 and ll. 22 ff. below.

12. *bridal bed* Cf. 4. 5. 35–9.

13. Staunton's punctuation.

thy canopy i.e. of thy bed.

14. *sweet water* Cf. Q 1 Entry (above).

15. *moans.* Q 2 'mones,'.

16. *keep* Q 2 'keepe:'.

17. S.D. Q 2 'Whistle Boy.', Q 1 'Boy whistles and calls. *My Lord.*'

18–120. *The boy...I die*   Once again the Qq links suggest that a corrected K1^{r,v} of Q1 served as copy for Q2. Cf. *Sh. Survey*, 1955.

18. *warning something* (Collier)   Q2 'warning, something'. Steev. (1773) 'warning;—something'.

20. *rite* (Pope, ed. 2)   Q2 'right'—a Sh. spelling.

21. S.D. (i) (Capell)   Qq om.; (ii) (Q1 at l. 18) Q2 'Enter Romeo and Peter.' Cf. Q2 sp.-hdgs. at 40, 43, 'Pet.'. Greg (*Edit. Prob.* p. 62, n.) suggests that this error 'may be due to a note by the book-keeper indicating that [Balthasar's] part could be doubled with that of the Clown [i.e. Peter]'. But Peter is the name of Rom.'s man in Brooke (ll. 2617 ff.), so that the error may be Sh.'s, though he had already written 'Balthasar' at 5. 1. 12 [G.I.D.].

25. *light. Upon*   Q2 'light vpon'.

26. *hear'st* (F.)   Q2 'hearest'   Cf. p. 116.

37. *savage-wild* (Steev.)   Q2 'sauage wilde'.

40, 43. sp.-hdgs.   Q2 'Pet.'   See n. on l. 21.

41. *friendship* (Q3)   Q2 'friendshid'.   S.D. (<Collier).

44. S.D. (Camb., after Hanmer)   F2 'Exit.'. He conceals himself behind a tree (a stage pillar): and, as he watches, he becomes drowsy, so that later he thinks he has dreamed what he has actually seen: cf. ll. 137–9.

45. *detestable*   Accented 'détestáble'.

womb. v. G.

47. S.D. (G.I.D.<Camb. 'Opens the tomb'—at l. 48). For the staging cf. Adams, pp. 206–7.

48. *in despite*='to spite thee—by making thee eat when thou art already gorged with food' (K.).

53. S.D. (Camb.).

55. ='Can you desire revenge from Tyb. any further than by killing him as you have already done?'

57. *must die*   See 3. 1. 193–4.

60. *Think...these gone* i.e. consider how I shall make you like one of these dead.

62. *Put* (Q2) A weak word. Capell conj. 'Pluck', which is attractive, since to 'pluck (disaster etc.) on one's head' is a Sh. idiom (cf. *All's Well*, 3. 2. 29; *R. II*, 2. 1. 205). Q1 'Heape'. The Q2 'Put' may be a correction of 'Puk' (i.e. 'Pluk' with 'l' omitted).

68. *conjuration* (Capell) Q1 'coniurations', Q2 'commiration' (misreading of 'coniuration'.).

70. S.D. (Q1).

71. *O Lord, they fight!* etc. (as in Q1) Q2 prints in italics, without sp.-hdg., and inset like a S.D. Greg (*Edit. Prob.* p. 61, n. 2) suggests that the line was added by Sh. in the margin of his orig. MS. without sp.-hdg.
S.D. (<Capell 'Exit Page.').

72. S.D. (Capell).

73. S.D. (Theob.).

84. *A grave? O no!—a* Q2 'A Graue, O no. A'. Many edd. read 'A grave? O no, a'.
lanthorn (Q2) v. G. The old form preserves the pop. association with 'horn' from which 'lanterns' and the windows of turrets and lighthouses were made.

86. *feasting presence* A room in a palace set out for a feast. Cf. l. 107.

87. *Dead* (Lettsom conj.) Q1, Q2 'Death'—prob. a common error; cf. p. 116, n. 3. To address Par. as 'Death' is very far-fetched, and with the occurrence of 'death' in l. 87 and l. 88 jars badly. The 'dead man'=Romeo.
S.D. (after Theob.).

88–9. *keepers*=either 'sick nurses' at death-beds, or 'jailers' of condemned prisoners.

90. *A...death!* Prov. exp. Cf. Tilley, L277; O.E.D. ('lightening', vbl. sb.² b) 'that exhilaration or revival of the spirits...supposed to occur...before death'.
light'ning Q2 'lightning'.

92–115. *Death...Death* Malone showed the close connexion between this and Henry's lament over the dead Rosamond in Daniel's *Complaint*, pub. 1592.

100. *his* i.e. Rom.'s own.

101. *cousin* Because Jul.'s. Cf. Brooke, 2660, 'Ah, cosin dere, Tybalt' (Romeus loqu.).

102–3. *Shall...amorous,* (Theob.) Q2, ending l. 102 with 'I will beleeue', prefixes 'Shall I beleeue' to l. 103. 'I will beleeue,' is prob. Sh.'s 'first shot' undeleted in the orig. MS. Cf. above p. 113 and Greg, *Ed. Prob.* 61, n. 2.

107. *palace* (Q3) Q2 'pallat'.   *night* (Q3) Q2 'night.'

107–8. Between these ll. Q2 has

Depart againe, come lye thou in my arme,
Heer's to thy health, where ere thou tumblest in.
O true Appothecarie!
Thy drugs are quicke. Thus with a kisse I die.

Whatever the 2nd line means, the passage almost certainly represents what the collator made of Sh.'s orig. ending to the speech, as Malone noted. Cf. ll. 102–3, n.

110. *set up...rest* See G. 'rest', and 4. 5. 6.

112. *world-wearied* Hyphen from Q3.

114. *seal...kiss* A very common legal quibble with Sh.; cf. *Gent.* 2. 2. 7; *Shrew*, 3. 2. 121; *K. John*, 2. 1. 20, etc.

116. *conduct* i.e. the potion, which now becomes pilot of the bark i.e. Rom.'s 'world-wearied flesh'.

119. S.D. (Camb., after Theob.).

120. S.D. (i) (Theob.); (ii) (<Q2, which reads 'Entrer' for 'Enter').

122. *stumbled* An ill omen. Cf. *R. III*, 3. 4. 84.

123. sp.hdg. Q2 'Man.'. so also at ll. 128–31, 137.

129. *One that you love.* Lined as by J. Appended to l. 128 in Q2.

136. *unthrifty* (Q2) v. G., and Spenser, *F.Q.* 1, iv. 35, 'Unmanly murder and unthrifty scath'. Many edd. read 'unlucky' (Q3).

137. *yew-tree* (Pope) Q2 'yong tree'. Cf. l. 3, n.

139. S.D. (Mal.).

140. Q1 here has S.D. 'Fryer stoops and lookes on the blood and weapons.'

143. *by* = beside. S.D. (Camb.), i.e. he goes into the inner stage.

147. S.D. (edd.) Q1 'Juliet rises', i.e. sits up.

150. S.D. (J.D.W. < Capell 'noise within').

151. *noise, lady. Come* Q2 'noyse Lady, come'. Many edd. read 'noise. Lady, come' < Q1's 'Lady come foorth, I heare some noise at hand,'.

160. S.D. Q2 'Exit'.

166. S.D. (Capell).

167. S.D. (J.D.W.) Q2 'Enter Boy and Watch.'.

168. sp.-hdg. (Capell) Q2 'Watch.'.

169. S.D. (Steev.).

170. *This* = her bosom. S.D. (Camb. < F 'kils herself').

rest (most edd. < Q1 'Rest in my bosome'). Q2 'rust' which makes sense of a kind, but one hideously unpoetical, and literally preposterous with 'and let me die' following, while 'rest' accords with 'happy' and the consummation she craves. [J.D.W. with help from A.W. Both she and G.I.D. note that a dagger naturally rests, rather than rusts, in its sheath.] 'This' and 'there' are emphatic. S.D. (Mal.) Q1 'She stabs herselfe and falles.'.

171. sp.hdg. (Capell) Q2 'Watch boy.'.

172. sp.-hdg. (Capell, subs.) Q2 'Watch.'.

173. S.D. (after Hanmer).

174–5. *slain:...dead,* (edd.) Q2 'slaine,...dead:'.

178. S.D. (after Capell).

181. S.D. (Dyce; after Rowe) Q2 'Enter Romeos man.'.

182. sp.-hdg. (Rowe, subs.) Q2 'Watch.'.

183, 187. sp.-hdgs. (Rowe) Q2 'Chief. watch.'.

183. S.D. Q2 'Enter Frier, and another Watch-man.'.

184. sp.-hdg. Q2 '3 Watch'.

186. *this churchyard's side* = this side of the church-yard (Hoppe).

187. *too.* (Q5, Ff.) Q2 'too too.' S.D. (<Q2 'Enter the Prince.' + 'and Attendants' (Rowe)).

189. S.D. (Q4) Q2 gives 'Enter Capels.' here, but the full (Q4) direction at l. 201, where it prob. represents a prompter's marginal clarification.

190. *should it be* = can it be.

is so shrieked (Daniel, > conj. by Camb.) Q2 'is so shrike' (misreading of 'is so shrikd'?). Many edd. read 'they so shriek' (Q3).

191. *O* (Q2) Edd. (<Pope) omit. Injures the metre, and looks like a player's connective, though not in Q1.

194. *our* (J. conj.; most edd.). Q2 'your'. We do not doubt that J. is right, since 'our' greatly eases the context and 'your' for 'our' is a common type of mis-print.

195, 199. sp.-hdgs. (Capell, subs.) Q2 'Watch., Wat.'.

199. *slaughtered* (Q3) Q2 'Slaughter'—app. taken as the name of Rom.'s servant.

201. Here Q2 gives S.D. 'Enter Capulet and his wife.'. Cf. l. 189 S.D. n.

204. *Montague* i.e. Rom.　　*house* sheath. 'The dagger was anciently worn behind the back' (Steev.).

205. *it* objective after 'lo'.

missheathed (F1) Q2 'missheathd'.

207. *warns* sc. tolls.   S.D. (Q2).

208–23. *Come...do least* After slight correction the lower half of K3ʳ in Q1 may well have served as copy for Q2 here.

209. *more early down* (Q1+most edd.) Q2 'now earling downe'. The words 'more' and 'nowe' were much alike in Sh.'s hand, while the antithesis 'early up' and 'more early down' has the authentic ring of his early rhetorical style.

211. *Grief...breath* Instead of this Q1 gives the line, 'And young Benuolio is deceased too', which may have been omitted by Q2. Ben. is Mont.'s nephew.

214. *thou* i.e. Rom.   *untaught* sc. in the rules of precedence.

216. *outrage* v. G.

219–20. *be general...to death* Military metaphor, which G.I.D. explains 'be the first to die of grief', and J.D.W. 'direct your woes towards the satisfaction of seeing their authors brought to justice and death'.

221. *And let* etc.=And submit to misfortune with patience.

222. S.D. (J.D.W.) None in Qq.

223. *greatest; able* Q2 'greatest able' (so also Q1). *greatest* refers to 'parties of suspicion'. *able to do least* Being old, feeble, and a man of God. .

225. *Doth* Cf. Franz, §156.

226–7. *to impeach and purge* etc. i.e. 'to accuse myself (being self-condemned) and to defend myself (being self-excused)' (G.S.).

229. *my short date of breath*—the short time I have to live.

232. *that Romeo's* (Q4) Balances 'that Juliet' in l. 231. Q2 'thats Romeo'.

241. *marriage* Trisyllabic. Again in l. 265.

243. (*so...art*) Brackets in Q2.

253. *hour* Q2 'hower'—two syllables.

258. *awakening* (Q2) Many read 'awaking' (Q3).

261. *patience* Trisyllabic.

265–8. Lined as by Pope. Three lines in Q2, ending 'priuie:', 'fault,', 'time,'.

266. *aught* (Theob. ed. ii) Q2 'ought'.

271. *to this* (Q2) Many read 'in this' (Q1).

274–5. *place, to...monument.* | *This* (F1) Q2 'place. To...monument | This'.

275. *early* goes with 'give'.

279. S.D. (<Collier 275 'forward').

292. *hate,* (F1) Q2 'hate?'.

294. *winking...discords* Cf. Tilley, F 123 'wink at small faults'.

297. *This* i.e. this handshake.   *jointure*=the portion the bridegroom brings the bride.

299. *raise* (Q4) Q2 'raie'. Not 'erect', but 'cause to be made'; cf. l. 303, which speaks of recumbent effigies.

303. *Romeo's* sc. effigy. Cap. will provide a golden figure of Rom.

304. *Poor* etc.='an inadequate atonement for our hatred' (Deighton).

310. S.D. Q2 om. F1 'Exeunt Omnes.' Both Q1 and Q2 print 'Finis' at the end of the text, which suggests that this last page of Q1 (K4ʳ) may have served as copy for Q2, or at least for ll. 296–310.

GLOSSARY

Note. Where a pun or quibble is intended, the meanings
are distinguished as (*a*) and (*b*)

'A (for 'ha'), he; 1. 3. 41;
1. 4. 80; 1. 5. 66; 2. 4. 114,
145, 146; 5. 1. 38
ABROACH, afoot; 1. 1. 103
ABROAD, (i) out of doors;
1. 1. 119; 3. 1. 2; (ii) far and
wide; 5. 3. 190
ABUSE (sb.), (i) misuse; 2. 3.
20; (ii) offence, crime; 3. 1.
192
ABUSE (vb.), mar, disfigure;
4. 1. 29
ACCENT, manner of speech; 2.
4. 29
ACCIDENT, event; 5. 2. 26
ACCORDING, consenting; 1.2.19
ACCOUNT, (i) reckoning; 1. 5.
118; (ii) store, number; 5.
1. 45
ACTED, put into (physical)
action, consummated; 3. 2.
16
ADVANCE, raise, lift up; 2. 3.
5; 4. 5. 72 (in social standing); 4. 5. 73; 5. 3. 96
ADVISE, reflect, consider; 3. 5.
190
AFFECTING, affected; 2. 4. 28
AFFECTION, (i) inclination,
feeling; 1. 1. 125, 146; (ii)
love; 2 Prol. 2; (iii) passion,
emotion, natural feeling; 2.
5. 12; (iv) partiality, biased
feeling; 3. 1. 176
AFFORD, 'manage to give,
spare' (O.E.D. 4a); 3. 1. 59

AFFRAY, startle, scare; 3. 5. 33
AFORE ME, by my soul; 3. 4. 34
AGATE-STONE, tiny figure cut
out in an agate set in a seal-
ring (cf. *Ado*, 3. 1. 65;
2 Hen. IV, 1. 2. 16); 1. 4. 55
AIM, (*a*) direct a weapon, (*b*)
guess; 1. 1. 204
ALLA STOCCATA (Ital.), the
thrust technique (v. note;
cf. à la=after the manner
of); 3. 1. 73
ALLIANCE, marriage; 2. 3. 91
ALLOW, grant; 2. 3. 86
ALLY, kinsman; 3. 1. 108
ALOOF, at a distance; 5. 3. 1,
26, 282
AMAZE, bewilder, astonish; 3.
1. 133; 3. 3. 114
AMBIGUITY, uncertainty; 5. 3.
217
AMBLING, dancing (contemptuous term); 1. 4. 11
AMBUSCADO, ambush; 1. 4. 84
AMERCE, punish by fining; 3.
1. 189
ANATOMY, bodily frame (contemptuous term); 3. 3. 106
ANON, (i) in a little while,
soon; 1. 4. 85; 5. 3. 283;
(ii) (as answer to a call)
'coming!'; 1. 5. 143; 2. 2.
137, 150; (iii) (do.) 'at your
service!'; 2. 4. 101, 208
ANTIC, grotesque; 1. 5. 56;
2. 4. 28

APT TO, UNTO, ready for; 3.
1. 40; 3. 3. 157

AQUA VITAE, any form of
ardent spirits; 3. 2. 88; 4. 5.
16

ARGUE, betoken, indicate; 2. 3.
33

ARGUMENT, subject of discussion; 2. 4. 97

ART, skill acquired by learning
or experience (as opposed to
'nature'); 2. 4. 88; 4. 1. 64;
5. 3. 243

AS, as on; 5. 3. 247

ASPIRE (trans.), mount up to;
3. 1. 116

ASSOCIATE, accompany; 5. 2. 6

ATOMI, tiny creatures; 1. 4. 57

ATTACH, arrest; 5. 3. 173

AURORA, name of classical goddess of dawn; 1. 1. 135

BACHELOR, young gentleman;
.1. 5. 112

BAKE, cake together; 1. 4. 90

BAKED MEATS, pies and other
pastry; 4. 4. 5

BALEFUL, deadly; 2. 3. 8

BANDY, (i) strike a ball to and
fro (a term of tennis, or
bandy, once a form of tennis); 2. 5. 14; (ii) give and
take (blows); 3. 1. 88

BANKROUT (Ital. 'banca rotta',
Fr. 'banqueroute'), bank-
rupt; fig. one who has lost
all; 3. 2. 57

BANQUET, dessert of sweet-
meats, fruit and wine (v.
Shrew, G.); 1. 5. 122

BATE (vb.), flutter. Of a hawk
trying to fly from its tamer's
wrist; 3. 2. 14

BAUBLE, (a) short stick, sur-
mounted by carved head,
carried by court fool, (b)
penis (cf. All's Well, G.);
2. 4. 90

BAWD, (a) procuress, (b) In
dial., North Midland = hare;
2. 4. 125

BECOMÉD, befitting, becoming;
4. 2. 26

BEDECK, adorn; 3. 3. 125

BEETLE-BROWS, overhanging
eyebrows; 1. 4. 32

BEGUILED, cheated; (i) pre-
vented from fulfilling proper
function; 3. 2. 132; (ii) dis-
appointed as regards hopes
for the future; 4. 5. 55,
56

BEHOVEFUL, needful, advantageous; 4. 3. 8

BENEDICITE. The 2nd pers. pl.
imperative of Lat. vb.
'benedico' = 'Bless you'—a
salutation, or an exclamation of surprise; 2. 3. 31

BENT, inclination (of the
mind); 2. 2. 143

BESEEMING, seemly, decorous;
1. 1. 92

BESHREW, curse; 2. 5. 51; 3. 5.
221, 227; 5. 2. 26

BETOSSÉD, agitated; 5. 3. 76

BIDE, endure; 1. 1. 212

BILL, 'an obsolete weapon
varying in form from a
simple concave blade with a
long wooden handle, to
a kind of concave axe with
a spike at the back and its
shaft terminating in a spear-
head; a halberd.' (O.E.D.
sb.¹, 2); 1. 1. 72

BIRD, maiden (cf. Cymb. 4. 2.
197; O.E.D. 1 d); 2. 5.
74

BIRTH, nature; 2. 3. 20

BITE, (i) 'bite the thumb at' = insult, 'threaten or defy by putting the thumb-nail into the mouth, and with a jerk (from the upper teeth) make it to knack' (O.E.D., cited from Cotgrave); 1.1.42–50; (ii) 'bite one by the ear' (i.e. as a sign of fondness, 'to caress fondly' (O.E.D.)); 2. 4. 77

BLAZE, proclaim, make known publicly; 3. 3. 151

BLAZON, describe fitly (lit. heraldic term); 2. 6. 26

BOOK, (i) 'without book' = by rote; 1. 2. 60; 'without-book' = recited by heart; 1. 4. 7; (ii) 'by th' book'— O.E.D. gives 'formally, in set phrase', but prob. = according to a book of rules, as if you had learned prescribed rules from a text-book or breviary (cf. 3. 1. 101, n.); 1. 5. 110

BOUT, round, turn, at any kind of exercise (here dancing); 1. 5. 18

BOW-BOY, boy archer (Cupid); 2. 4. 16

BOWER, embower; 3. 2. 81

BOY, (i) familiar address to fellow-servant; 1. 5. 11, 15; (ii) reproving term for recalcitrant junior; 1. 5. 77, 83; (iii) insulting term applied by one young enemy to another; 3. 1. 129; 5. 3. 70

BRAIN, 'I do bear a brain' = I have a fine memory; 1. 3. 30

BRAVE, fine, splendid, noble; 3. 1. 115

BREACHES, i.e. in the walls of besieged towns; 1. 4. 84

BRIEF (adv.), quickly; 3. 3. 173

BROAD, (a) 'plain, evident' (Schmidt; cf. O.E.D. 5), (b) indecent; 2. 4. 85

BUCKLER, small round shield; 1. 1. head S.D.

BURDEN, weight (a) of toil, (b) of a husband; 2. 5. 76

BURN DAYLIGHT, waste time (cf. Tilley, D 123); 1. 4. 43

BUTT-SHAFT, 'unbarbed arrow used in shooting at the butts' (O.E.D.), ludicrously applied to Cupid's dart (cf. L.L.L. 1. 2. 168); 2. 4. 16

BY AND BY, very soon, shortly; 2. 2. 151; 3. 1. 169; 3. 3. 77; 3. 4. 35; 5. 3. 284

CAGE, 'anything resembling a cage in structure or purpose' (O.E.D. 4), in this case a basket; 2. 3. 7

CAITIFF, 'expressing commiseration: a wretched miserable person, a poor wretch, one in a piteous case' (O.E.D. 2), used as adj.; 5. 1. 52

CAKE OF ROSES or ROSE-CAKE, 'a preparation of rose-petals in the form of a cake, used as a perfume' (O.E.D.); 5. 1. 47

CALL IN QUESTION, 'make the object of thought or of notice' (K.); 1. 1. 228

CANDLE-HOLDER, an attendant who lights others in a ceremony at night (cf. O.E.D.); 1. 4. 38

CANKER, worm that destroys plants; 2. 3. 30

CANKERED, (i) of weapons, 'cankered with peace' =

rusted, corroded, through disuse; 1. 1. 94; (ii) of persons or sentiments = malignant; 1. 1. 94

CAREFUL, concerned for someone's welfare; 3. 5. 107

CARELESSLY, with indifference; 'held him carelessly' = did not value him highly; 3. 4. 25

CARRIAGE, power of bearing a weight (v. *burden*), with quibble on bodily deportment and/or moral character; 1. 4. 94

CARRION, applied in contempt to a living person, as being no better than a decaying corpse; 3. 5. 156

CARRY, endure, put up with (O.E.D. 39); 4. 5. 117

CARRY COALS, 'do dirty or degrading work', hence 'submit to humiliation or insult' at the hands of one's enemies (v. O.E.D. 'coal', 12, and Tilley, C 464); 1. 1. 1

CASE, (i) mask; 1. 4. 29; (ii) (*a*) state of affairs, (*b*) case for musical instruments (or perhaps set of instruments; cf. *Hen. V*, 3. 2. 4); 4. 5. 99

CAST BY, throw aside; 1. 1. 92

CATLING, 'a small lute-string made of catgut' (Steevens), as a personal name; 4. 5. 122

CHANGE (sb.), succession, passage; 1. 2. 9

CHAPLESS, without lower jaw; 4. 1. 83

CHARGE, importance, weight; 5. 2. 18

CHARM, (*a*) magic spell, (*b*) attractive quality; 2. Prol. 6

CHARNEL HOUSE, 'a vault or small building attached to a church and used as a depository for such skulls and bones as came to light in digging new graves' (K.); 4. 1. 81

CHASTE, unmarried; 1. 1. 216

CHECK'RING, diversifying with a different colour, variegating; 2. 3. 2

CHEER, fare, provisions, viands; 4. 5. 87

CHEVERIL, kid leather, capable of being stretched (cf. *Tw. Nt*. G.); 2. 4. 82

CHINKS, coins (from the sound made by their striking against one another); 'have the chinks' = have plenty of money; 1. 5. 117

CHOP-LOGIC, sophistical argumentation ('chop' = 'bandy', not 'mince'); 3. 5. 149

CHORUS, Presenter or Prologue, to 'make plain' the action (cf. *V.A.* 360; Creizenach, pp. 276, 389); acts 1 and 2

CHURL, niggard, stingy person; 5. 3. 163

CIRCLE, (*a*) magic ring, circular area within which a conjuror recited his spells, (*b*) female pudenda; 2. 1. 24

CIRCUMSTANCE, details, detailed information; 2. 5. 36; 5. 3. 181

CIVIL, (i) belonging to citizens; Prol. 4; (ii) occurring among fellow-citizens; 1. 1. 88; (iii) seemly, decorous, in attire (and perh. behaviour); 3. 2. 10

CLASP, metal clasp to keep a book shut (with quibble on 'embrace of a lover'), 1. 3. 93

CLOSE (adj.), (i) reserved, private; 1. 1. 148; 2. 2. 188; (ii) shut fast, *or* concealing; 3. 2. 5

CLOSE (adv.), at close quarters, hand to hand; 1. 1. 106

CLOSE (vb.), (i) enclose; 1. 4. 110; 5. 2. 29; 5. 3. 161; (ii) join; 2. 6. 6.

CLOSELY, secretly; 5. 3. 255

CLOSET, private room; 4. 2. 33

CLOUT, rag, piece of cloth (cf. *dishclout*); 2. 4. 198

CLUBS, 'the regular weapon of the London journeyman and apprentices. The cry "Clubs!" was the citizens' watchword, whether in raising a riot or [as here] in rallying to keep the peace' (K.; cf. O.E.D. 1 c); 1. 1. 72

COCK-A-HOOP, 'set cock-a-hoop'='cast off all restraint, become reckless' or 'give a loose to all disorder, set all by the ears' (O.E.D.). Origin obscure; 1. 5. 81

COCKATRICE, mythical creature hatched from a cock's egg by a serpent, able to kill with its breath or by a look, also called 'basilisk'; 3. 2. 47

COIL, fuss; 2. 5. 65

COLDLY, coolly, calmly; 3. 1. 51

COLLAR, hangman's halter (but O.E.D. queries), with quibble on 'choler'; 1. 1. 5

COLLIER, 'one who carries coals for sale', 'often used with allusion to the dirtiness of the trade in coal, or the evil repute of the collier for cheating' (O.E.D. 2 and 3); 1. 1. 2

COMBINE, (i) 'all combined' ='everything has been brought into harmonious union' (K.); 2. 3. 60; (ii) unite; 2. 3. 60

COME ABOUT, turn out to be true; 1. 3. 46

COME NEAR, affect intimately; 'touch closely' (O.E.D.); 1. 5. 21

COME UP (v. *marry come up*); 2. 5. 62

COMES WELL, is welcome; 1. 5. 30

COMFORTABLE, comfort-giving, supporting; 5. 3. 148

COMMISSION, a delegated authority for the performance of a judicial function (O.E.D. 2); 4. 1. 64

COMMON, (i) public, 1. 1. 101; (ii), ordinary; 1. 4. 18

COMPLAIN, utter laments, express grief, 'address pathetic words of love' (K.); 2. Prol. 7

COMPLIMENT (early edd. 'complement'), formal civility; 2. 2. 89; 2. 4. 20

CONCEIT, thoughts, imagination; 2. 6. 30 (v. note); 4. 3. 37

CONCEIVE, understand; 2. 4. 48

CONDUCT, (i) conductor, guide; 3. 1. 123; 5. 3. 116; (ii) guidance; 3. 3. 131

CONDUIT, fountain, 'often in the form of a human figure (hence allusively)' (On.).

Several in London in Sh.'s day; 3. 5. 129

CONFIDENCE, blunder for 'conference'; 2. 4. 122

CONFOUND, destroy; 2. 6. 13

CONFUSION, (i) calamity, disaster (K.); 4. 5. 65; (ii) (plur.) disorderly behaviour, lamenting commotions; 4.5. 66

CONJURATION, solemn appeal; 5. 3. 68

CONJURE, utter magical words to summon up a spirit; 2. 1. 6, 16, 17, 29; 'conjure down'=dismiss by magical words (with indelicate quibble); 2. 1. 26

CONSORT (intrans.), (i) associate; 2. 1. 31; 3. 1. 44; (ii) (with quibble on (i)) 'combine in musical harmony; play, sing or sound together' (O.E.D. 7); 3. 1. 45, 48; (trans.), attend, accompany; 3. 1. 129

CONTAGION, poisonous influence; 5. 3. 152

CONTENT, (a) pleasure, satisfaction, (b) 'contents'; 1. 3. 85

CONTRADICT, oppose; 5. 3. 153

CONTRARY (vb.), oppose; 1. 5. 85

CONVERT, change, be changed; 1. 5. 92

CONVOY, 'a conducting medium, channel, way, or path' (O.E.D. sb. 9). Quibbling on the nautical sense; 2. 4. 184

COPE WITH, encounter, engage, (O.E.D. 2); 4. 1. 75

CORDIAL, stimulant for the heart; exhilarating, restora-

tive, or comforting drink; 5. 1. 85

CORSE, corpse; 3. 2. 54, 128; 4. 5. 80, 89, 93; 5. 2. 29

COT-QUEAN, lit. housewife of a cot or labourer's hut; but 'to play the cot-quean' was said of a man who meddled with matters properly a housewife's concern. (Cf. O.E.D. 1, 3); 4. 4. 6

COUNSEL (sb.), (i) 'good counsel'=effective plan resulting from deliberation or consultation; 1. 1. 141; (ii) private talk; 1. 3. 10; 2. 2. 53; (iii) advice 2. 2. 81; 3. 3. 160; 4. 1. 61; (iv) 'keep counsel'= maintain secrecy; 2. 4. 190

COUNSEL (vb.), advise; 3. 5. 208

COUNSELLOR, secret advisor, confidant(e); 1. 1. 146; 3. 5. 239

COUNT (sb.), reckoning; 1. 3. 72; 3. 5. 46

COUNT (vb.), (i) reckon; 2. 6. 32; (ii) consider; 3. 5. 143; 4. 1. 9

COUNTERVAIL, equal, counterbalance; 2. 6. 4

COUNTY, title of nobility, Count; 1. 2. head S.D., and *passim*

COURSE, (i) (a) voyage, (b) life; 1. 4. 112; (ii) line of action, method or procedure; 4. 1. 5; 5. 3. 27; (iii) 'their course of love'=the progress of their love; 5. 3. 287

COURT-CUPBOARD, 'movable sideboard or cabinet used to display plate, etc.' (O.E.D.); 1. 5. 7

COURTSHIP, 'the state be-
fitting a court or courtier'
(O.E.D. 2), with quibble on
'courting, wooing'? (O.E.D.
6); (cf. *A.Y.L.* 3. 2. 340);
3. 3. 34

COUSIN, used in full, or abbreviated Coz, *passim* in ord.
mod. sense; but can indicate
any 'collateral relative more
distant than a brother or
sister' (O.E.D.), and =
nephew at 1. 5. 65; 3. 1.
145, 149

COVER, (i) binding of a book.
Quibbling on law-French
feme couvert=married woman (O.E.D. 'feme'); 1.
3. 89; (ii) hood of vehicle; 1.
4. 63

COVERT, concealment, shelter;
1. 1. 124

CROSS (adj.), perverse; 4. 3. 5

CROSS (vb.), go counter to,
interfere with; 4. 5. 95; 5.
3. 20

CROTCHET, (*a*) a note in music,
(*b*) silly notion (same quibble in *Ado*, 2. 3. 55); 4. 5.
117

CROW, crowbar; 5. 2. 21; 5. 3.
120 S.D.

CROW-KEEPER, boy with bow
and arrows, employed to protect a cornfield from crows;
1. 4. 6

CRUSH, 'crack', drink, quaff;
1. 2. 83

CRY, (i) 'cry a match'=
'claim the match as mine;
claim the victory' (K.); 2.
4. 70; (ii) 'cry mercy'=
beg pardon; 4. 5. 137; (iii)
'cry on'=exclaim against;
3. 3. 101

CUNNING (adj.), skilful; 4. 2. 2

CUNNING (sb.), artfulness; 2. 2.
101

CURE (intrans.), be cured; 1. 2.
49

CURFEW BELL. Orig. bell rung
in evening to indicate time
when domestic fires were to
be extinguished or covered
over (Fr. 'couvre feu'); but
also, as here, a bell rung at
3 or 4 a.m. (v. O.E.D.
'curfew' 1c); 4. 4. 4

CURIOUS, carefully observant;
1. 4. 31

CYNTHIA, the moon personified
as a goddess; 3. 5. 20

DAINTY (sb.), fastidiousness;
hence 'make dainty'=be
chary or loth; 1. 5. 20

DANGER, harm, damage; 5.2.20

DARE, (*a*) show courage, (*b*)
challenge; 2. 4. 12

DATE, duration, term of existence; 1. 4. 3, 108; 5. 3. 229

DATELESS, without term, end-
less; 5. 3. 115

DEAR, (i) valuable; 1. 5. 47;
3. 1. 182; (ii) hard, grievous; 1. 5. 118; (iii) fond,
affectionate; 2. 2. 115; 2. 3.
57; 3. 3. 128; (iv) fortunate,
happy; 2. 2. 189; (v) '? rare,
unusual, or ? loving, kind'
(O.E.D.), or great ('empha-
sizing' word) (K.); 3. 3. 28;
(vi) important, momentous;
5. 2. 19; 5. 3. 32

DEATH-MARKED, marked out
by Fate for death; Prol. 9

DEBT (fig.), 'someone's debt'
=at someone's mercy. (Cf.
O.E.D. 'debt' 20; 'danger'
1); 1. 5. 118

DEFENCE, means of defence, arms or armour; 3. 3. 134

DEFY, (i) challenge a person or power to do the worst; 5. 1. 24; (ii) reject; 5. 3. 68

DEMESNES, (i) regions; 2. 1. 20; (ii) estates; 3. 5. 180

DENY, (i) refuse; 1. 1. 156; 1. 5. 20; (ii) disown; 2. 2. 34

DESCENT, source, origin; 5. 3. 218

DESPERATE, (i) violently reckless; 3. 3. 108; 5. 3. 117, 263; (ii) bold, rash; 3. 4. 12

DESPISED, (i) despicable, 1. 4. 110; 3. 2. 77; (ii) 'hateful' (Schmidt); 4. 5. 59

DEVISE, (i) contrive, arrange; 2. 4. 173; 5. 3. 240; (ii) imagine, conceive, guess; 3. 1. 68

DEW-DROPPING, 'rainy' (Schmidt); 1. 4. 103

DIAL, clock; 2. 4. 109

DIAN, Diana, Latin goddess, early identified with the Greek Artemis, virgin huntress, regarded as a symbol of chastity, celibacy; 1. 1. 208

DIDO, Queen of Carthage, who slew herself when Aeneas deserted her (Virgil, *Aeneid*, iv); 2. 4. 41

DIFFERENT, 'opposed, hostile', (K.); 1. 5. 90

DIGNIFIED, made worthy, ennobled; 2. 3. 22

DIGNITY, worthiness, nobility, social position, Prol. 1

DIGRESS, depart, deviate; 3. 3. 127

DIRE, DIREFUL, dreadful, horrible; 5. 3. 225, 247

DISCOVER, reveal, 2. 2. 106; 3. 1. 141

DISCOVERY, exploration, investigation; 1. 1. 149

DISCREET circumspect, 'sanely discriminating' (K.); 1. 1. 192

DISHCLOUT, dishcloth (freq. used in contemptuous comparison); 3. 5. 219

DISLIKE, displease; 2. 2. 61

DISMAL, (i) gloomy, dreadful, 'striking the mind with dismay' (Schmidt; cf. O.E.D. 4); 3. 2. 44; (ii) dreadful, horrifying; 4. 3. 19

DISPLANT, uproot; 3. 3. 60

DISPOSITION(s), (i) inclination; 1. 3. 66; (ii) mental constitution or temperament; 3. 3. 115

DISPUTE OF, discuss; 3. 3. 64

DISTANCE (in fencing), 'a definite interval of space to be observed between two combatants' (O.E.D. 5 b); 2. 4. 21

DISTEMPERATURE, mental disturbance; 2. 3. 40

DISTEMPERED, disordered, distracted; 2. 3. 33

DISTILLED, extracted; 4. 1. 94; 5. 3. 15

DIVINE (sb.), ecclesiastic; 3. 3. 50

DIVISION, (a) 'execution of a rapid melodic passage' (O.E.D. 7); (b) separation; 3. 5. 29

DO GOOD (to someone), benefit, assist (esp. with money); 3. 5. 194

DOCTRINE, instruction, lesson; 1. 1. 237

Doom (sb.), (i) judgement, sentence; 3. 3. 4, 8, 9, 60; (ii) 'general doom' = Day of Judgement; 3. 2. 67

Doom (vb.), adjudge; 3. 1. 133

Doomsday, last day of life; 3. 3. 9; 5. 3. 234

Doting, violently in love; 3. 3. 68

Doubt (sb.), hesitation; 4. 1. 87

Doubt (vb.), suspect; 5. 3. 44

Down, (i) abed; 3. 5. 66; 4. 5. 12; (ii) brought low in death (with quibble on (i)); 5. 3. 209

Drawer, tapster; 3. 1. 9

Drift, (i) meaning; 2. 3. 55; (ii) intention, or perhaps scheme (O.E.D. 5); 4. 1. 114

Drivel, (a) slaver, (b) talk nonsense; 2. 4. 89

Drum, drummer; 1. 4. 114

Dry-beat, thrash severely (properly, beat with blows which bruise but do not draw blood); 3. 1. 78; 4. 5. 122

Ducat, silver Ital. coin worth about 3s. 6d.; 5. 1. 59

Dull, heavy; 1. 4. 21; 2. 1. 2

Dump, tune (properly, melancholy tune); 4. 5. 105, 107

Dumps, low spirits; 4. 5. 126

Dwell on, stand on, be punctilious for; 2. 2. 88

Earth, body; 1. 2. 15; 3. 2. 59; (quibble on 'the earth', 'clay'), 2. 1. 2; 3. 3. 120

Effect, fulfilment; 1. 5. 106

Ell, 45 inches; 2. 4. 83

Endart, shoot as if a dart; 1. 3. 99

Engross, gain exclusive possession; 5. 3. 115

Enpierce, pierce through; 1. 4. 19

Entertain, conceive (the idea of); 3. 1. 170

Envious, (i) malicious; 1. 1. 150; 3. 1. 167; 3. 2. 40; 3. 5. 7; (ii) jealous; 2. 2. 4, 7

Estate, situation, condition; 3. 3. 64

Ethiop, Ethiopian, with black skin; 1. 5. 46

Excuse, defer with excuses (cf. O.E.D. 3b); 2. 5. 34

Exhale, draw forth (v. *meteor*); 3. 5. 13

Expire, bring to an end; 1. 4. 109

Extremes, terrible (utmost) difficulties; 4. 1. 62

Extremity, desperate condition; 1. 3. 103

Fair (adj.), (the freq. sense of 'beautiful' occurs *passim*); (i) bright, broad; 1. 1. 138 (O.E.D. 12b); (ii) used conventionally in polite address; 1. 1. 206 ('fair coz'); 2. 2. 98; 2. 4. 106; (iii) (in 'fair mark') (a) beautiful, (b) plainly to be seen, obvious (cf. O.E.D. 17); 1. 1. 206; (iv) favourable; 1. 2. 19; (v) fine, excellent; 1. 2. 74; 3. 5. 180; (vi) peaceable, agreeable; 1. 5. 73; (vii) civil, courteous; 2. 1. 11; (viii) decent, clean; 1. 1. 220; 2. 1. 28; (ix) benign; 2. 3. 19

Fair (adv.), courteously; 3. 1. 152

GLOSSARY

FAIR (sb.), (i) beautiful woman; 1. 1. 235; 2 Prol. 3; (ii) (a) fair complexion, (b) (i); 1. 1. 230; (iii) beauty; 1. 3. 91

FAIRLY, completely; 2. 4. 45

FALL BACKWARD, sc. in embrace of husband; 1. 3. 43, 57

FANTASTICO, ridiculous person; 2. 4. 29

FANTASY, imagination; 1. 4. 98

FASHION-MONGER, one who studies and follows the latest fashions; 2. 4. 33

FAST, sound asleep; 4. 5. 1

FATAL, (i) fraught with evil destiny; Prol. 5; (ii) producing death, destruction; 3. 1. 142, 165; 5. 1. 65

FAULT, lack, want; 2. 4. 118

FAY, faith; 1. 5. 126

FEARFUL, (i) dreadful, terrible; 1 Prol. 9; 1. 4. 108; 2 Prol. 8; 4. 3. 32; (ii) timorous, apprehensive; 3. 3. 1; 3. 5. 3; 5. 2. 16

FEARFULLY, dreadfully, terribly; 5. 3. 133

FEELING, deeply felt; 3. 5. 74

FEE-SIMPLE, absolute possession (lit. estate in perpetual possession of owner and his descendants); 3. 1. 31, 33

FETTLE, make ready; 3. 5. 153

FIELD, place of combat; 3. 1. 57

FIELD-BED, (a) camp-bed, (b) resting-place on open ground; 2. 1. 40

FILM, 'fine thread or filament, as of gossamer, silk, etc.' (O.E.D.); 1. 4. 66

FIND (abs.), discover (game) in hunting (O.E.D. 9b); 2. 4. 126

FISH, female flesh (lit. 'harlot'; cf. 'fishmonger', *Ham.* 2. 2. 174, n.); 1. 1. 30

FLASK, powder-horn, carried on the belt not far from the 'match' (a piece of slow-burning rope, used to ignite the powder in the lock of the match-lock musket); 3. 3. 132

FLATTERING, (adj. and adv.), pleasing, pleasingly (with idea of deception); 2. 2. 141; 5. 1. 1

FLECKED. (a) dappled with bright spots (O.E.D. 3); (b) flushed or blotchy (O.E.D. 2 cites Burton, *Anat. Mel.* 'red and flect ...as if they had been at a Mayor's feast'); 2. 3. 3

FLEER, grin contemptuously; 1. 5. 57

FLESH (vb.), to get oneself in flesh = to grow plump (O.E.D. 3); 5. 1. 84

FLIRT-GILL, giddy or loose woman; ('Gill' short for Gillian); 2. 4. 148

FLOW, abound; 2. 4. 39

FOND, (i) unwisely affectionate; 2. 2. 98; (ii) foolish; 3. 3. 53; (iii) combining i and ii; 4. 5. 82

FOOL, (i) term of endearment; 1. 3. 32, 49; (ii) dupe; 3. 1. 135

FOOL'S PARADISE, state of happiness based on illusion; 2. 4. 159

FOOT IT, dance; 1. 5. 27

FOR. Unusual senses: (i) 'for

FOR (*cont.*):
you'=ready to join issue
with you; 1. 1. 53; (ii) as
concerns; 3. 1. 98

FORFEIT, penalty; (here) loss
of life; 1. 4. 111

FORM, (i) formal manners, conventional etiquette; 2. 2.
88; (with quibble on 'form'
=bench) 2. 4. 34; (ii) likeness; 5. 3. 246

FRANK, generous, bountiful; 2.
2. 131

FRENCH SLOP or 'trunk hose',
short loose hanging breeches;
2. 4. 44

FRIEND, (i) lover, paramour (cf.
Meas. 1. 4. 29); 3. 5. 43,
77; (ii) kinsman; 3. 3. 151;
3. 5. 75

GALL, (i) bitter poison; 1. 1.
193; (ii) bitterness; 1. 5. 92

GAPE (vb.), long. Commonly
used with 'heir'; 2. Prol. 2

GEAR, orig.=clothes, (hence)
stuff, goings-on, etc.; 2. 4.
98, 5. 1. 60

GENERAL, universal; 3. 2. 67

GENTLE, used before proper
name or title as complimen-
tary term in polite address;
1. 2. 16; 1. 4. 13; 1. 5. 65;
2. 2. 93; 3. 1. 83; 4. 3. 1; 5.
3. 59;

GHOSTLY, spiritual; 2. 2. 188;
2. 3. 45; 2. 6. 21; 3. 3. 50

GIVE YOU THE. . ., call you. . .;
(cf. *Macb.* 1. 3. 119); 4. 5.
114. 115

GLEEK, gibe; 'give someone
the gleek'=mock him, make
a jest at his expense; 4. 5.
113

GLOOMING, dark, dismal; 5. 3.
305

GO, 'go to' = come, come!
(expressing 'disapprobation,
remonstrance, protest, or de-
risive incredulity', O.E.D.);
1. 5. 77, 78, 82; 2. 4. 178

GO TO THE WALL, 'give way,
succumb in a conflict or
struggle' (O.E.D. wall, 13);
1. 1. 14

GOD-DEN or GOOD-DEN, good
evening, good afternoon; 1.
2. 57; 2. 4. 107; 3. 1. 37

GOD GI' GOD-DEN, GODIGO-
DEN, GOD YE GOOD-DEN,=
God give you good evening;
1. 2. 58; 2. 4. 106; 3. 5.
172

GOD'S BREAD! Oath=by the
bread consecrated for Com-
munion; 3. 5. 176

GOD SAVE THE MARK. Prob.
orig. a formula to avert an
evil omen, hence used by
way of apology when some-
thing horrible etc. has been
mentioned (O.D.P.); 3. 2.
53

GOD YE GOODMORROW, God
give you good morning; 2. 4.
105

GOLDEN, (i) fine, excellent; 1.
3. 93; (ii) happy, refreshing;
2. 3. 38

GOOD-DEN, see *God-den*

GOOD HEART, (i) familiar or
affectionate form of ad-
dress; 1. 1. 183; (ii) oath,=
'by God's heart'; 2. 4. 167

GOODMAN, 'prefixed to names
of persons under the rank of
gentleman, esp. yeomen or
farmers' (O.E.D. 3 b), hence
applied here ironically to

a presumptuous young gentleman; 1.5. 77.

GOOD MORROW, (a) good morning; 1. 1. 159; 2. 3. 31; 2. 4. 46; (b) good-bye; 2. 3. 34

GORE BLOOD, clotted blood; 3. 2. 56

GOSSAMERS, threads of spiderweb; 2. 6. 18

GOSSIP, (i) familiar friend; 2. 1. 11; (ii) tattling woman crony; 3. 5. 171, 174

GOWN, dressing-gown; 1. 1. 73 S.D.

GRACE, (i) favour; 1.3.60; 2. 3. 86; (ii) beneficent virtue, efficacy; 2. 3. 15; (iii) divine grace; 2. 3. 28

GRAVE, (i) dignified; 1. 1. 92; (ii) (a) solemn, (b) in, or ready for, a grave; 3. 1. 97

GRAVITY, weighty speech, serious talking (used ironically); 3. 5. 174

GREAT CHAMBER. Corresponded to modern drawing-room; 1. 5. 13

GREEN, pale, sickly; 2. 2. 8

GREEN IN EARTH, freshly laid in the grave; 4. 3. 42

GREEN-SICKNESS (as adj.), afflicted with the green-sickness (v. note on 2. 2. 8), hence miserably pallid; 3. 5. 156

GRIEVANCE, (i) trouble, distress; 1. 1. 156; (ii) cause of complaint; 3. 1. 51

GRIPING, agonizing; 4. 5. 125

GROUND, (i) earth; 5. 3. 179; (ii) cause; 5. 3. 180

GRUDGE, ill-will; Prol. 3

GYVES, fetters; 2. 2. 179

HA, 'An inarticulate vowel-sound, expressing hesitation or interruption in speech' (O.E.D. 3); 3. 3. 12; 3. 4. 19

HAI (It. lit.=you have it), home-thrust in fencing; 2. 4. 26

HAIR, 'against the hair'= contrary to my inclination (with quibble on pubic hair); 2. 4. 93

HALL, 'a hall!'=cry to make room (for a dance or the like); 1. 5. 27

HAND, 'at my hand'=from me; 3. 3. 5

HAP, fortune; 3. 3. 171; 'dear hap'=good fortune; 2.2.189

HAPPY, opportune; 5. 3. 169; 'in happy time', phrase expressing pleasure at good fortune, here = 'à propos' (Schmidt, On.), or 'how opportune, fortunate!' (spoken with concealed irony); 3. 5. 111

HARE, (a) the animal, (b) prostitute; 2. 4. 127–132

HARLOTRY, good-for-nothing wench; 4. 2. 14

HASTY, quick-acting; 5. 1. 64

HAVE AT THEE (YOU), 'App. 1st pers. plural, but often singular in sense, announcing the speaker's intent to get at or attack' (O.E.D. have, 20); 1. 1. 71; 4. 5. 122; 5. 3. 70

HAVE IT, have been given a home-thrust (cf. HAI); 3. 1. 106

HEAD, source of a river; fig. (as here) origin; 5. 3. 218

HEARTLESS, spiritless, cowardly; 1. 1. 65

HEARTS, good fellows; 1. 5. 86, 88

HEAVINESS, sadness; 3. 4. 11;
3. 5. 108

HEAVY, (i) sad; 2. 2. 157;
(in quibbling contrast to
'light') 1. 1. 136, 177; 1.
4. 12; (ii) grievous; 3. 3.
157; 4. 5. 18; (with quibble
on heavy in weight) 1. 1.
185; 3. 3. 60; (iii) sluggish;
2. 5. 17

HELEN. In classical mythology
the most beautiful woman of
her time, wife of the Greek
Menelaus, seduced and carried off to Troy by the
Trojan Paris, whence arose
the Graeco-Trojan War; 2.
4. 42

HERO. In classical mythology
a beautiful priestess of the
goddess Aphrodite at Sestos
on the European side of the
Hellespont; she was loved by
Leander who belonged to
Abydos on the opposite
shore; he was wont to
swim to her at night,
guided by a torch held up
by her; one stormy night he
was drowned, and she threw
herself into the water; 2. 4.
42

HIGH-LONE, 'quite alone, without support' (O.E.D.). Prov.
expr. (Tilley, G 157); 1. 3.
37

HILDING, jade, baggage
(O.E.D. 2 b); 2. 4. 42; 3. 5.
168

HIND, menial; 1. 1. 65

HIT (sb.), striking of target
with arrow, hence fig. guess;
1. 1. 207.

HIT (vb.), (i) strike; 3. 1.
167; (ii) (a) strike with

arrow, (b) copulate with
(v. mark); 1. 1. 207; 2. 1.
33; (iii) 'hit it'=strike
target with arrow, hence
fig. guess; 2. 3. 41; 2. 4.
55

HOAR (adj.), (a) mouldy, (b)
grey- or white-haired with
age (with quibble on
'whore'); 2. 4. 128, 129,
130, 132

HOAR (vb.), (a) become
mouldy, (b) become grey- or
white-haired (with quibble
on 'whore'); 2. 4. 134

HOLIDAME. Corruption of
'halidom'=holiness, (hence)
relics upon which oaths
were sworn, (hence) the
formula 'by my halidome'
which by association with
'dame' became 'holidame',
so that the phrase was
popularly taken as 'by our
Lady' (v. O.E.D.); 1. 3. 44

HOLP, helped, remedied; 1. 2.
48

HOMELY, simple, straightforward; 2. 3. 55

HONEST, (i) honourable; 1. 5.
124; 2. 5. 55, 60; 3. 2. 62;
(ii) respectable, seemly; 2.
1. 28; (iii) worthy; 2. 5. 78;
4. 5. 97

HOOD (? sb.); v. note; 4. 4. 13

HOOD (vb.), blindfold a hawk;
3. 2. 14

HOODWINKED, blindfolded; 1.
4. 4

HOT, (i) eager; 2. 5. 62; (ii)
quick-tempered; 3. 5. 175;
(iii) violent, raging; 3. 1.
159

HOUSE (fig.), sheath; 5. 3. 203

HUMOROUS, (a) moist, damp,

(b) whimsical, capricious, moody; 2. 1. 31

HUMOUR, (i) inclination; 1. 1. 128, 140; (ii) caprice; 2. 1. 7; (iii) morbid fluid; 4. 1. 96

HUNT'S-UP. Orig. a song entitled 'The Hunt Is Up', used to awaken huntsmen; hence, an early morning song, esp. one for the newly married (cf. Cotgrave, 'Resveil'); 3. 5. 34

HURDLE, 'a kind of frame or sledge on which traitors used to be drawn through the streets to execution' (O.E.D. 1c); 3. 5. 155

IDLE (adj.), foolish, silly; 1. 4. 97

IDLE (vb.), move lazily or uselessly; 2. 6. 19

ILL-BESEEMING, (i) inappropriate; 1. 5. 74; (ii) ill-sorted; hence, monstrous; 3. 3. 113

ILL-DIVINING, prophesying evil; 3. 5. 54

IMAGINED, in thought, inner; 2. 6. 28

IMPORT (sb.), importance; 5. 2. 19

IMPORT (vb.), signify; 5. 1. 28

IMPORTUNE, interrogate urgently and persistently; 1. 1. 144

IN, under, liable to; 1. 2. 2

INDITE, intentional blunder for 'invite' —satirizing the unintentional blunder of the previous speaker (cf. 2 Hen. IV, 2. 1. 27); 2. 4. 124

INHERIT, receive, enjoy the possession of; 1. 2. 30

IRON WIT, dull or stupid wit; (cf. R. III. G.); 4. 5. 123

JACK, (i) lad, chap; 3. 1. 11; (ii) rude fellow, knave; 2. 4. 147; 4. 5. 143

JAUNCE (sb. and vb.), prance. Cf. R. II. 5. 5. 94, and D.D. 'jance' (Suss. dial.) =weary or tiring journey. K. quotes 'jaunce' from Seneca's Ten Tragedies; 2. 5. 26, 52

JEALOUS, suspicious; 5. 3. 33; 'jealous hood' (v. note); 4. 4. 13

JOINED-STOOL, 'stool made by a joiner, as distinguished from one of more clumsy workmanship' (O.E.D.); 1. 5. 6

JUST (adv.), exactly; 3. 2. 78; 3. 3. 86

JUSTLY, (a) exactly, (b) honourably; 3. 2. 78

KEEP, (a) inhabit, (b) guard (fig. from notice, observation); 3. 2. 74

KINDLY, aptly, exactly. (Cf. as adj. in 1 H. VI, 3. 1. 131); 2. 4. 55

KNAVE, (i) servant; 1. 5. 28; (ii) rogue; 2. 4. 148, 150, 156; 4. 5. 142

LABEL, lit. a supplementary note or codicil to a legal document (O.E.D. 2), hence (here), such a note cancelling 'another deed'; 4. 1. 57

LACE, 'mark as with (gold or silver) lace or embroidery; diversify with streaks of colour' (O.E.D. 6); 3. 5. 8

LADY, (i) wife; 3. 3. 98; (ii)
'God's Lady'=the Virgin
Mary; 2. 5. 61; (iii) 'By
'r Lady', oath=by the
Virgin Mary; 1. 5. 34

LADY-BIRD, (a) term of endearment, 'sweetheart', (b)
light o' love (cf. O.E.D. 2,
quot. 1700, and *Dict. Slang*);
1. 3. 3

LAMB, term of endearment,
'pet'; 1. 3. 3; 4. 5. 2

LAMMAS EVE, 31 July (day
before Lammas-tide); 1. 3.
18, 22

LANGUISH, sickness, suffering;
1. 2. 49

LANTHORN, (i) a lighthouse
(O.E.D. 3); or windowed
turret on the roof of a
(college) hall (O.E.D. 4);
5. 3. 84; (ii) lantern; 5. 3.
120 S.D.

LARGE, (a) lengthy, (b) licen-
tious, gross, (c) (indelicately)
large in size; 2. 4. 94

LAURA, lady to whom Petr-
arch (q.v.) wrote his love-
sonnets; 2. 4. 39

LAY, (a) prevent (spirit) from
'walking', cause (spirit) to
disappear, (b) (indelicately)
cause (erection) to subside;
2. 1. 26

LAY HAND ON HEART, ref. to
'gesture used in protesting
the reality of the feeling expressed' (Deighton); 3. 5.190

LEARN, teach; 1. 4. 93; 3. 2.
12; 4. 2. 17

LEAVE, 'give leave'= kindly
leave (us/me) alone, undis-
turbed; 1. 3. 8; 2. 5. 25;
'by your leaves'= with your
permission; 2. 6. 36

LENTEN PIE, properly pie containing no meat and thus
suitable for consumption in
Lent; here perhaps meat pie
consumed bit by bit sur-
reptitiously in Lent and
therefore mouldy before it
is all eaten; 2. 4. 127–8

LETTERS, plur. with sing.
sense; 4. 1. 114, 124; 5. 1.
13, 31

LEVEL, 'aim, line of aim'
(K.); 3. 3. 103

LIGHT, (i) active, nimble, swift;
2. 2. 66; (with quibble on
opposite of 'heavy') 1. 4.
20; (ii) immodest; 2. 2. 99;
(with quibble on opposite of
dark) 2. 2. 105; (iii) trivial,
worthless (with quibble on
opposite of 'heavy'); 2. 6. 20

LIGHTLY, joyfully; 5. 1. 3

LIGHTNESS, (a) light weight,
(b) levity, frivolity; 1. 1.
177

LIST, please, wish; 1. 1. 41

LIVING, property, estate; 4. 5.
40

LODGING, night's resting-place
(O.E.D. 3); 3. 2. 2

LOLL, stick out (sc. (a) the
tongue, (b) the 'bauble',
q.v.); 2. 4. 90

LONG SWORD, old fashioned
two-hand sword (cf. *Wives*,
2. 1. 203; *Sh. Engl.* ii. 394,
with picture on p. 393); 1.
1. 74

LOST, beside oneself, (here)
love-lorn; 1. 1. 196

LURE (vb.), falconry term; used
of a falconer recalling a
hawk from flight by holding
up to its sight a 'lure', i.e.
a kind of leather frame,

decked with feathers and garnished with pieces of meat, which the falconer carried in his hand (v. *Shrew*. G.); 2. 2. 159

LUSTY, vigorous, lively, merry; 1. 2. 26; 1. 4. 113; 2. 4. 146

MAKE AGAINST, provide evidence against; 5. 3. 225

MAMMET, doll, puppet; 3. 5. 184

MANAGE (sb.), conduct, 'course, rise and progress' (K.); 3. 1. 142

MANAGE (vb.), handle, wield; 1. 1. 68

MANDRAKE, poisonous plant, with forked root which was thought to resemble the human form; the plant was believed to utter shrieks when pulled from the ground, which shrieks were fatal to the hearer or drove him mad; 4. 3. 47

MANNERLY, seemly, decent; 1. 5. 98

MARCHPANE, marzipan, kind of sweetmeat; 1. 5. 8

MARGENT, (lit.) margin, (hence) marginal note, interpretation (cf. *Ham*. G.); 1. 3. 87

MARK (sb.), (i) target (with indelicate *double entendre*); 1. 1. 206; 2. 1. 33; (ii) 'God save the mark', phrase used by way of apology for mentioning something disagreeable, prob. orig. a formula to avert an evil omen (cf. O.E.D. 'mark', sb.¹, 18); 3. 2. 53

MARK (vb.), 'mark to', designate for; 1. 3. 60

MARRIED, harmoniously blended; 1. 3. 84

MARRY (interj.), to be sure, indeed (orig. name of Virgin Mary used as oath); 1. 1. 37 and *passim*

MARRY COME UP, An exp. of 'indignant or amused surprise or contempt="hoity-toity"' (O.E.D.). Cf. Tilley, C 740; 2. 5. 62

MARTYR, afflict with grievous pain; 4. 5. 59

MASQUE (sb.), ball attended by masked visitors; 1. 4. 48; 1. 5. 34

MASQUE (vb.), attend ball or assembly wearing masks; 1. 5. 38

MASS, mild oath, 'by the Mass' (church service); 4. 4. 19

MASTERLESS, without its owner (cf. *F. Q.* 1, vii. 19, 'His silver shield, now idle, maisterlesse'); 5. 3. 142

MATCHED, (i) compared; 2 Prol. 4; (ii) married; 3. 5. 178

MAW, stomach, 5. 3. 45

MEAGRE, thin, starved; 5. 1. 40

MEAN, means, method. With quibble; 3. 3. 46

MEASURE (sb.), (i) dance; 1. 5. 50; (ii) (a) dance, (b) standard; 1. 4. 10

MEASURE (vb.), (i) estimate; 1. 1. 125; (ii) (a) estimate, (b) mete out, (c) dance; 1. 4. 10

MEAT, (i) food (not flesh); 3. 1. 22; see also *baked*

MEAT (*cont.*):
  meats; (ii) food (flesh);
3. 1. 106; (iii) (*a*) food
(flesh), (*b*) flesh of whore,
and hence whore; 2. 4. 131

MEDICINE, the physician's art;
2. 3. 24

MEDLAR, a fruit 'with a
large cup-shaped "eye" between the persistent calyx-
lobes. It is eaten when
decayed to a soft pulpy
state' (O.E.D.); here (*a*)
with quibble on 'meddle'=
to have sexual intercourse
(O.E.D. 5), and (*b*) by allusion to its obscene synonym (v. note); 2. 1. 34, 36

METEOR. Supposedly engen-
dered from vapours drawn up
by the sun and then ignited;
3. 5. 13

MEW (vb.), shut up (as hawks
were shut in their 'mews'
or cages); 3. 4. 11

MICKLE, great; 2. 3. 15

MIND, pay attention to, brood
over; 4. 1. 13

MINION, hussy; 3. 5. 151

MINISTER, provide; 4. 3. 25

MISADVENTURED, unfortunate;
Prol. 7

MISSHAPEN, ill-directed
(O.E.D., 4 < Johnson's
Dict. Cf. *Ham.* 5. 2. 10,
'shapes our ends'; *Lear*, 1.
1. 190, 'shape his course');
3. 3. 131

MISTA'EN, gone astray (v.
O.E.D. 'mistake' vb. 3);
5. 3. 203

MISTEMPERED, tempered for
an evil purpose (with quibble
on sense of 'bad-tempered,
angered'); 1. 1. 86

MODERN, ordinary, common-
place; 3. 2. 120

MONUMENT, burial vault; 3.
5. 201; 5. 1. 18; 5. 2. 23;
5. 3. head S.D., 127, 193,
274

MOOD, anger; 3. 1. 12

MOODY, angry; 3. 1. 12, 13

MOUSE-HUNT, pursuer of women by night (v. note); 4.
4. 11

MOVE, (i) make angry; 1. 1.
6, 87; 3. 1. 13; 4. 5. 95;
(ii) impel; 1. 1. 7, 10; 3. 1.
12; 4. 3. 4; (iii) (*a*) (i), (*b*)
(ii); 1. 1. 8, 11; (iv) cause,
call forth; 1. 3. 98; 3. 2.
120; (v) take the initiative;
1. 5. 105; (vi) make a pro-
position to; 3. 4. 2

MUCH, (i) approximately; 1.
3. 73; (ii) 'much in years'=
advanced in age; 3. 5. 46

MUFFLE, (i) blindfold; 1. 1.
170; (ii) cover up, conceal;
5. 3. 21

MUTINY, strife, discord; Prol.
3; 1. 5. 80

NATIVE, (i) original, where you
were produced; 3. 2. 102;
(ii) natural, normal; 4. 1. 97

NATURAL (adj.), kindly; 2. 3.
12

NATURAL (sb.), congenital
idiot; 2. 4. 89

NATURE, natural affection (v.
Ham. G.); 4. 5. 82

NAUGHT, wicked; 3. 2. 87

NAY (in asseveration), indeed;
1. 3. 30, 79; 3. 1. 15; (in
protest), now then; 2. 5. 28

NEAR, (*a*) near the bull's-eye,
(*b*) accurately; 1. 1. 204; see
also *come near*

Needly, of necessity; 3. 2. 117

Neighbour, neighbouring; 2. 6. 27

Nice, trivial; 3. 1. 153; 5. 2. 18

Nïess, or 'nyas', a young hawk in the aerie (<Fr. niais = nestling, an innocent girl (v. note)); 2. 2. 167

Nightly, at night; 4. 1. 81

Note (sb.), marginal comment (v. note); 1. 1. 234

Note (vb.), (a) furnish with notes, (b) find fault with (O.E.D. 7); 4. 5. 119

Numbers, verse; 2. 4. 39

O (as sb.), lament (v. also *circle*); 3. 3. 91

Occupy, (a) dwell upon, (b) have to do with sexually (cf. *2 Hen. IV.* 2. 4. 143 and G.); 2. 4. 97

O'erperch, fly over; 2. 2. 66

Office, duty; 4. 5. 85; 5. 1. 23

Old, (i) vague epithet implying familiarity; 1. 4. 60; (ii) inveterate, hardened (cf. O.E.D. 5; with quibble on 'aged'); 3. 3. 94

Omit, miss, neglect; 3. 5. 49

Once, at any time, ever; 1. 3. 62; 'at once' = once for all (note by J. C. Maxwell in *M.L.R.* xlix, p. 464); 3. 2. 57

Open-arse, medlar (v. note); 2. 1. 38

Oppression, (i) distress, affliction; 1. 1. 183; 5. 1. 70; (ii) pressure, burden; 1. 4. 24

Orison, prayer; 4. 3. 3

Ornaments, equipment, attire; 1. 1. 92; 4. 2. 34

Osier, made of willow twigs; 2. 3. 7

Out, (i) at an end, expired; 1. 4. 3; (ii) exclamation expressing reproach, indignation, or anger; 3. 5. 156; (with 'upon you') 2. 4. 110; (with 'on her') 3. 5. 168; (iii) exclamation of lament; 4. 5. 25

Outrage, (i) disgraceful tumult; 3. 1. 86; (ii) passionate outcry; 5. 3. 216

Overwhelming, overhanging; 5. 1. 39

Owe, possess, 2. 2. 46

Pains, trouble, labour; 2. 4. 176, 185

Palmer, 'pilgrim who had returned from the Holy Land, in sign of which he carried a palm-branch or palm-leaf; also, an itinerant monk who travelled from shrine to shrine, under a perpetual vow of poverty; often simply an equivalent of *pilgrim*' (O.E.D.), with quibble on the sense of one who clasps another's palm with his own; 1. 5. 100, 101

Pardon, to give one his congé (cf. *Gent.* 3. 2. 98); 3. 5. 187

Part (sb.), (i) side (in a quarrel); 1. 1. 113; 'on part and part' = some on one side, some on the other; 1. 1. 113; (ii) (plur.) abilities, endowments, personal qualities; 3. 3. 2;

PART (cont.):
3. 5. 181; (iii) share; 4. 5. 69, 70; 'had part in'= shared; 4. 5. 67

PARTIES OF SUSPICION, persons suspected (of crime); 5. 3. 222

PARTISAN, spear with broad head (v. *Ham*. G.); 1. 1. 71 S.D.; 93

PASSADO, It. thrust in fencing, with one foot forward; 2. 4. 25; 3. 1. 84

PASSAGE, course; Prol. 9

PASSION, 'passionate speech or outburst' (O.E.D. 6d); 2. 2. 104

PASSING, pre-eminently; 1. 1. 233, 235

PASTRY, place where pastry is made, 4. 4. 2

PEEVISH, perverse, obstinate; 4. 2. 14

PENCIL, paintbrush; 1. 2. 41

PENNYWORTHS, allowances (here, of sleep); 4. 5. 4

PENSIVE, sorrowful; 4. 1. 39

PENTECOST, Whitsuntide; 1. 5. 37

PEPPER (vb.), 'give (one) his death-blow, "do for"' (O.E.D. 5b), make an end of; 3. 1. 98

PETRARCH, 14th cent. Ital. poet who wrote famous love-sonnets; 2. 4. 39

PHAËTON, in Gk. mythology, son of the sun-god Phoebus; he begged, and was allowed, to drive his father's sun-chariot on one occasion, but he drove it too near the earth, and Zeus, chief of the gods, slew him with a thunder-bolt to save the world from conflagration; 3. 2. 3

PILCHER. App. an extension of 'pilch'= an 'outer garment of skin or leather', here fig. (contemptuous) = scabbard (O.E.D.); 3. 1. 79

PIN, stud in centre of the archer's target; 2. 4. 15

PINK, acme, perfect example (with quibble on (a) name of flower and (b) 'pink'= rapier-thrust); 2. 4. 57

PIPE, 'put up one's pipes'= cease from action, speaking, etc., desist, 'shut up' (O.E.D. 1e); 4. 5. 96

PITCH, height (a falcon's 'pitch' is the height to which it soars before swooping down on its prey); 1. 4. 21

POISE, weigh; 1. 2. 98

POOR JOHN, salted and dried hake, 'a type of poor fare' (O.E.D.), applied fig. to a person; 1. 1. 31

POPERIN PEAR, variety of pear named from Poperinghe, a town in West Flanders (with an indelicate quibble); 2. 1. 38

PORTENTOUS, foreboding misfortune, of evil omen; 1. 1. 140

PORTLY, dignified; 1. 5. 66

POST, (i) 'take post'=start out with 'post horses' (q.v.); 5. 1. 21; (ii) 'in post'=in haste by means of post horses 5. 3. 273

POST HORSES, horses for rapid travel, available for hire at post-houses or inns; a long journey would involve the use of post horses in relays; 5. 1. 26

Pox, 'the pox of'=a plague on; 2. 4. 28

Practise, contrive, plot; 3. 5. 209

Prating, idly chattering; 2. 4. 193

Presence, (i) aspect, demeanour; 1. 5. 73; (ii) presence-chamber, room of state; 5. 3. 86

Present, immediate; 4. 1. 61; 5. 1. 51

Presently, immediately; 4. 1. 54; 5. 1. 21

Pretty, not inconsiderable; 1. 3. 11

Prevail, avail, have effect; 3. 3. 61

Prick (sb.), (a) point on clock face, (b) penis; 2. 4. 109

Prick (vb.), (i) (a) torment, grieve (O.E.D. 2), (b) stimulate, excite (O.E.D. 10); 1. 4. 28; (ii) remove by pricking with needle; 1. 4. 69

Pricking, (a) hurting, (b) copulation; 1. 4. 28

Pride, splendour; 1. 2. 10; (with quibble on 'pride'=sexual desire); 1. 3. 90

Princox, saucy youngster; 1. 5. 86

Procure, (i) cause; 2. 2. 145; bring; 3. 5. 67

Prodigious, monstrous, deformed, ill-omened; 1. 5. 140

Profaner, one who puts something to an unworthy use; 1. 1. 81

Promise, assure; 3. 4. 6

Proof (sb.), (i) 'in proof'=by the test of experience; 1. 1. 169; (ii) proved or tested armour; 1. 1. 209

Proof (adj.), invulnerable; 2. 2. 73

Propagate, augment (cf. *Tim.* 1. 1. 67); 1. 1. 186

Proper, handsome; 2. 4. 197

Proportion, rhythm; 2. 4. 21

Proportioned, formed, shaped; 3. 5. 182

Prorogue, postpone; 2. 2. 78; 4. 1. 48

Proud, elated, gratified; 3. 5. 143

Proverbed, supplied with a proverb; 1. 4. 37

Puling, whimpering; 3. 5. 183

Pump, light shoe; 2. 4. 60, 62

Punto reverso, (Ital.) backhanded thrust in fencing (lit. sword-point reversed); 2. 4. 25–6

Purblind, quite blind (cf. *L.L.L.* 3. 1. 178); 2. 1. 12

Purchase out, buy off, buy immunity for; 3. 1. 192

Purge, purify; 1. 1. 190

Question, converse, talk; 5. 3. 158

Quit; requite; 2. 4. 185

Quote, notice, observe; 1. 4. 31

Rage, frenzy, madness; 4. 3. 53

Rearward, rearguard; (fig.) 'with a rearward'=as a subsequent event (with poss. quibble on 'rearword'— v. note); 3. 2. 121

Reason of, discuss; 3. 1. 51

Rebeck, early kind of fiddle; used as personal name; 4. 5. 132

RECEPTACLE, sepulchre (cf. *Titus*, G.); 4. 3. 39

RECKONING, estimation, repute; 1. 2. 4; (with quibble on 'counting, enumeration'); 1. 2. 33

RECLAIM, reduce to obedience; 4. 2. 47

REEKY, 'that emits vapour; steamy; full of rank moisture' (O.E.D. 1a); 4. 1. 83

REFLEX, reflection; 3. 5. 20

RESIGN, submit oneself; 3. 2. 59

RESPECTIVE, 'discriminating, partial' (O.E.D. 2b), having respect to who a person is; 3. 1. 122

REST, (i) 'rest you merry'= God keep you happy; 1. 2. 63, 84; (ii) 'set up one's rest'=properly, in card game of primero, stake one's all; hence fig. be firmly determined; 4. 5. 6 (with quibble on 'rest'=stake); 5. 3. 110

RETORT (of a blow), return; 3. 1. 163

ROOD, cross on which Christ was crucified; 1. 3. 37

ROPERY, 'trickery, knavery' (O.E.D.), '(here) "rascally talk"' (K.); [Q1 'rope-ripe'=fit for the gallows]; 2. 4. 141

ROSEMARY. Used at both weddings and funerals as a symbol of remembrance; 2. 4. 199, 205; 4. 5. 79

RUDE, (i) violent, disorderly; 1. 4. 26; 3. 1. 188; (ii) rough, coarse; 1. 5. 51; (iii) ungoverned, unrestrained;

2. 3. 28; (iv) churlish, boorish, barbarous; 3. 3. 24

RUNAGATE, vagabond; 3. 5. 89

RUSH ASIDE, force out of place (O.E.D. v²); 3. 3. 26

SADLY, seriously; 1. 1. 200

SADNESS, seriousness, earnest (with quibble on 'sorrow'); 1. 1. 198, 201, 203

SAINT, adored one, mistress (cf. p. xx, Introd. *1 H. VI*); 1. 1. 213; 1. 5. 101; 2. 2. 55

SAUCY, insolent, impudent. A stronger term than in the mod. sense; 1. 5. 83; 2. 4. 140

SAVE-YOUR-REVERENCE. Orig. an apology for introducing an offensive word or expr. Here a sb. used attributively= human dung (cf. O.E.D. 'sir-reverence', 2); 1. 4. 42

SCANT, scarcely; 1. 2. 102

SCAPE, escape; 3. 1. 3; 4. 1. 75

SCATHE, injure; 1. 5. 84

SCOPE, area, 'field'; 1. 2. 18

SEARCHER, 'a person appointed to view dead bodies and to make report upon the cause of death' (O.E.D. 2 e); 5. 2. 8

SEASON (vb.), (*a*) preserve (by salting), (*b*) give a flavour, relish, zest, to; 2. 3. 72

SECRET, reticent, secretive; 2. 4. 184

SENTENCE, pithy saying, maxim; 2. 3. 79

SENTENTIOUS, speaker's blunder for 'sentences' or 'sententias' (=Lat. *sententiae*), pointed, witty sayings; 2. 4. 204

SERVE GOD (v. note); 2. 5. 45

SET, (i) stationed, posted; 3. 3. 148, 167; (ii) valued; 5. 3. 301

SETTLED (of the blood), congealed or 'ceased to flow' (O.E.D. 'settle' 22b), or 'flown back to the heart' (cf. *R. III*, 1. 2. 59, n.; *Caes.* 2. 1. 289, n.); 4. 5. 26

SHAKE, (*a*) quake, (*b*) bestir oneself (v. O.E.D. 6 g); 1. 3. 34

SHANK, shin-bone; 4. 1. 83

SHARP (adj.), (i) pungent in taste; 2. 4. 80; (ii) hungry; 5. 1. 41

SHARP (sb.), shrill high note; 3. 5. 28

SHIELD, 'God shield'=God forbid; 4. 1. 41

SHRIFT, (i) confession; 1. 1. 158; 2. 4. 174; 2. 5. 66; 4. 2. 15; (ii) absolution; 2. 3. 56

SHRIVE, give absolution after confession; 2. 4. 176

SIEGE, fig. assault; 1. 1. 211; 5. 3. 237

SIMPLE (adj.), (i) foolish; 2. 5. 38; 3. 1. 33; (ii) plain, mere; 3. 2. 16

SIMPLE (sb.), medicinal herb (called 'simple' because used in the production of medicinal 'compounds'); 5. 1. 40

SIMPLENESS, foolishness; 3. 3. 78

SINGLENESS, (*a*) fact of being one, (*b*) simplicity, silliness (cf. *2 H. IV*, 1. 2. 180); 2. 4. 66

SINGLE-SOLED, (*a*) (of footwear) 'having a single thickness of material in the sole' (O.E.D.), (*b*) (fig., of persons, here of a jest) 'poor, mean, of little account or worth' (O.E.D.); 2. 4. 65

SINGULAR, unmatched, unique; 2. 4. 64, 65

SKAINS-MATES. Meaning uncertain; various conjectures, e.g. 'cut-throat companions' (Malone), 'sempstresses, a word not always used in the most honourable acceptation' (Douce), etc.; 2. 4. 149

SLIP, (*a*) counterfeit coin, (*b*) evasion; 2. 4. 48

SLOP, v. *French slop*; 2. 4. 44

SLUG-A-BED, one slow to arise (cf. *R. III*, G. 'slug'); 4. 5. 2

SMALL, thin, fine; 1. 4. 64

SMATTER, chatter; 3. 5. 171

SOFT (interj.), stay!, stop!, wait a minute!; 1. 1. 194; 2. 2. 2; 3. 4. 18; 3. 5. 141

SOLACE IN, be happy in; 4. 5. 47

SOLELY, absolutely; 2. 4. 63, 65

SOLEMN, pertaining to a ceremony (here the marriage ceremony), hence 'festive, joyful'; 4. 5. 88

SOLEMNITY, 'occasion of ceremony; observance or celebration of special importance' (O.E.D.); (i) ref. to Capulet's ball; 1. 5. 57, 63; (ii) ref. to the (projected) nuptials of Juliet and Paris; 4. 5. 61

SOON-SPEEDING, *either* of quick effect *or* rapidly fatal; 5. 1. 60

SORT, choose, select; 4. 2. 34; 'sort out', choose, select, contrive; 3. 5. 109

SOUND, (i) (a) utter, express, (b) measure the depth of; 3. 2. 126; (ii) make music; 4. 5. 134

SOUNDING, (i) measuring of depth, investigation (by others of his innermost feelings); 1. 1. 149; (ii) making music; 4. 5. 139

SOUNDLY, thoroughly; 3. 1. 107; (with quibble on 'in musical sounds'); 4. 5. 111

SOUNDPOST, 'small peg of wood fixed beneath the bridge of a violin or similar instrument, serving as a support for the belly and as a connecting part between this and the back' (O.E.D.); as a personal name; 4. 5. 135

SPARING, (a) refraining, (b) thrift; 1. 1. 217

SPED, dispatched, done for; 3. 1. 90

SPEED, 'be my speed'=be my assistance, prosper me; 5. 3. 121

SPENT, (i) (a) consumed, (b) worn out; 2. 4. 128, 134; (ii) shed; 3. 2. 130

SPINNER, spider; 1. 4. 62

SPITE (sb.), (i) contemptuous defiance; 1. 1. 77; 1. 5. 62; (ii) vexation; 2. 1. 27; (iii) injury; 4. 1. 31

SPITE (vb.), injure; 4. 5. 55

SPLEEN, fiery temper, impetuosity; 3. 1. 156

STAIR, ladder; 2. 4. 182

STAND, (i) (a) make a stand, fight, (b) stand still; 1. 1. 10, 11; (ii) (a) hold one's own, (b) stand in a row; 1. 2. 33; (iii) stand upright (with indelicate quibble);

1. 1. 28; 2. 1. 25; (iv) 'stand on'=attach importance to, insist on; 2. 3. 93; 2. 4. 33–4; (v) 'stand to'= maintain; 2. 4. 144; (vi) 'here stands'=herein consists; 3. 3. 166; (vii) 'stand aloof'=keep away, withdraw to a distance (cf. *Merch.* 3. 2. 42; O.E.D. 3); 5. 3. 1, 26

STAR-CROSSED, thwarted by adverse influence of the stars; Prol. 6

STATE, (i) pomp, splendid array; 1. 4. 70; (ii) high rank; 3. 3. 34; (iii) fortunes; 3. 3. 166; (iv) condition; 4. 3. 4; (v) ceremony; 4. 3. 8

STAY, (i) undergo (cf. *Caes.* 5. 1. 106); 1. 1. 211; (ii) wait, await; 2. 5. 36; 4. 5. 144; (with 'on') 1. 2. 37; (iii) stop; 2. 3. 26; 4. 3. 57; 5. 3. 187, 251

STEAD, help, benefit; 2. 3. 54

STILL, ever, always; 1. 1. 170, and *passim*

STILL-WAKING, always awake; 1. 1. 180

STINT, cease; 1. 3. 49, 58, 59

STONE, testicle; 1. 4. 54

STORE, property, capital; 1. 1. 215

STOUT, brave, valiant; 3. 1. 168, 172

STRAIGHT, straightway; 1. 3. 104, and *passim*

STRAIN, (i) force; 2. 3. 19; (ii) 'strain courtesy'='act with less than due courtesy' (On.); 2. 4. 50; (iii) utter in song (O.E.D. 22b); 3. 5.

28; (iv) tax one's resources;
4. 1. 47

STRANGE, (i) distant, reserved;
2. 2. 101, 102; (ii) (a) shy,
(b) unfamiliar; 3. 2. 15

STRATAGEM, deed of violence;
3. 5. 209

STREAM, emit beams of light;
2. 2. 21

STUFFED (WITH), (a) full (of)
(cf. *Ado.*, 1. 1. 53); (b) with
an indelicate reference (cf.
Ado, G. on 'a maid and
stuffed'); 3. 5. 181

SUBTLY, craftily, treacher-
ously; 4. 3. 25

SUDDEN, (i) immediate; 2. 3.
93; 3. 5. 136; (ii) quickly
effective; 3. 3. 46; (iii) soon
to come; 3. 5. 109

SULLEN, mournful; 4. 5. 88

SUPPLE GOVERNMENT=power
of motion; 4. 1. 102

SURCEASE, cease; 4. 1. 97

SWEET, (a) savoury, (b) dear
(cf. '*sweet* fellow'); 2. 4. 81

SWEET WATER, perfumed water;
5. 3. 14

SWEETING, sweet kind of
apple; 2. 4. 79

SWITCH AND SPURS! To ride
'switch and spur'=to gallop
at full speed (O.E.D. 'spur',
2a). Cf. Tilley, S 1046; 2.
4. 69

SWOUND, swoon; 3. 2. 56

SYMPATHY, agreement in feeling; 3. 3. 86

TACKLED, made of rope; 2. 4.
182

TAKE DOWN, *either* humiliate,
abate the arrogance of, *or*
rebuke (v. O.E.D. take,
80c); 2. 4. 145–6

TAKE ME WITH YOU, be explicit
so that I can follow your
meaning (cf. *1 H. IV*, 2. 4.
451); 3. 5. 141

TAKE THE WALL, keep, as one
walks, beside the wall, this
being the safest and cleanest
part of the street, since the
gutter was in the middle
(cf. O.E.D. 'wall', 16); hence,
fig., 'take the wall of someone'=get the better of him
(as if forcing him to walk
on a portion of street less
safe and clean). London
streets were very narrow
and without side-pave-
ments; 1. 1. 12

TALE, story (with quibble on
'tail'= penis); 2. 4. 92, 94,
96

TALL, valiant; 2. 4. 30

TALLOW-FACE, pale wretch; 3.
5. 157

TARTAR'S BOW, (v. note); 1. 4.
5

TASSEL-GENTLE or tercel-
gentle, male peregrine falcon; 2. 2. 159

TEAR, burst; 2. 2. 161

TEEN, sorrow; 1. 3. 14

TEMPER (sb.), (a) disposition,
(b) the quality of steel;
3. 1. 114

TEMPER (vb.), (i) modify;
2 Prol. 14; (ii) mix, compound; 3. 3. 115; (iii) (a)
(ii), (b) (i); 3. 5. 97

TENDER (sb.), offer (of love or
marriage); 3. 4. 12; 3. 5.
184

TENDER (vb.), value, have regard for; 3. 1. 70

TETCHY, fretful, peevish; 1. 3.
33

TEXT, 'a certain text'=a very true quoted saying; 4. 1. 21

THINK LONG, yearn, be impatient for (v. O.E.D. 'think', vb.², 10 c); 4. 5. 41

THISBE, in classical mythology, a maiden beloved by Pyramus, a youth of Babylon. (Their story, told in Ovid, *Met.* bk. iv, bears certain resemblances to that of Romeo and Juliet; and forms the subject of the mechanicals' play in *M.N.D.*); 2. 4. 42

TILT, thrust; 3. 1. 157

TIME, 'in good time'= at the right moment, well met; 1. 2. 44–5.

TIMELESS, untimely; 5. 3. 162

TITAN, classical sun-god who travels through the sky in his chariot; 2. 3. 4

TITHE-PIG, pig paid as tithe; 1. 4. 79

To, in comparison with; 2. 4. 39; 3. 5. 219

TONIGHT, last night; 1. 4. 50; 2. 4. 2

TOOL, (a) weapon, (b) penis; 1. 1. 31

TOPGALLANT. 'Top'=platform near the head of a mast (O.E.D. 'top' 9); 'top mast'=the second section of a mast above the deck; 'top gallant mast'=a mast above that; 'top gallant'= the platform for this top mast; 2. 4. 183

TOWARDS, in preparation, about to take place; 1. 5. 122

TOY, whim, fancy; 4. 1. 119

TRAFFIC, business, occupation; Prol. 12

TRANSPARENT, (a) (lit.) clear, (b) (fig.) manifest; 1. 2. 94

TRICK, capricious piece of behaviour; 1. 5. 84

TRIUMPH, exultation, 'rapturous delight' (O.E.D. 5); 2. 6. 10

TRIUMPHANT, magnificent, glorious; 5. 3. 83

TROW, 'I trow'=(i) I'm sure; 1. 3. 34; (ii) a surprised or indignant expletive; 2. 5. 62

TRUCKLE-BED, 'low bed running on truckles or castors, usually pushed beneath a high or "standing" bed when not in use' (O.E.D.); 2. 1. 39

TRUDGE, 'undignified equivalent of "walk"' (O.E.D. 1); 1. 2. 34; 1. 3. 35

TRUST, trustworthiness; 3. 2. 85

TRUTH, honesty (cf. *Lucr.* 1532, *Son.* 48. 14, etc.); 5. 1. 1

TRY, (i) find out by testing; 4. 2. 3; (ii) test; 4. 2. 5; (iii) prove by experience; 4. 3. 29

TWAIN, separated; 3. 5. 240

TYRANNOUS, cruel, pitiless; 1. 1. 169

TYRANT, cruel, pitiless person; 1. 1. 21; 3. 2. 75

UMPIRE. Legal term='a third person called upon to decide a matter submitted to arbitrators [here, 'my extremes and me'] who cannot agree'; 4. 1. 63

UNACCUSTOMED, not customary, strange; 3. 5. 90

UNADVISED, unconsidered; 2.
2. 118

UNATTAINTED, not infected
(cf. 1. 2. 50); 1. 2. 88

UNBOUND, (a) without a
binding, (b) unmarried; 1.
3. 88

UNBRUISED, unbattered; 2. 3.
37

UNCOMFORTABLE, 'causing
or involving discomfort'
(O.E.D. 1), bringing sorrow,
'cheerless' (Schmidt); 4. 5.
60

UNEVEN, not smooth, (fig.) full
of difficulties; 4. 1. 5

UNFURNISHED, unprovided; 4.
2. 10

UNMANNED, (term in falconry), unused to the presence
of a man, 'not trained or
broken in' (O.E.D. 3), with
quibble on sense of 'husband-
less'; 3. 2. 14

UNSTUFFED, 'not clogged with
cares' (K.); 2. 3. 37

UNTHRIFTY, unfortunate, un-
toward, not bringing
'thrift' (=success); 5. 3.
136

UP, (i) aroused, up in arms; 3.
1. 132; (ii) come along!; 3.
1. 138; (iii) completely;
4. 2. 41, 45; (iv) afoot (with
quibble on 'out of bed');
5. 3. 188; (v) 'up and down'
=hither and thither, all
over the place; 2. 4. 90;
2. 5. 52

URGE, (i) mention, speak,
speak of; 1. 1. 202; 1. 5.
109; 3. 1. 153; (ii) provoke;
5. 3. 63

USE, (i) be accustomed; 2
Prol. 10; 3. 5. 189; (ii)

treat; 2. 4. 150; (iii) have
sexual intercourse with
(O.E.D. 10 b); cf. Per. 4. 6.
150, 'use her at thy
pleasure'; 2. 4. 151

UTTER, put on the market, sell;
5. 1. 67

VAIN, empty, foolish; 1. 4. 98

VALIDITY, value, worth; 3. 3.
33

VANITY, (i) frivolity; 1. 1. 177;
(ii) the delights of this world;
2. 6. 20

VAST, (a) extensive; (b) de-
solate; 2. 2. 83

VAULTY, arched; 3. 5. 22

VERSAL, 'Illiterate or colloq.
abbrev. of "universal"'
(O.E.D.); 2. 4. 199

VESTAL, chaste; 2. 2. 8; 3. 3.
38

VEX, (i) agitate; 1. 1. 191;
(ii) annoy; 2. 4. 155; (iii)
distress; 3. 5. 95

VIEW, (i) appearance; 1. 1.
168; (ii) eyesight; 1. 1. 170

VILE, (i) worthless; 1. 4. 111;
2. 3. 17; 3. 2. 59; (ii) evil,
base, filthy; 3. 1. 72, 140;
3. 2. 83; 3. 3. 106; 5. 3. 54

VILLAIN, term of address to a
servant, without implication
of bad qualities; 3. 1. 93

VIRTUE, beneficial power,
medicinal quality; 2. 3. 13

VISOR, (i) mask; 1. 4. 30;
1. 5. 23; (ii) face; 1. 4. 30

VOICE, vote; 1. 2. 19

WALK, step aside, come with
me in private; 3. 1. 74

WANNY, pallid; 4. 1. 100

WANT, WANT OF, lack; 2. 2.
78, 155; 5. 3. 15

WANTON (adj.), (i) *either* 'luxuriant' (Schmidt) *or* 'ungoverned, uncontrolled' (K.); 2. 5. 70; (ii) sportive, frolicsome; 2. 6. 19

WANTON (sb.), (i) trifler, unrestrained merrymaker; 1. 4. 35; (ii) spoiled or playful child; 2. 2. 177

WARRANT, assert as true, declare; 1. 3. 47, 53; 2. 5. 56; 3. 1. 98; 4. 5. 5; with 'him' or 'her',='concerning him or her'; 2. 5. 44; 4. 5. 1; with 'you',='to you'; 2. 4. 197; 4. 2. 40

WASHING, swashing, 'slashing with great force' (O.E.D. cf. Jonson, *Staple*, 5. 5. 15); 1. 1. 62

WASTE, expend, use up; 1.4.45

WATCH (sb.), watchmen, night-police; 3. 3. 148, 167; 5. 3. 71, 158, 279, 285

WATCH (vb.), (i) watch for the moment of; 4. 1. 116; (ii) stay awake; 4. 4. 8, 9, 12; (iii) prevent by vigilance; 4. 4. 12

WATERY, *either* 'controlling the tides' (On.), *or* 'pale' (O.E.D. 3); 1. 4. 65

WAX, (i) 'a man of wax'= a man perfect in beauty, like a wax model (O.E.D. 3c, doubtfully); 1. 3. 77; (ii) 'a form of wax'=a wax figure, lacking in essential human attributes; 3. 3. 126

WAYS, 'go thy ways'=go on your way (adverbial genitive sing.); 2. 5. 44

WEAK, 'stupid' (Schmidt), unworthy of a gentleman' (K.), but v. n.; 2. 4. 163

WEEDS, clothes; 5. 1. 39

WERADAY, alas. A variant of 'well-a-day'; 3. 2. 37; 4. 5. 15

WHAT, how; 1. 5. 55

WHORESON, coarse term of abuse, but sometimes (as here) of jocular familiarity; fellow, 'dog'; 4. 4. 19

WILD-GOOSE CHASE, 'a kind of horse-race or sport in which the second or any succeeding horse had to follow accurately the course of the leader (at a definite interval), like a flight of wild geese' (O.E.D.); here fig., and with a suggestion of 'flighty, foolish, fantastic person' in 'wild-goose'; 2. 4. 71

WILFUL, willing, eager; 1. 5. 89

WINDOW, shutter (v. *Caes*. G.); 1.1.138; "eyes' windows"= eyelids; 4. 1. 100

WINK, lit. shut, shut the eyes; hence, wink at, connive at (O.E.D., 5, 6.); 3. 2. 6; 5. 3. 294

WIT, (i) wisdom, prudence; 1. 1. 208; 1. 4. 49; (ii) wisdom, understanding, intelligence; 1. 3. 43; 3. 3. 122, 125, 130; 3. 5. 73; (iii) (plur.) mental faculties; 2. 4. 67, 71, 73; 4. 1. 47; (iv) wittiness, power of witty invention, 'mental quickness or sharpness' (O.E.D. 5); 2. 4. 79, 82; 4. 5. 121, 122, 123; (v) 'five wits'='usually, the five (bodily) senses; often vaguely, the perceptions or mental faculties generally'

(O.E.D. 'wit', 3b); 1. 4. 47;
cf. also 2. 4. 71–3

WITHAL, (i) thereby; 1. 1.
111; (ii) with; 1. 5. 115,
143; 3. 1. 77; (iii) in addition; 3. 1. 153

WOES, (i) pitiful objects; 5. 3.
179; (ii) sorrows; 5. 3. 180

WOMB, belly; 5. 3. 45

WORD, motto; 1. 4. 40

WORSHIPPED, venerated; 1. 1.
117

WOT, know; 3. 2. 139

WREAK, avenge; 3. 5. 101

WRETCH, term of endearment;
1. 3. 45

WROUGHT, prevailed upon
(O.E.D. 'work', 14); 3. 5.
144

ZOUNDS, an oath, short for
'God's wounds', i.e. the
wounds of Christ on the
cross; 3. 1. 48, 99